PHILIP BAGWELL, who is Professor Emeritus in History at the Polytechnic of Central London, is a recognised authority on transport history and the history of industrial relations. He has been a consultant on these subjects for BBC schools television. His principal published writings include *The Railwaymen: a history of the NUR* (two vols. 1963 and 1982): *The Railway Clearing House in the British Economy 1842-1922* (1970): *The Transport Revolution from 1770* (1974): *Industrial Relations* (1974) and (with G.E. Mingay) *Britain and America: a study of economic change 1850-1939*. He has been a London commuter (by London Transport) for over thirty years and has also used and studied the transport systems of many overseas countries.

Philip S. Bagwell

Verso

End of the Line?

**The Fate of Public Transport
Under Thatcher**

First Published 1984
© Philip S. Bagwell 1984

Verso Editions and NLB
15 Greek Street London W1V 5LF

Filmset in Times Roman by
Red Lion Setters, London

Printed in Great Britain by
The Thetford Press Ltd
Thetford, Norfolk

ISBN 0 86091
     86091 (Pbk.)

Contents

Contents

Introduction

A comprehensive and efficient system of public transport is a great national asset. The Victorian economist John Stuart Mill considered that 'countries which at a given moment are not masters of their transport will be condemned to ruin in the great economic struggles of the future'. The UK's first Minister of Transport, Sir Eric Geddes, told the Commons on 17 March 1919: 'The railway interest is a community interest. ... We must not commit the folly of our predecessors and allow the development ... of every system according to the whims and notions of those who introduce it.'

By the 'folly of our predecessors' he meant the unbridled competition in canal and railway construction which resulted in the UK's railways being among the most expensively constructed and operated in the world.

The Royal Commission on Transport in 1930 found that competition had not produced the much needed coordination of transport under which freight and passenger traffic is moved by that form of transport whose real economic costs are lowest. It reported that 'without unification – however it may be accomplished – no attempt to bring about coordination would be successful'.

The Thatcher government has rejected the above weighty advice. David Mitchell, Under Secretary of State for Transport, told a *Financial Times* conference on 15 November 1983: 'Our philosophy and principle is that the pattern of transport should be decided by customer choice with competition providing the options.'

This is a seemingly unexceptionable statement until the meaning of 'customer choice' is examined. Mitchell clearly equated it with demand expressed in money terms. He was certainly not equating it with a personal or social 'need' for transport.

In an article in *The Times* a few days earlier Professor Hayek, the Austrian economist, whose teachings have profoundly influenced the policies of the Thatcher government, wrote that he had 'no idea of what "social market economy" could possibly mean.' Four days later a correspondent to the same newspaper enlightened him. 'A social market economy', he wrote, 'is one which supplies those needs of individuals which the market fails to provide.'

The Attlee government which introduced the Transport Act of 1947 was of the opinion that public ownership of the principal forms of transport was needed in order to provide minimum standards of service in both urban and rural districts. Such thinking is anathema to the Thatcher government. From May 1979 market forces, rather than social needs, have determined the level of transport services provided.

The aim of this book is to examine the application of the philosophy of the market economy and privatisation in the transport sphere since May 1979. The impact of four transport acts passed by the Thatcher government is considered and the plans for the future, as expressed in the Serpell Report, are examined. The changes in policy proposed for London transport and for the Passenger Transport Authorities have been far-reaching. They are the subject of investigation in chapter ten. The Thatcher government has achieved some credibility through propaganda which stresses that 'There is no alternative'. In the concluding chapter an attempt is made to demonstrate that, at least in transport policy, there *is* an alternative.

In the preparation of this book I have been given unstinted help by many people. The assistance given by Mike Evans, Laurie Harries and the research department of the NUR has been invaluable. Tom Millman and Colin Sheehan of the union's publicity department have been most helpful. I have benefited from the advice and experience of Tom Ham, NUR President, and Russell Tuck, former Senior Assistant General Secretary of that union. Conversations with past and present members of the executive committee, including John Cogger, Bill Fordham, Ann Laverick, Jim Milligan, Jock Nicolson, Jim Stevenson and Ken Turton have been most useful in giving me a first hand impression of recent events. Keith Hill and Richard Faulkner have read through parts of the typescript and saved me from many pitfalls. Sandra Barr provided me with much useful information on the policies of TSSA. To Robert Shooter I am indebted for reports on country bus services. Len Shackleton gave guidance on recent trends in economic thought and Mick Hamer provided insight on happenings in Whitehall. I wish to thank them all. They are not responsible for any errors which may remain in this book.

This is the third time that Irene Ellis has typed out the entire manuscript of one of my books. I hope this fact will demonstrate how greatly I value her skill and patience.

To my wife, Rosemary, I am grateful for her understanding and tolerance in the face of the ever mounting piles of books and papers that accompany the preparation of a work of this kind.

Acknowledgement

I am grateful to Jimmy Knapp, General Secretary of the NUR, for giving me every encouragement and help in the writing of this book.

P.S.B.

Glossary

ACAS	Advisory Conciliation and Arbitration Service
AGM	Annual General Meeting
AMOS	Associated Minibus Operators
ABP	Associated British Ports
ASLEF	Associated Society of Locomotive Engineers and Firemen
BR	British Railways
BRB	British Railways Board
BREL	British Railways Engineering Ltd
BTDB	British Transport Docks Board
BTH	British Transport Hotels
CSEU	Confederation of Shipbuilding and Engineering Unions
EFL	External Financing Limit
EFR	External Financing Requirement
FL	Freightliner Ltd
GLC	Greater London Council
LDC	Local Departmental Committee
LRT	London Regional Transport
LT	London Transport
LTE	London Transport Executive
MMC	Monopolies and Mergers Commission
NBC	National Bus Company
NFC	National Freight Corporation
NTA	National Transport Authority
NTDB	National Transport Docks Board
NUR	National Union of Railwaymen
OMO	One Man Operation
PSO	Public Service Obligation
PTA	Passenger Transport Authority
PTE	Passenger Transport Executive
RSJC	Railway Staff Joint Council
RSNC	Railway Staff National Council
RSNT	Railway Staff National Tribunal
SGM	Special General Meeting
TSSA	Transport Salaried Staffs' Association

Do We Need Public Transport?

I

Until May 1979 it would have been considered a waste of time to pose this question. Before Margaret Thatcher came to power Conservative and Labour governments alike accepted the fact that publicly owned bus, railway and shipping services were essential for the economic and social well-being of the nation. It is true that in the 1960s and 1970s there was a serious deterioration in many public transport services, especially within the Celtic fringe areas of Scotland, Wales and the South West. Nevertheless, successive cabinets of varying political complexions accepted the case for subsidisation of some bus and railway services from government funds, knowing that it was impossible to run them purely on a commercial basis.

From 2 May 1979 when the Tories won an overall victory in the general election and Margaret Thatcher became Prime Minister the era of consensus came to an abrupt end. The new leader was brought up in a household which regarded the possession of a private motor car as a symbol of personal and family success; buses and trains, inferior forms of transport, were for those who had not 'made it' in society. Unlike the Prince and Princess of Wales, the Prime Minister chooses not to travel by rail. On the one occasion she met the members of the British Railways Board the atmosphere was decidedly chilly. By her remarks she implied that Board members could not be very capable persons or they would have found jobs as directors of private companies. For her it was impossible to conceive that talented men and women might aspire to serve a great public industry and make it a success.[1]

Immediately on assuming office the Premier appointed as her Parliamentary Private Secretary, Ian Gow, Conservative MP for Eastbourne, who during the preceding Labour administration made his reputation as the foremost advocate of de-nationalisation. On 26 October 1976, when asking leave in the House of Commons to bring in a Bill 'to restore the National Freight Corporation and its subsidiaries to private ownership' he confessed:-

> If I had my way I would continue the process of de-nationalisation of all projects under his (i.e. the Secretary of State for Transport's) control so that he too would become redundant.[2]

Despite the extreme statements of her backbencher, Margaret Thatcher, then Leader of the Opposition, followed him into the division lobby, though Norman Fowler, her front bench spokesman on transport, was notably absent.

Also strongly influencing the Premier's thinking were Professor Alan Walters, her economic adviser, and his friend Alfred Goldstein of the accounting firm of R. Travers Morgan and Partners, and Alfred Sherman of the Centre for Policy Studies. All three, with Gow, are noted for their dislike of British Rail and for their determination to minimise its role in the British economy. In a BBC Panorama programme on 24 January 1983 Sherman claimed that there would be an improvement in transport efficiency if the railway tracks were torn up and roads constructed in their place. In October 1981 Walters told the Adam Smith Institute in London: 'I would love to see many railway lines in private hands. They may do wonders. It would be very nice to get out of railways. The real wages you need to pay railway drivers are very low. People would almost pay you to drive a railway train.'

It is this small group of extremists centred on the Prime Minister, rather than the Secretary of State for Transport, which has had the final say in transport policy over the last four years. Its members incline to the belief that publicly owned transport is an unnecessary extravagance in present day Britain.

It is essential, therefore, for those who take a contrary view to state their case in no uncertain terms.

II

In 1981 thirty-nine per cent of all households had no car. This is of course, an average figure. In one of the regions most threatened with rail closures, Scotland, forty-nine per cent of households are without cars. At the other extreme, in the relatively prosperous South East (excluding Greater London) the figure is as low as thirty per cent.[3] It is obvious that unless some form of bus or train service is available in all the regions, even in those where less than a third of the number of households are without cars, millions of people will be largely immobilised. In 1982 over thirteen million young people were below the legal minimum age for driving a car. Perhaps half this number were of an age to travel on their own. Many teenagers over seventeen years old have not yet passed the driving test. Though some may have followed Norman Tebbit's advice and taken to two wheels, riding a bicycle in modern traffic conditions can be very dangerous. Inexpensive, reliable and frequent public transport services are essential if teenagers are to become aware of a larger environment than their home town or village, attend school, college or university or take part in recreational or educational activities in the evening. At the other end of the life span, a large proportion of the more than nine million men and women of pensionable age are no longer driving or have never learned to drive. Thus many millions within the UK population are heavily dependent on public transport for their mobility. To be dependent on relatives or friends offering lifts in private cars is often a very unreliable alternative. Many older people are reticent about asking for a lift. The wishes of the driver and the passenger may well coincide for the outward journey: finding agreement on the timing of the return is generally more difficult.

The argument that where there are no publicly owned buses or trains private enterprise will do the job will not hold water. It is true that examples can be cited of bus and coach routes served profitably by private companies as in the case of the Oxford-London route following the removal of licensing restrictions on services exceeding 30 miles under the Transport Act of 1980. However, in this instance there is a large potential market already well served by British Rail and the National Bus Company (NBC). The emergence of new competition on this popular route did not serve to improve transport facilities in those parts of the country where they were most needed. Indeed the opposite was the case. In order to beat off competition from the newcomers on the commuter routes the NBC diverted resources from its unprofitable country services, with the result that

areas already poorly served in 1979 were in an even worse position in
1983. Between 1980 and 1981 the NBC route mileage fell by eight per
cent.[4] Private bus operators did not fill in the gaps.

A much canvassed suggestion made by the critics of the railway is
that bus services should be provided as a substitute for trains. The
rail-bus has distinct possibilities and is being developed by British
Rail in so far as its limited funds permit. However, recent history
shows that where bus services have been provided to take the place
of the closed railway, passengers have not taken kindly to the new
mode of public transport. Mayer Hillman and Anne Whalley, who
examined the social consequences of ten post-Beeching rail closures
spanning the years 1963-76 in widely scattered parts of the UK,
found that less than half the former rail users switched to the substitute bus after their line had been closed. Bus services were found to
be slower, less frequent, less reliable and less comfortable than the
train.[5] For disabled persons the bus is often seen as less convenient
than the train since there is generally no opportunity to stand up,
stretch one's legs or visit the toilet. As a letter-writer to *The Times*
expressed it on 3 February 1983: 'One may be quite incapable of
folding up in order to get into a car or of holding one position for
any length of time as necessitated by bus or coach journeys, and yet
be perfectly able to travel even long distances by train because of the
possibility of standing up and walking about from time to time.'

In some parts of the UK topographical conditions make the bus
alternative to the railway even less attractive. When the Cambrian
Coast line, a 57 mile long link between Pwllheli and Machynlleth,
was under threat of closure in 1971 the Crossville Bus Company was
asked to submit plans for an 'alternative' bus service. It was found
that it would take the bus one hour 50 minutes to cover the route
between Towyn and Barmouth. By train the journey takes 31
minutes. The reason for the huge discrepancy in journey times is
that the train crosses the Mawddach estuary by means of a 1½ mile
long railway bridge; the bus has to make a 17¼ mile long detour
inland to reach the first road bridge at Dolgellau.[6]

III

Each working day of the year some 400,000 commuters travel into the central London area by British Rail. An even larger number, some 600,000 persons, use London Transport's underground trains or buses to get to work. By comparison, less than 160,000 private cars are driven into inner London in the rush hours. They carry only 20 per cent of the commuter traffic.[7] Radial roads leading into central London from the suburbs are already heavily congested during the daily head-to-tail rush hour crawl – and increasingly at other times as well. If only a sizeable proportion of the number of commuters who now travel by public transport opted for travel by private car, the main roads of London would form one big traffic jam from before the start of the working day until well after its end. That this is no exaggerated statement is shown by what has happened on the rare occasions when no buses or tube trains are running. When all London Transport services were halted by a strike on 10 March 1982 the evening rush hour 'lasted until late at night – eight hours after it started'; and this despite the fact that thousands of commuters stayed at home anticipating prolonged delays if they attempted the journey to work.[8] The other big conurbations such as Greater Manchester, Merseyside or Glasgow have similar problems though lesser in magnitude than those of London.

Official figures of the number of journeys made by private car are inflated through a bias in tax law which induces many people to use this form of transport rather than the train or bus. These figures show that in 1981 84 per cent of all passenger journeys were made in private motor vehicles, whereas only eight per cent of journeys were made by bus and seven per cent by train.[9] However, an uncounted, but almost certainly large, number of journeys by road were made in company cars. Between one half and two thirds of all new cars coming on to Britain's roads each year are bought by businesses as employees' perks, the companies offsetting the cost of the vehicles against their tax liabilities. It is estimated that one fifth of all car commuting is done in company cars; that six per cent of all petrol consumed is acquired as a free perk from the driver's employer; and that the aggregate value of tax subsidies to the company car owners is about £2,000 million a year, or roughly twice the amount of government support for the passenger railway. No other country subsidises car travel in this way. No doubt many a private car owner who does not run a company car feels unfairly treated by comparison with the railway user. He has to pay VAT on the purchase of his vehicle, the road licence, insurance and petrol duty while the railway user is subsidised out of taxation (though less so in Britain than in almost any other country). However, estimates show that there are wider disparities between different classes of car user (in terms of relative taxes and subsidies) than exist between the motorist and the user of public transport. In 1976 company car users enjoyed a subsidy of 2.3 pence per mile compared with the rail passenger's 1.9 pence.[10]

An additional perk which, by widespread practice, is enjoyed by many car owners is free parking near the place of work. The introduction of street parking meters in the 1960s was designed to make the motorist pay for congesting the highway and slowing down the movement of traffic, including buses. To be effective the scheme required the employment of sufficient staff – traffic wardens and fixed penalty office employees – to ensure compliance with the law. But in London the situation has become wholly farcical for the reason that successive Secretaries of State for Transport have failed to ensure the recruitment of the 4,000 traffic wardens the Metropolitan Commissioner of Police considers necessary to do the job. For reasons of 'economy' the Metropolitan Police were ordered to reduce the number of wardens to 1,500. In fact they had fallen to 1,300 by 1981. The result has been a widespread evasion of the law. In September 1981 the consultancy firm TEST found that in London's inner West End (WC1, WC2 and W1) 86 per cent of vehicles were parked illegally and that only 10 per cent of these were likely to receive a ticket ordering payment of a fine. It has become the rule, rather than the exception, for commuters who drive to town to park illegally on the yellow lines and take a calculated risk that they will not be served with a ticket. Even if they are unlucky and the traffic warden places the small piece of paper under one of the windscreen wipers, the odds are that the fixed penalty office will not have sufficient staff or time to summon the offender if he fails to pay. The commuter finds that over a year, his outgoings in penalties actually paid are less than he would have had to pay for garaging. He is therefore induced to continue to depend on his car rather than on public transport.[11] Meanwhile nearly empty buses crawl down the road he has helped to congest, the tube trains attract ever fewer passengers and Mrs. Thatcher's advisers assert that labour employed in public transport is unproductive and that increasing numbers of the public prefer to travel by private car.

IV

Energy conservation, environmental and safety considerations all underline the advantages of rail as compared with private motor car transport.

The more fully loaded the vehicle – of whatever type – the more economical it is in its use of fuel. It is as misleading to assert that the private car is more fuel-efficient than the train as it is to maintain that the train always has the advantage, irrespective of other circumstances. It all depends on the load factor, i.e. how many available passenger seats are occupied. A small car with a 100 per cent load factor, i.e. four passengers, uses 0.8 mega joules of energy per passenger mile and is more energy efficient than an electric train with only a 45 per cent load factor (1.0 mega joules). But since the private car averages only 1.3 passengers per journey, the electric train, even with less than half its seats occupied, is more energy efficient. To carry one passenger one mile a car needs two to five times (depending on its miles-per-gallon performance), and an aeroplane four to eight times, more energy than an electric train. The diesel scores even more marks for energy conservation than the electric locomotive, but its maintenance costs are higher and it can use only one, non-renewable, type of fuel – diesel oil. By contrast, electric power can be generated from a variety of sources: domestic supplies of coal or oil or the harnessing of the energy in the wind, rivers or tides.[12] These facts point the way to certain priorities in transport policy. A government committed to long-term energy conservation should sponsor railway electrification. At the same time, by means of an attractive fare structure, it should encourage the fuller use of the passenger train.

The nineteenth-century steam train polluted the environment. Smoke from the locomotives made a handsome contribution to the smog that enveloped the big cities, and housewives obliged to live near the railway depots and termini, found it virtually impossible to keep their washing clean. Railway company management was sensitive to criticism of smoke emission and punished, with fines, footplatemen who unnecessarily created a 'smoke nuisance'. From the 1960s onwards it was not only the Clean Air Act, 1956, but also the replacement of steam by diesel and electric traction which transformed, for the better, the urban atmosphere. However, no sooner had the evil arising from the burning of coal been largely eliminated than a new threat to health emerged in the form of emissions from millions of car exhausts of carbon monoxide, hydrocarbons, lead and other chemical pollutants. At the same time, with the growth of car ownership, and particularly with the increase in the number of heavy lorries on Britain's roads, the noise problem in cities and towns has increased to an almost unbearable extent. Market and Opinion Research International, which has conducted annual surveys, has found that respondents consider traffic noise to be one of the three or four most serious problems of modern Britain. Older town dwellers know that a quarter of a century ago it was possible to have a chat with a friend on the pavement. This is scarcely feasible now. Those who value the quality of urban life believe that, where there is a choice, rail transport should be encouraged and road transport minimised. Railways have a very low nuisance factor; they are quieter than road traffic and segregated from shops, business premises and most people's homes. At 20 yards distance a train transmits between 65 and 70 decibels of noise. Even a private car creates 70 to 90 decibels, whilst a single heavy lorry transmits 100 decibels.[13] This being the case what can be said of those who would bring yet more vehicles on to our overcrowded roads by closing down a large part of the rail network.

There is no doubt at all that travelling by train is much safer than travelling by car. Each year over 700 million passenger journeys, covering over 30,700 million passenger miles, are made by train.[14] In some years, as in 1976 and 1977, there were no deaths resulting from train accidents. An average of 30 passengers a year die on railway premises, though not from train accidents.[15] Between 1975-9, inclusive, an average of 6,546 persons were killed on Britain's roads each year. Considerable satisfaction was expressed when the figures for 1981 revealed fewer than 6,000 fatalities – 5846 – and it was emphasised that Britain's record was far better than that of France or the Federal Republic of Germany. Nevertheless deaths on the roads, per passenger mile travelled, were ten times of those of the railways.[16] In the Falklands war of 1982 255 British servicemen were killed.[17] The outcry that would have arisen if the fatalities had been 23 times that number can well be imagined. And yet the nation regards with some complacency an annual death toll of that magnitude on its roads.

The cost of supporting the passenger services of British Rail is constantly under the searchlight of criticism. Questions are rarely asked about the cost of road accidents. When one was asked in the House of Commons on 1 July 1980 the minister, Kenneth Clarke, replied that, at June 1979 prices, the cost of a fatal road accident was estimated at £113,400. Multiplying this figure by the number of such accidents in 1981 we arrive at a total sum of over £663 million. Serious accidents, the minister said, cost £6,100. There were 78,000 of these in 1981, making an annual cost of nearly £476 million. In that year slight accidents numbered 241,000 which, at an estimated average cost of £790, added more than £190 million to the nation's road accident bill. Thus adding together the cost of fatal, serious and slight accidents, and other aspects such as loss of production, we reach the staggering total of £1,730 millions annually.[18] Many accidents are not reported. The cost in terms of the anguish of the bereaved and the distress caused to those maimed for life cannot be measured in pounds and pence.

It cannot be imagined that transferring traffic from the safer railways to the more dangerous roads will do anything but increase the number and cost of road accidents. By slashing the size of the rail network and reducing the Public Service Obligation grant to the railways the government will ensure that yet more millions will be added to the already huge sum the nation pays for its road accidents.

V

The volume of freight traffic carried by rail has been steadily decreasing over the last quarter of a century. In 1981 only 14.1 per cent of the ton mileage of goods was railborne compared with 64.3 per cent which went by road. (The greater part of the remainder was carried in coastal vessels.)[19] Opponents of public transport have therefore been led to argue that since rail transport's share is so small the traffic could be transferred to the private road hauliers without making any very noticeable difference to road congestion. However the rail traffic is still substantial. In 1981 it amounted to 154 million tonnes of which 95 million tonnes was coal and coke. Furthermore the average haul by rail is longer than that by road.[20]

Should government policies be so misguided as to cause more freight traffic to be sent by road the prospect for the private motorist and for citizens living near the main lorry routes would be yet more forbidding than they are now. Many thousands more heavy lorries would clutter up our already congested roads. More jack-knife style accidents would occur. The strains of motoring for the car driver would increase.

More, not less, freight should be going by rail. That railways carry such a small proportion of the traffic is in part due to the injustices of fiscal policies over many decades. Department of Transport estimates for 1982-3 reveal that the 76,000 articulated lorries of 32 gross tonnes will pay £86 million less in taxation than their proper share of road costs.[21] British Rail, by contrast, is expected to pay for the maintenance and renewal of the permanent way. The consequence is that BR's market share of freight haulage is only about a third of that of Swedish railways; less than half that of the SNCF (the French state railway system) and well below the performance of the German, Norwegian, Belgian and Italian railways. Only in the case of the Dutch and the Danish, who have the advantage of cheap internal waterway transport, is the proportion of freight carried by rail smaller than it is in Britain.[22]

VI

So what is to be said of the 'solution' of concreting over the rail bed and converting it to motorway? Were it not for the fact that its advocate, Alfred Sherman, is a member of Mrs. Thatcher's inner circle of advisers it would not be worth spending time in exposing the impracticalities of such a harebrained scheme.

In the early 1920s Britain had over 21,000 route miles of railway, nearly half of which have since been closed to traffic. What a magnificent opportunity this has provided Ministry of Transport road planners to convert the rail bed into road surfaces. How has it happened, then, that only 70 miles of former railway have been so converted? It is not because, as might be thought, most closures were in rural areas where there was no great call for new roads. Most of the mileage closed is within big cities or on main routes which unnecessarily duplicated inter-city communications. (A relic of the days of competing railway companies.) Lines passing through the heart of Glasgow, Liverpool, Birmingham, Nottingham, Leicester and

Bristol have been abandoned. None has been converted to roads though new roads have often been built close by.

The reason is that disused railway lines are unsuited to road conversion. Drainage is one problem. Railway track is self draining, as water can penetrate the stone ballast. Roads being impermiable, require much bigger drains which are placed at the sides, whereas many railways are drained in the centre – a system quite unsuited to road construction.

A second major problem is that railways are built on narrower ribbons of land than are needed for modern roads. Over 90 per cent of British Rail's network is double or single track. Only seven per cent of the route has four or more tracks. Yet even a four-track rail route is only 60 feet wide, whereas a six lane motorway spans 130 feet. The present railway network is crossed by 51,000 bridges and threads its way through 700 tunnels. Trains have a rounded profile so that they can pass through the brick arches with only a few inches to spare. Most road freight vehicles do not have a rounded profile and would not be able to pass safely under many bridges which cross the railway track. The theoretical headroom maintained over British roads is five metres; but the springing of a typical railway double track brick arch starts to curve inwards at no more than three metres high. There are already far too many accidents caused by road vehicles hitting railway bridges. A survey conducted in 1972-4 revealed that an average of 500 such accidents were happening annually. It can well be imagined that this figure would be multiplied several times if the Sherman plan were to be adopted.

A third problem would be that of linking the new roads with the existing road network. Astronomical sums would have to be spent making access from the rail termini, such as Waterloo or Paddington, to the main roads of the capital and other big cities.[23]

What would be the point of undertaking the vast expenditure which conversion of rail into road would involve? Properly utilized railways are more energy-efficient, safer, faster and more economical of land use than road transport. Why spend billions of pounds on such a scheme when the existing rail network is under-utilized? Why must it be the case that only in Britain government seems bent on wrecking the railway system, either through the slow attrition resulting from under investment or the more drastic surgery seriously proposed by the Railway Conversion League and Alfred Sherman? In

France, Germany, Italy and Holland new lines are being built and in these countries and elsewhere the investment in railways per head of population is higher than it is in Britain. Those concerned to see developed a more rational transport system are led to conclude that the Prime Minister and her closest advisers have such strong prejudices against public transport that they outweigh any other considerations.

2

The Economic Philosophy of Thatcherism: Its Consequences for the Rail Business

I

Activity in the railway industry has often been considered a barometer of the prosperity or depression prevailing in industry as a whole. After 2 May 1979 the British Railways Board was aware that if the new Tory government succeeded in fulfilling its leader's general election promises of reviving British industry there would be good prospects of increasing traffic and revenues. If, on the other hand, the new government's policies failed, the prospects for the Board and its work force would be decidedly bleaker.

In their general election manifesto, published on 11 April 1979, the Conservatives promised 'proper monetary discipline' to master inflation. It was 'vital', they claimed, to reduce the size of the government's borrowing requirement. Because the state took too much of the nation's income, 'taxes, interest rates, prices and unemployment rise'. It was 'especially important to cut the absurdly high marginal rates of tax at the bottom and the top of the income scale'. If this was done the people would have an incentive to work harder and produce more wealth.

Margaret Thatcher returned to this theme on 15 May 1979 when making her first Commons speech as Prime Minister. She expressed sympathy with an old lady she had met just before the election who was paying £1.15 a week tax out of her £25 a week income and promised: 'That is the kind of person who will benefit from the reductions in income tax that we propose'.

The outcome was very different. The actions of Sir Geoffrey Howe, Chancellor of the Exchequer, which quickly followed, were in sharp contrast to the honeyed words of his leader – though they were fully endorsed by her. They also made a mockery of the Premier's invocation of the spirit of St. Francis – 'Where there is despair may we bring hope' – on the steps of number 10 Downing Street on 4 May. That part of the election manifesto which promised drastic reduction in the 'absurdly high marginal rate of tax' at the *top* of the income scale was immediately implemented in the budget of June 1979. The Chancellor cut the rate of income tax on the wealthiest from 83 per cent to 60 per cent. However, to meet the cost of this change, VAT, the biggest proportion of which is paid by wage and salary earners, was raised from 8 per cent to 15 per cent and government spending on the publicly owned industries and the social services, which provide the 'social wage', was cut by £4,000 million.

The result of these and subsequent budget changes was the exact opposite of the objective proclaimed by Mrs Thatcher on 15 May 1979. The *Financial Times*, in its issue of 20 February 1982, revealed that the poorest taxpayers, those on half average weekly earnings or less, were then paying 18.6 per cent of their gross incomes in tax and National Insurance contributions, a rate roughly half as much again as they were paying in 1978-9. At the other end of the scale a £77,000 a year executive with a wife and two children was substantially better off. Whereas in 1978-9 he paid 66.1 per cent of his income in tax, in 1982 the proportion had fallen to 52.4 per cent.

The justification given for easing the burden of taxes on the rich was that the private enterprise sector – which Mrs. Thatcher chose to call 'the wealth creating part of the economy' – needed encouragement and expansion while the public sector needed 'rolling back' since, according to Sir Keith Joseph, 'high state spending crowds out enterprise and threatens freedom'. It was assumed that money put back into the pockets of the wealthier classes would soon be transferred to productive investment. This belief is largely a myth. When Chancellor Barber cut taxes with a similar objective in the early 1970s the result was a speculative property boom. The long unoccupied Centre Point skyscraper by St. Giles' Circus, London, stands as a monument to the fiscal follies of those years. A decade later the result of similar policies pursued by Sir Geoffrey Howe was even more damaging to Britain's interests. In the early 1980s there were fewer plums to be picked in the property market; but exchange controls were greatly eased in the budget of 1979 and a huge exodus of investment funds took place. Much of this investment went directly to foreign firms competing with British manufacturers. Central Statistical Office figures reveal that the total of British private investment overseas rose from £6,555 million in 1979 to £10,637 million in 1981, while over the same span of time investment in Britain from overseas *fell* from £4,361 million to £3,356 million. It is not difficult to discover why such investment was taking place abroad rather than at home. The monetarist policies of the government, with minimum lending rate at an all-time high of 17 per cent in the winter of 1979-80, made the cost of borrowing to finance improvements, or even to warehouse stocks, so exorbitant that there was an unprecedented number of bankruptcies.

In June 1979 Sir Geoffrey Howe said: 'We need to enlarge freedom of choice by reducing the role of the state'. Four years later there is no denying that the role of the state has been reduced. At the same time certain types of freedom have been increased. The more than two million persons added to the numbers of the unemployed now enjoy freedom from work, freedom to try and make ends meet on their social security benefits, and freedom to contemplate how nice it would be to be able to afford a trip on a British Rail train.

Britain's economic performance over the last four years has been, by a substantial margin, the worst of all the leading industrial nations.[1] Trends in industrial production and unemployment in the UK are shown in Figure 1. The production graph indicates the output of all industries, including North Sea oil. The performance of manufacturing production alone, excluding North Sea oil, has been even more dismal, with a decline of 20 per cent.[2] The excuse has been made that Britain's economic decline has been due to circumstances beyond our control, a world recession of trade. This would be more convincing were it not for the fact that in the UK the sharp decline in economic activity and the rapid rise in the number of jobless began more than a year *before* the peak of world trade was reached in 1980. Unemployment in Britain rose from 5.8 per cent of the work force at the end of 1979 to double that rate in May 1981. In none of the other major industrial countries was the rate of increase more than half in the same period of time.[3] The increase of unemployment under the Thatcher government was particularly alarming in that it devastated a number of major industries such as construction, mechanical engineering, the car industry and metal manufacture. Figure 2 shows the extent of the job loss in the one year 1982 and the percentage of the work force in each industry rendered idle.

The appalling unemployment problem bequeathed to the nation

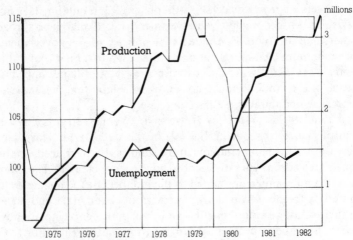

FIGURE 1
The record of decline
Trends in Industrial Production and Unemployment in the UK

NOTE: Unemployment is total registered unemployment (including school leavers) UK.
NOTE: Production is index of industrial production (all industries), 1975 = 100.
SOURCE: CSO

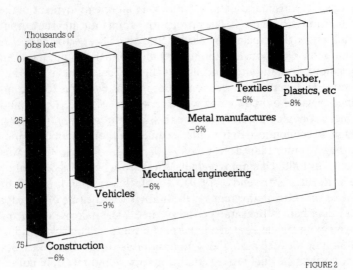

FIGURE 2
The worst hit industries in 1982

NOTE: All figures October 1981 to October 1982. SOURCE: *DE Gazette*

by the Conservative government bears the hall mark 'Made in Britain'. The aim of cabinet policy from May 1979 was clearly expressed in the White Paper on public expenditure issued in November 1979: 'It is essential to contain and reduce progressively the growth of the money supply. This means that government borrowing must in turn be firmly controlled. It is a main determinant of monetary growth.'[4]

Consistent with this aim, substantial reductions in expenditure on the main public industries and services were put in hand at once. A £22 million pound reduction in the Public Service Obligation (PSO) grant to BR was announced in November 1979. The stated purpose of all the cuts in the Public Sector Borrowing Requirement (PSBR) was to reduce the money supply, curb inflation and restore business confidence. However, contrary to the government's assumption, there is no certain co-relation between the growth of the money supply and the rate of inflation. The evidence available at the time of the publication of the White Paper was that for the five year period up to 1978 the rate of growth of money supply in West Germany, Belgium, Switzerland and the UK – on an agreed definition (M3) of what constitutes the money supply – rose, in each case, by around ten per cent. But the rate of inflation in Switzerland was four per cent, in West Germany 4¾ per cent, in Belgium nine per cent in the UK 15 per cent. The remarkable fact was that whereas the money supply in the UK amounted to 34 per cent of gross national income, in the case of Germany it was 67 per cent in Switzerland 125 per cent, and yet the rate of inflation in those two countries was less than a third of what it was in Britain.

The Treasury's claim that government borrowing 'is a main determinant of monetary growth' is false. Some three-quarters of the PSBR is financed by borrowing from individuals and pension funds, a harmless enough arrangement since it involves *transfers*, rather than the creation of new money. At the same time as exchange controls were relaxed in 1979 the control over private sector borrowing from the banks – 'the corset' – was also lifted. Thus, simultaneously, severe restraints were imposed on the public sector and removed from the private borrower – provided of course he could meet the high prevailing interest rates. What becomes clear is that what was advanced as a highly principled economic and fiscal 'cure' for inflation in fact emerged primarily as a politically motivated plan to 'roll back the public sector'.[5]

In cutting back public expenditure the government aggravated the depression in private industry rather than alleviated it. Public spending on education, training and health boosts demand for the products of private industry. The wages and salaries paid to teachers, social workers, nurses and others employed in the public sector are spent mainly on the products of private firms.

Writing in *The Guardian* in December 1980, Sir Peter Parker, Chairman of British Rail, recalled that a National Economic Development Office (NEDO) study in 1975 showed that Britain's six major national industries (coal, gas, electricity, steel, railways and the Post Office) accounted for one third of all UK industries expenditure on plant and machinery and took, on average, 19 per cent of the total output of their main suppliers. 'Because of this', he wrote, 'the national industries have taken a very positive view in their purchasing policy so as to give every assistance to suppliers in the development of overseas sales'.[6] In 1980 BR and its subsidiaries alone spent £1,242 million on goods and services. About 80 per cent of this huge sum was spent in private sector industries.[7]

In so far as the Thatcher government has succeeded in pushing back the frontiers of publicly owned industry in a time of severe economic depression it has most probably reduced the demand for the products of British private industry. Publicly owned industries have generally pursued a policy of buying British (as Sir Peter Parker stressed). There is no guarantee that the private corporations that have taken over the hived off parts of these industries will follow that example.

Another myth sedulously advanced by the Thatcherites is that an important reason for our poor economic performance and heavy unemployment is the payment of excessively high wages. Workers, it is claimed, have priced themselves out of jobs. However, in March 1981 the US Bureau of Labour Statistics revealed that the UK's hourly wage costs were, in 1980, lower than those of the other nine leading industrial nations, with the exception of Japan. The same report examined wage costs in 80 US subsidiary companies operating in Wales and found that 91 per cent of the companies recorded higher output per unit wage cost than obtained in comparable industries in the US.[8] Nevertheless, prevalent opinion in government circles is that British workers are overpaid and that wages must come down if Britain is to meet the challenge of her overseas competitors. Sir Geoffrey

Howe constantly pleaded for lower wage settlements. This has important repercussions for the workers in the publicly owned industries, such as the railways. Sir Peter Parker has been under great pressure from No. 10 Downing Street to reduce the level of wage settlements, even though 'Britain's railwaymen are Europe's lowest paid'.[9] Being desperate for more investment if the railway industry is to survive, he has hardened his stance against the claims of railway labour in the hope of keeping on favourable terms with the government. The outcome was that in 1982 more working days were lost from industrial disputes on the railways than in the previous 50 years of the industry's history.

II

Since the early summer of 1979 the steep decline in manufacturing production and the rapid rise in the number of the unemployed was bound to affect adversely BR's business activity and its financial stability. There was a fall of almost one fifth in the output of British manufacturers between 1979 and 1982 inclusive. The BRB's *Annual Report and Accounts* for 1981 commented that the freight market continued to be characterised by 'too much transport chasing too little tonnage'.[10] BR's freight traffic is predominantly in the bulkier items such as coal, steel, chemicals, heavy engineering products and the timber, cement and other heavy materials used in the construction industry. These were precisely the sectors of industry most adversely affected by the slump. Between 1979-81 inclusive UK crude steel production fell from 21 million to 15 million tonnes, or by 29 per cent; construction industry output and orders, at 1975 prices, fell from £2,892 million to £2,418 million, or by 16 per cent and total sales in engineering fell from an index of 100.5 to 89 (1975 = 100), or by 11½ per cent, and coal production fell from 129.6 million tonnes to 118.5 million tonnes, or by 8.5 per cent.[11]

In the circumstances BR's freight carrying stood up well as Table 1 indicates:

Table I
BR Freight Traffic: Tonnes carried by commodity[12]

| | | million tonnes | |
	1979	1980	1981
Coal and coke	93	94	95
Iron and steel	25	13*	18
Oil and chemicals	21	18	16
Building and construction	19	19	16
Freightliner	8	7	7
Other traffics	3	2	2
Total	169	153	154

* Low carryings in 1980 due to three months' steel strike.

Freight traffic in coal and coke was well sustained because two thirds of it was carried largely in 'merry go round' trains to the Central Electricity Generating Board's (CEGB) power stations. The volume of iron and steel rail freight fell by slightly less than the decline in national production of those commodities. The fall in the volume of building and construction industry materials carried matched the 16 per cent downturn in that industry's orders.

It was, thus, the depression in Britain's basic industries which brought an aura of gloom to BR's *Annual Report* for 1980 and obliged Sir Peter Parker, for the first time in five years, to announce a failure to keep within the government's contract price for running the railway. The group loss was £79.9 million, £53 million of which was attributable to the 10 per cent decline in the volume of freight carried.[13] Although losses from freight were halved in 1981 as a result of improved productivity, the Board was obliged to postpone important investment projects in order to stay within the Government's External Financing Limit (EFL).[14]

It might have been expected that, with the sharp rise in the number of unemployed from 1979 onwards, passenger traffic on British Rail would have been adversely affected. That this was not the case was largely due to the success of BR's marketing initiatives in the sale of Senior Citizen, Student and Family Railcards. The volume of rail passenger travel actually showed a marked increase in the early life of the Thatcher government. In 1979 the 32,000 million passenger kilometers travelled were the greatest since the pre-Beeching year 1961, when the rail network was 30 per cent larger and there were only half as many private motor cars on the roads.[15] In 1980 the number of passenger journeys made was the highest for nine years and the figure for passenger kilometers travelled was only one per cent down on 1979.[16] This good record could not be sustained in 1982 because of the cumulative effects of the economic depression and the damaging impact of strikes in the first seven months of the year.

Despite these gallant efforts to sustain and improve passenger revenues the economic recession acted remorselessly on the general financial position of BR. In his *Annual Report and Accounts* for 1980, Sir Peter Parker 'estimated a loss of receipts of between £100 and £120 million attributable to the effects of the recession'. Owing to the niggardliness of financial support from successive governments (Labour and Conservative) the BR Board had begun to look round for alternative sources of finance long before the Thatcher government's monetarist policies aggravated the Board's financial plight. Since at least 1977 the Annual Reports make reference to the possibility of 'joint ventures' or 'joint operations' with the private sector in one or more of BR's subsidiaries. It was by no means envisaged then that such arrangements would in any way result in a loss of control by BR: but it is an indication of the Board's awareness of under-investment, particularly in British Transport Hotels. However, these were small clouds on the horizon. They were as nothing compared with the storms to come after 1979 when Tory transport policy began to have its full effect.

3
Tory Transport Policies – How Far Have They Deviated from *The Right Track* (1977)?

I

In the Conservative General Election Manifesto published on 11 April 1979 there were few references to transport policy. There was a promise 'to sell shares of the National Freight Corporation (NFC) to the general public in order to achieve substantial private investment in it', but no suggestion that any other of BR's subsidiaries would be denationalised. There was no hint of any plans to sell off British Transport Hotels or Sealink UK Ltd. or to disturb 'Travellers Fare' business in buffet and restaurant services. After reading the Manifesto one could be forgiven for concluding that, apart from the injection of private capital into the NFC and a strong hint of the need for increased productivity – 'the key to the future of industries like BR' – Sir Peter Parker and his team would be left largely undisturbed to manage their business. For road passenger transport there was a clear commitment 'to relax the Traffic Commissioner's licensing regulations to enable new bus and other services to develop – particularly in rural areas'. There was no indication of any plan to disturb ownership or management of the efficiently run and profitable British Transport Docks Board (BTDB).

If, before 1979, a major disintegration of the BR organisation had been intended once the Tories returned to power, one would have expected to see some indication of these plans from the party's leaders. Norman Fowler was their front bench spokesman on transport matters from 1976 until Margaret Thatcher appointed him Secretary of State for Transport in 1979. Obligingly, he expressed his views in a book *The Right Track*, published by the Conservative Political Centre in 1977. Much of what he wrote comprises unexceptionable generalisations: transport policy should recognise that 'nearly everyone needs access to public transport at some time'; it should take account of 'vital environmental interests'; it must take account of 'those employed in the transport industries'; it must aim at providing railway services 'with maximum efficiency and minimum cost'; it should result in 'improving transport in rural areas' and it should acknowledge 'that for millions without cars – in particular the elderly, the young and the housewife – the bus is essential for mobility'.

Fowler believed that these desirable objectives would best be achieved 'by giving the user maximum choice and allowing the maximum of competition'. For the bus industry his proposals were broadly the same as those contained in the 1979 Manifesto. He advocated the relaxation of traffic licensing regulations, the encouragement of locally organised minibus services, car and van sharing and the introduction of privately run commuter coaches. The complete denationalisation of the NFC was envisaged neither in *The Right Track* nor in the election Manifesto. In the former Fowler wrote: 'One proposal is for NFC and private companies to join together in joint venture projects. That is a useful advance. However, we want to go further than this. Another proposal is that some of the companies of the NFC should be sold to the private sector. Our preferred solution, however, is to seek private investment in the NFC, and provide a corporation similar (although not necessarily identical) in make up to BP.'[1]

His statements in the Commons when he was opposition spokesman were complimentary to the NFC and its chairman, Sir Dan Pettit. On 12 May 1976 he declared: 'The NFC is not run as some over-centralised nationalised industry. The corporation is broken down into a federated structure, and maximum independence is given to the separate companies . . . the management in NFC seems genuinely in no way to wish to avoid commercial realities.'[2]

Neither in March 1977 during the proceedings on the Transport (Financial Provisions) Bill, nor in early 1978, in the committee stage of the Transport Bill, 1978, did Fowler take up the frequent invitations from Ian Gow to endorse the selling off of the NFC. Regarding National Carriers Limited (NCL), a subsidiary of the NFC, he stated quite categorically that he was 'not advocating that it should go into the private sector.'[3]

II

The implementation of Tory transport policy after May 1979 was, in part, through ministerial decisions which did not require fresh legislation and in part through the passage of the Transport Acts of 1980, 1981, 1982 and 1983. Since the new legislation was to a considerable degree concerned with the transference to private ownership of undertakings formerly publicly owned it will be considered in Chapter 4. In the remaining part of this chapter policies concerned with BR will be examined.

An examination of BR's Annual Reports of the late 1970s and early 1980s, reveals that the Chairman and Board regarded the provision of adequate financial support from the government as of paramount importance for the successful operation of the railways. Major re-equipment took place under the Railway Modernisation Plan of 1955 when a rapid change from steam to diesel traction took place. By the later 1970s the Diesel Multiple Units (DMUs), diesel locomotives and much passenger rolling stock were nearing the end of their useful lives. If an acceptable standard of service to the public was to be maintained this essential replacement of nearly 'clapped out' equipment had to be carried out as a matter of utmost urgency. Sir Peter Parker's *Annual Report* of 1979 spotlighted the problem.

> The results of under-investment are now showing through in the deteriorating quality of service in parts of the system. We are replacing our assets at a slower rate than any other European railway and we are not investing in the new opportunities which railways and governments elsewhere see as necessary to the long term future of their countries. Through Transmark, our Queen's Award winning consultancy, we are hard at work on railway developments in 29 countries; at home we are running the railway very hard just to stand still.
>
> The signs are clear. Without increasing investment, standards will continue to drop at an ever accelerating rate and profitable freight traffic – £10 million to £15 million of it in 1979 – turned away. Only 16 locomotives were built in 1979, out of a total fleet of 2000 which needed replacement. The peak spending in the late 1950s and early 1960s is creating a bow wave of investment which is still building up ahead of us.
>
> Unless our investment levels are lifted by some 30 per cent just to replace worn out assets, the consequences will be lower standards of speed, frequency, comfort and reliability on rail services.

The Board reiterated its pleas for more government support for investment in 1981 in its publication *Rail Policy*: 'If BR is to take the path of progress we must also have a new financial regime. Under the prevailing system it has been impossible to undertake the long term investment programme which the railway requires. Financial ceilings, shortage of cash, the need to divert 'investment' money to meet shortfalls on current account have all militated against such a course.'

In the light of these unequivocal statements the questions need to be answered. Have British railways been starved of necessary capital and revenue support? Has BR been treated in a niggardly fashion by comparison with other European railway systems?

Before considering government financial assistance to BR it needs to be pointed out that this is on a small scale compared with that received by other leading European railways. A study conducted by economists of Leeds University with the help of some officers of BR, revealed that in 1977 71.2 per cent of BR's total costs were financed from its own revenues; only 28.8 per cent came from outside sources. Only the Swedish railways were more self-supporting, meeting 83.1 per cent of their total costs internally. (From 1983, however, the Swedish government increased its financial aid to its railways thus causing them to be less self-supporting than BR.) For the eight other national railway systems examined, dependence on help from state funds was substantially greater than was the case in the UK. Deutsche Bundesbahn (West Germany), for example, raised only 61.2 per cent of its finance internally. In France, SNCF could manage to meet only 55.5 per cent of its costs from its own revenues.[4] A later study comparing the performances of the French, West German and British railways in 1981 showed that the French and the Germans were still receiving a larger proportion of their total costs from Government grants than were the British.[5]

III

The greatest contribution to the finances of BR from government funds comes from the Public Service Obligations (PSO) grant. This had its origins, in a different guise, in Barbara Castle's Transport Act of 1968. By this date it had become apparent that the pruning of routes, services and equipment under the Beeching Plan of 1963 did not result in BR 'breaking even' as Dr. Beeching had anticipated. The Act therefore provided that where BR was able to demonstrate that a particular line was not commercially viable, the minister might make a grant to enable it to be kept open if it was meeting a social need. Under the Transport Act 1974 the payments which had been particularised for each line supported were now generalised as the PSO for the 'social railway'. A second element within the total PSO grant is the payment made by Passenger Transport Executives (PTEs) to BR for rail services which they require to be operated within their geographical boundaries. The remaining grants available to BR are much smaller. Under EEC Regulation 1192 of 1969, payments are made from Community funds for part of the cost of installation and maintenance of automatic level crossing barriers. Under Section 56 of the Transport Act, 1968, grants are available for capital inprovements in public transport, including rail and bus services. Section 57 of the same Act provided for research and development grants to be made available to public transport authorities. At the Derby research centre of BR these funds were used to develop the Advanced Passenger Train and other projects.[6]

Since January 1976 BR has been subject to an External Financing Limit (EFL) or ceiling of expenditure of funds from outside sources. Included within the limit are all moneys obtained from central and local government and the EEC. If the Board fails to keep within the EFL, i.e. if its External Financing Requirement (EFR) exceeds the EFL, the money it is obliged to borrow has to be paid back in the ensuing financial year and its PSO grant for that year is reduced by a corresponding amount until repayment is made.

Finally, since the early 1960s BR has been subjected to an annual investment limit. Apart from the special grants for level crossings, research and development and special items of capital replacement the Board has to finance its investment from its own revenues.[7]

If the onset of economic depression or the impact of strikes makes it impossible for the Board to keep within the PSO grant the shortfall has to be made good by cutting back investment. Nevertheless there are strict limits to such action. Failing to replace worn out track or rolling stock, with consequent deterioration in train services, will lead to declining revenues and a further aggravation of the Board's financial difficulties.

When comparison is made with the German and French railways BR has suffered from underlying government attitudes less sympathetic to its role and its financial requirements. Financial support from central government funds has been given grudgingly, as a regrettable necessity, rather than positively. On the continent, by contrast, railways are accepted as 'a vital element in the infrastructure of the economy'[8] and accordingly are given more generous, though not uncritical, support.

So when we compare the Tory government's record of financial support for Britain's railways with the performance of the preceding Labour administrations of Callaghan and Wilson we are starting from a none too generous base.

The keynote of the new government's approach to the railways, was struck in June 1979 when the EFL was cut from £730 million to £715 million. On 12 November that year Norman Fowler announced a further cut of £9 million to take effect in the financial year 1980-1. Just over a month later, however, he felt obliged to raise the limit 2.3 millions 'in recognition of the difficult trading conditions facing the Board's passenger operations'.[9]

Table 2 shows the Thatcher government's record of financial support for the railways over the four years.

As has been emphasised earlier in this chapter, it was already clear in 1979 that BR was withholding necessary investment in order to

Table 2
Government Financial Support for BR, 1979-82

	£s millions				Amount needed in 1982 to equal 1979 allocation in real terms	% excess or shortfall
	1979	1980	1981	1982		
Public Service Obligation (PSO)	543	635	812	804	798	+ 1
External Financing Limit (EFL)	715	750	920	897	1051	− 15
External Financing Requirement	707	790	959		−	−
Retail Price Index (1974 = 100)	219.6	265.7	295.8	322.9		+ 47

Source: CSO and BR *Annual Report and Accounts*

stay within the financial limits imposed by the government. Table 2 makes clear that the already inadequate EFL fell by 15 per cent over the four years 1979-82. To keep within this ever-tightening straight-jacket BR felt obliged to make even more drastic cuts in its invest-ment programme. The alarming extent of this curtailment is shown in Table 3.

Table 3
BR Investment Performance 1979-82

	£s millions				Amount needed in 1982 to equal 1979 allocation in real terms	% excess or shortfall
	1979	1980	1981	1982		
Investment ceiling	387	398	398	398	569	− 30
Total investment (BR + subsidiaries)	379	366	310	265	557	− 48
of which railways	290	309	263	242	426	− 43

Source: Report by Secretary of State for Transport (Derek Fowler) to British Rail Council, 30 April 1982

The Leeds University/BR investigating team discovered that BR capital expenditure in 1977 at £0.264 per train kilometre (at purchas-ing power exchange rates) was lower than that of any of the nine other European railway systems examined.[10] Since then BR invest-ment levels have fallen to little more than half the already disgrace-fully low levels of 1977. The contrast with France and Germany is seen most strikingly when plans for investment in 1983 are com-pared. Whereas BR's expected investment is £200 millions the Bundesbahn (West Germany) will allocate the equivalent of £1,300 millions and the SNCF (France) £900 millions, that is, in the one case over six times and in the other four and a half times the British figure.[11]

From Table 2 it might be concluded that the Goverment has done well in maintaining the real value of the PSO. However, the fact that between 1979-82 the sums allocated to the social railway have kept pace with inflation does not mean that the level of support is satis-factory. Expressed as a percentage of Gross National Product (GNP) the PSO grant in 1979 was nearly 12 per cent below the level of 1975. In 1977 only the Danish government devoted a smaller percentage of GNP to railways than did the British.[12]

IV

On his appointment as Secretary of State for Transport, Norman Fowler was immediately confronted with a terrible dilemma. As a young member of the new government he was keen to make a success of his job. Through his contact with the BR board and the trade unions he was soon presented with the case for an increase in the size of the PSO and the investment allowance. On the other hand one of the cornerstones of Thatcherite policy was a sharp reduction in government spending. To win favour with the Premier and the Treasury he needed to demonstrate success in pruning expenditure on the railways. Tom Ham, NUR President, 1981-83, watched his performance at meetings of the British Rail council where representatives of the Board and of the unions considered how to tackle the problems of the industry. At the first such meeting the new minister referred repeatedly to his civil service team for information and advice. At the second meeting he was fully the master of his brief. At the third he appeared won over to the case being made by the unions and the Board and was especially enthusiastic for the electrification programme.[13] In the meantime, however, the unsympathetic attitude towards public industries at No. 10 Downing Street, became intensified with the appointment of Professor Alan Walters as special economic adviser to the Premier. Thenceforward, until his promotion to head of the Department of Health and Social Security in 1981, Fowler was obliged to resort to delaying tactics with regard to the claims of BR and the unions, maintaining that progress in improving the performance of the railways depended primarily on the co-operation of the workforce in reducing 'over-manning', and conveniently overlooking the fact that it was well placed investment that could make the biggest contribution to increased productivity.

Inconvenient decisions were passed to the Board rather than shouldered by the minister. When the claim was made in a front page article in *The Guardian* on 7 November 1979 that there were plans for the closure of 900 route miles of the railway network, the minister assured MPs that the article was 'untrue'. He had 'no list of passenger services for closure' and he deplored the 'groundless anxiety caused by such inaccurate reports'. Later during the same question time, however, he admitted that, the week before, the PSO had been cut by £22 millions. He also admitted that Sir Peter Parker had sent him 'an option for closing some services'. Although he (Fowler) had 'made it clear that there was no case for a further round of Beeching cuts' it was 'obviously . . . a matter for BR to decide how it should live within the cash limits.'[14] The minister was clearly taken aback by the furore created by the suggestion that some hundreds of miles of railway might be closed. Two days after being subjected to the above mentioned barrage of questions on the subject, he wrote to Sir Peter Parker to inform him that the option of closing 40 passenger services, included in BR's 1979 Corporate Review was unacceptable to the Government[15] Neither the Chairman of the Board nor the minister was keen to endorse any substantial cuts in rail services. Back in October 1976 the Chairman rejected the Beeching thesis that you could achieve a viable railway by 'hammering away at the feeder lines'.[16] But he was being driven into a corner. The minister knew that one of the strongholds of support for the Conservative Party was the commuter belt of the South East. Not for him the odium of being responsible for cutting commuter – or other – rail services. But on the same day on which he suggested that it was Sir Peter Parker, Chairman of the nationalised railways, who was threatening the commuters' lifelines to the capital, he announced a substantial reduction in the grant – the PSO – which kept branch lines and commuter services open.

V

For more than a decade BR has been well aware that the UK was falling behind other industrial nations in its railway electrification programme. By 1977 only 20.8 per cent of BR route miles of track has been electrified whereas the French had electrified 28 per cent, the West Germans 37.2 per cent, the Italians 52 per cent, the Norwegians 57.5 per cent, the Netherlands 61.0 per cent and the Swedes 61 per cent of their systems. In 1978 Sir Peter Parker went to William Rodgers, Secretary of State for Transport in the Callaghan Labour government with a shopping list of railway lines to electrify. Satisfied that there was a prima facie case for the programme, the minister set up a joint British Rail/Department of Transport inquiry. No less than forty organisations, including the Association of County Councils, the Association of Municipal Authorities, pressure groups, such as the British Road Federation and Transport 2000, professional groups such as the Institute of Electrical Engineers, conservation societies and trade unions, gave written and/or oral evidence. The NUR presented its case for railway electrification in a printed booklet of 16 pages. The Final Report *Review of Main Line Electrification* appeared under the joint signatures of Sir Peter Parker and Norman Fowler early in 1981. The steering group, which examined practice in overseas countries, as well as hearing evidence from interested parties within the UK, comprised representatives of the Treasury, the Department of Energy and other government departments. Despite the fact that the Department of Transport is by no means noted for a pro-rail bias, the Report concluded that 'a substantial programme of main line electrification would be financially worthwhile'.[17] It was estimated that all the larger electrification options would produce a real rate return of about 11 per cent. Endorsement of a major programme would have the benefits of reducing the country's dependence on oil and boosting manufacturing industry, since commitment to a large domestic programme would be likely to increase overseas, as well as home market, orders. A strong case was made for a strategic decision to be taken covering policy over a 20 or 30 year period. This would secure commitment from the supply industry, labour and management. The policy of ad hoc approval of individual projects was not favoured since it created uncertainty about future business prospects and precluded the long term deployment of a skilled work force.[18] Once expensive capital equipment and specially trained labour had been mobilised it made sense to employ them on a long term programme.

Even before the publication of the above *Review* Norman Fowler was on record for supporting a programme of railway electrification. Answering questions in the Commons on 20 June 1979 he said 'I accept that there is a strong case for electrification.'[19] When the minister met the members of the British Rail Council for the first time in the ministry's Marsham Street headquarters on 29 January 1981 he conceded that 'many of the problems of the industry were the inheritance of lack of investment over a long period of time', but he made no promise about electrification.[20] At the next meeting of the Council on 22 June 1981 he said that the government had accepted a commitment to electrify certain routes with a profitable future, profitability being identified in terms of the freight and inter city traffic; but he mentioned nothing more specific than that. In the Commons on that day he was even less encouraging. He said he was 'not prepared to give an unconditional commitment to the electrification of an extensive network'.[21] For the first of a number of times the Board was asked to go back and re-work its sums. (The consensus of opinion at Rail House regarding the delays in 1981 and 1982 is that the most influential members of the government, particularly the Prime Minister, were seeking to find reasons why no more money should be spent and that as soon as BR had completed one set of calculations and presented these to the minister they were told, after some delay, to make further calculations based on different assumptions regarding the volume of traffic.)

On 18 March 1982 the Board sent the new Secretary of State, David Howell, a fully worked out scheme for East Coast main line electrification; but the members of the British Rail Council were told three months later that Sir Peter Parker was still awaiting a reply. If the minister needed new evidence to strengthen his case against the obstructionists at No. 10 Downing Street he was given it in the *Report* of the House of Commons Select Committee on Transport published on 12 May. BR described this as 'a positive endorsement of the case for electrification'. The Committee found that it was 'incumbent on the government to come to a decision on the Board's proposals'. Meanwhile, however, the opposition to the electrification plans within the cabinet and at No. 10 was strengthened by the argument that the 17 days of ASLEF strikes in January-February 1982 had lost BR important freight and passenger traffic and that therefore the estimates of traffic on which the plans for electrification were based, were outmoded. With Alan Walters pouring cold water on investment plans for the railways it is a matter for conjecture whether even without the strikes an imaginative long-term plan of electrification would have been approved. There is no doubt that the strikes made it less, rather than more, likely that any such plan would see the light of day.

The government's approach to electrification has been, to say the least, unimaginative. Viewed in a less favourable light its policy has been deadening and obstructive. Its unimaginative character is shown by its failure to take sufficiently into account the traffic *generating* effect of a new and exciting means of transport. The boost to passenger revenues brought by the electrification of the Euston-Liverpool line was well beyond expectations. The introduction of the High Speed Train on the Western Region brought a 35 per cent increase of passenger traffic in two years. Much more consideration, also, should be given to the importance of the morale of the workforce. Nothing would do more to reassure railway workers that they are employed in an industry which the government sees as important and has an assured future than an unequivocal pronoucement from the Secretary of State that a long term plan of electrification had been approved.

Compared with this need, the government's announcement, on 3 November 1982, that it had approved BR's proposals for the electrification of the line from London, through Harwich, to Norwich, at a cost, over the years to 1987, of £60 million had a minimal impact. It reflected that same piecemeal approach which the Final Report of the *Review of Main Line Electrification* had found so unsatisfactory.

The reduction in the real value of BR's investment programme by forty-three per cent over the years 1979-82 and the Thatcher government's shilly-shallying for over two years on railway electrification was bound to have disastrous consequences for the work load of the railway workshops whose problems will be examined in chapter eight.

4
Privatisation and Its Consequences

If the Trade Descriptions Act, 1968, applied to legislation there would be a strong case for prosecuting the Thatcher government for misleading traders and the travelling public about the Transport Acts of 1980, 1981 and 1982. The label on the package in each case was 'Transport Act'; the contents, for the most part, suggest 'Asset Stripping Act' as a more appropriate title. A close examination of the legislation and the record of proceedings in parliament reveals that the government's motivation was ideological. The leading objectives were to reduce the public sector borrowing requirement, roll back the frontiers of state-owned industry and sell off the most profitable parts of some of the nation's most important public enterprises to a limited number of private investors. Incidental advantages which, it was believed, would spring from reducing the size of the public sector were the discrediting of nationalised industry, as compared with private enterprise, and the better disciplining of labour employed in the public service. Shorn of some of its more promising or profitable subsidiaries, the Board of British Rail would be under even stronger pressure to extract more productivity from the work force.

The Transport Acts must be seen in the context of the government's policy of across the board de-nationalisation. In the Queen's speech of 20 November 1980 it was stated that measures would be taken 'to reduce the scope of state industry and increase competition', but the process had been begun at least a year earlier. The tactics of de-nationalisation varied from industry to industry and even within different sectors of the same industry, but three principal approaches were adopted. Where a state corporation was in a healthy economic condition, the entire enterprise was converted into a company under the Companies Acts and the shares sold off to private investors. The outstanding example of this approach in the transport industry was the conversion of the National Freight Corporation (NFC) into the National Freight Company under the Transport Act, 1980. The second case is where an enterprise as a whole is not profitable, but important parts of it are; the tactics then being to sell off the profitable, or potentially profitable, subsidiaries, leaving the main organisation under the old management but, clearly, in a less viable situation. The sale of the hotels in British Transport Hotels, a subsidiary of the British Railways Board, under the Transport Act, 1981, is an important example of the use of this tactic. The third possible line of attack, exemplified in the telecommunication and electricity supply industries, is to encourage new private enterprise competitors. The National Bus Company has been subjected to such an onslaught under the terms of the Transport Act, 1980.[1]

The underlying assumption of the assault on the nationalised industries was that they are vast, monopolistic, inefficient and unprofitable. However, gas, electricity and coal are, at least in some areas, competitive with each other. British Rail is subject to the fiercest competition from private road hauliers, from the National Bus Company's, and other companies', express road passenger services and from domestic air flights. It is simply untrue that most state undertakings have been unprofitable. Early in 1980 a survey conducted by *The Economist* found that only two out of 18 state companies were currently in the red.[2]

The campaign against public enterprises, waged with such determination since May 1979 had as its objective the switching of *profitable* undertakings from public to private ownership and control. Although it was asserted that under private enterprise the businesses would be more efficiently run, this was certainly not the prime motive for the changes made, as it is hoped to show in the remainder of this chapter.

II

When he introduced the Thatcher government's first Transport Bill in the House of Commons on 27 November, 1979, Norman Fowler,

Secretary of State for Transport, claimed that the Bill's purpose was 'to increase freedom of choice for the public, to provide a better range of transport services and to take the state out of activities which it should not be in'. The Bill was in two main parts: Part I concerned road passenger services and Part II road haulage, with special reference to the NFC. The minister claimed that the Road Traffic Act, 1930, under which route licensing of bus and coach services was maintained, had outlived its usefulness. The aim of the Act was 'not to encourage operators but to prevent them', with the result that 'there were now fewer passengers and fewer services at increasing cost to the public, not only through fares but through rates and taxes'. The Transport Bill, therefore, removed all restrictions, except those concerning safety, on express bus and coach services covering over thirty miles between stops, and on excursions and tours. It also did away with all restrictions on car sharing. Under the Labour government's Transport Act, 1978, it was lawful to advertise a car-share on notice boards in churches, clubs, works or factories. The new Bill extended this freedom to newspapers and local newsagents. The minister placed great hopes on this reform. If only a small proportion of the 130,000 cars entering London in the morning rush hour offered to share their cars, he said, there would be 'a reduction in road congestion and a saving of energy'. To encourage the growth of local bus services the traffic commissioners were always to grant route licenses to new applicants unless they were satisfied that to do so would be against the public interest. As a further stimulus to the provision of local bus services the minister was given the power – it was to be an enabling Act – to designate certain 'trial areas' in the UK where all restrictions on licensing would be removed. Even before the Bill was debated in the Commons, the minister was reported (*Surveyor* magazine, 29 November 1979) to be in negotiation about the creation of 'trial areas' with ten county councils: Buckinghamshire, Devon, East Sussex, Kent, Lincolnshire, Norfolk, Northamptonshire, Nottinghamshire, Oxfordshire and Suffolk. Apart from East Sussex and Buckinghamshire, all were counties characterised by an exceptionally low level of support for public transport. In fact only three 'trial areas' eventually materialised.

The second part of the Act provided for the transference of the NFC, with all fifty of its subsidiary companies, from large concerns like Pickfords and National Carriers Ltd, to much smaller road haulage, waste disposal and parcel delivery firms – from public to private ownership. In his speech introducing the Bill, Norman Fowler revealed that the government had no intention of retaining any financial interest in the NFC's successor. This disclosure came as a surprise to MPs. The decision to sell off the organisation in its entirety must have been taken abruptly and, one suspects, under direction from the 'Think Tank'. As late as 22 August 1979 Norman Fowler was still only talking about disposing of 'a majority share-holding' of the new company's assets. The minister claimed that the change to private ownership was necessary as the NFC lacked the commerical freedom and opportunities for raising capital open to private firms.[3]

Albert Booth, from the opposition front bench, gave a very different interpretation of the purposes of the Bill and of its likely effects. It would, he asserted, 'pose a serious threat of damage, possibly irreparable, to bus services in many parts of the country'. The expansion of bus services based on competition between private operators existed 'only in a Tory dream world'. The reality of experience was that 'when unregulated competition is tried it results in a serious deterioration in public services to the point at which many parts of the country are left without any bus services at all'. The reason for the decline in bus services and bus usage had nothing to do with the licensing system. It was the result of widespread car ownership and the inability of either public or private bus operators to make a profit on many of the routes. It was not true, as the minister asserted, that the licensing system was unduly restrictive. During 1977-8 in the Northern traffic area, for example, 792 licences were granted, of which 177 were new ones. Only five applications were refused. It was much the same in the Eastern traffic area where 139 of the 841 licences granted in the same time span were new ones and only three applications were refused. Under the new law applicants would not seek licences to operate on loss making routes: they would compete in the profitable ones. He described the likely action of the existing major operators – the National Bus Company concerns – as follows: 'If the major operator on the route is using it to cross-subsidise another route, he must then decide whether to compete on his profitable route by reducing his fares and abandoning the route that he is cross-subsidising. He is almost certain to take

38

this course. He will fight, not to stay in the area where he is losing, but to stay in the profitable area.'[4]

Ken Weetch, the moderate Labour MP for Ipswich, said that although the government had stressed the competitive principle, it scarcely applied to what was proposed in the case of the NFC which controlled only 10 per cent of the road haulage market (though its share of the market and its profits were increasing). In fact it was the subsidy principle which had been applied. To give the new privately owned company an enhanced opportunity for success, a subsidy of £100m was proposed, £58.7m of which was to wipe out the NFC's commencing debt and the remaining £41.3m to cancel outstanding loans. UK taxpayers would lose not only the £100m paid out by government but also £8m in interest revenue annually, simply in order that private investors could be offered an attractive bargain. He said that none of the arguments put forward by spokesmen from the government front bench had anything to do with transport, the objective being simply to diminish publicly owned, and increase privately owned, capital.[5]

III

On 1 July 1980, the day after the Transport Bill received royal assent, Norman Fowler issued a press notice in which he stated that the new Act would 'reshape the system in ways specifically designed to benefit the travelling public' and that 'it would encourage ... new operators to come forward, especially in the rural areas'. On the other hand Albert Booth had said that there would be 'a serious threat of damage, possibly irreparable to bus services in many parts of the country'. They could not both be right. It is therefore worth examining the evidence of what has happened since the Act came into force on 6 October 1980.

Early in 1983 the Bus and Coach Council noted: 'Thus far, there has been little response to the changes as far as conventional rural bus services are concerned. The hopes of the legislators have not been realised because the market has invariably not justified the commercial investment.'[6] In explanation, it has been suggested, that running a smaller bus of the type used on many rural routes is less cost effective than is sometimes imagined. Drivers' wages do not vary with the size of the vehicle and the bigger bus has a far longer life than the smaller one, thus, to some extent, offsetting its higher initial capital cost.

Immediately the Act came into force there was a rush of operators wanting to take advantage of the relaxation of licensing controls on express services (with 30 miles or more between stops). The view of the Lord Shepherd, Chairman of the National Bus Company, was that privatisation of coaching operations 'must necessarily impact on the remainder'.[7] In 1981 the NBC made an all out effort to beat off the challenge of the private express coach operators appearing on the scene after October 1980, by expanding its own express coaching services. In this it was highly successful. Its express coach mileage increased from 46 million in 1980 to 62 million in 1981, an increase of 35 per cent, while the number of express coach passengers it carried rose from 9.2 million to 14 million, or by 43 per cent.[8] In the first six months of operation of the Transport Act, 1980, 29 private coach operators contemplated exploiting the London commuter market. Twenty of these actually ran services but only six were still functioning in November 1981, just over a year after the Act came into force.[9] The NBC had largely beaten off its challengers. The irony of the situation was that an Act designed to increase private operators participation and profits had given a mighty boost to the profits of the publicly owned undertaking. However its success was not achieved without cost. In order to meet the challenge of competition on the lucrative express services it cut back on its less profitable country routes. Within the twelve months its route mileage fell by eight per cent. This was broadly equivalent to the total operations of a 1000 vehicle bus undertaking.[10] As its chairman commented in his Foreword to the 1981 *Annual Report*, 'little consolation' could be drawn from 'a cut of that magnitude'; but the change was imperative if the company was to meet – as it did – the more stringent financial targets set by the Secretary of State.

An important outcome of this battle between the coach operators on the express routes was that many thousands of passengers, including commuters, were induced, by the cheaper fares, to desert British Rail, which suffered a loss of revenue in 1981, estimated at £10 millions, from this cause. To this extent BR was less able to live within the PSO grant. The Minister, by creating new competition in road passenger services, was aggravating the problem of BR's finances.

There is little doubt that the new operators' and NBC's concentration on the express services led to a deterioration in the extent and frequency of the country bus services. What happened in West Cumbria is a case in point. In the Whitehaven area a private company, Yeowarts, applied for a road service licence for well-frequented routes in the town and neighbourhood already served by the buses of Cumberland Motor Services, a subsidiary of the NBC. Initially the application was for services to operate only at times of peak demand, with no Sunday service, no early morning and evening services and no services on early closing day. The Traffic Commissioners rejected the application and their decision was upheld by the Inspector appointed by the Secretary of State. However, Mr. Howell over-rode his Inspector's ruling and allowed Yeowarts to run its buses. The response of Cumberland Motor Services was precisely as Albert Booth had predicted would happen in such circumstances; it concentrated on beating off the challenge on its most profitable routes and cut its costs by withdrawing services from five of its surrounding rural routes.[11] Meanwhile, in the House of Commons, an irate D. Campbell-Savours, MP for Workington, pilloried the minister whose actions had deprived many villagers in his constituency of their only form of public transport.[12]

There was no sudden burgeoning of private bus companies in the 'Trial Areas' designated under the Transport Act, 1980. After a small bus operator in the Norwich area went into liquidation there was little further talk of new privately run services being started. In Herefordshire, operators were freed from any control by Traffic Commissioners, only to be subjected to a much more rigid control by the county authorities. This was a negation of the purposes of an Act intended to promote free competition between operators.[13]

Car sharing, on which the minister placed great store, has been a flop. One would have imagined that large work places would be ideal for its introduction. And what better place than the Department of Enviroment and Transport headquarters in Marsham Street, London? When the Act came into operation Michael Heseltine, the Secretary of State, waived an earlier edict that the Department's house magazine *Environment and Transport World*, should pay its way, advertisers being charged commercial rates. Free advertising of car sharing proposals was permitted. The column had ten advertisers in December 1980; by April 1981 there were only two

and by June of that year only one. One South coast resort newspaper which tried to cash in on car sharing in October 1980 established a new classified advertisement section; but the maximum
number of adverts it secured was four. In one case the advertiser
wished to share his car with an attractive woman. In another there
was appeal to share in the cost of running a Rolls Royce.[14] More seriously, there are considerable difficulties in establishing a coinci-
dence of travel times between users from different households.
According to the Transport and Road Research Laboratory, 'it
takes a doubling of motoring costs to achieve a ten per cent increase
in car occupancy.[15]

By 1981, under the terms of the Transport Acts of 1978 and 1980,
there were 174 post bus services operating in the UK, most of them in
Scotland. These are a boon to thousands of people living in remote
areas, and, indeed, the Swiss example should have been followed
much earlier. A considerable number of Community Bus services
including, for example, the Fellrunner Community Bus linking Carlisle and Penrith with remote Cumbrian villages, have been established by local initiative. These are sometimes run with the help of
the local NBC subsidiary and sometimes operate quite independently.

Regrettably, the sum total of all new ventures, including community buses, car sharing and post buses, does not add up to the loss
of regular stage coach services which has sprung from the primacy
given to commercial profit rather than public service. What has happened in the Southdown Bus Company area of Sussex and parts of
Hampshire may serve to illustrate the trends. Since 1955 the company has withdrawn services from 34 villages. In 1983 six of these
villages were served by independent operators, five had community
buses, three had postal buses, one had a railway station and two
were occasionally served by a special ramblers' bus. The other 17 villages had no public transport service at all.[16]

Norman Fowler declared that the 'litmus test' of the success or
failure of his Act would be whether the travelling public benefited
by the changes it introduced. Undoubtedly many thousands of commuters and inter-city passengers were pleased to take advantage of
the cheaper fares arising from the competition in express coach services. However, public transport was already available on those
routes in 1979. Its users had a legitimate complaint about the high

fares they were charged. But the remedy lay in government raising the level of support to public transport to something like that given by other European governments to their public transport services. To those country dwellers who since 1979 have lost all public transport services the Fowler 'remedy' must be seen as worse than the disease. The Transport Act of 1980 has resulted in a decline in cross subsidisation which in many cases exceeded the revenue support grants from county councils.[18] The phasing out of the new bus subsidy by 1984, decreed by Norman Fowler in 1979, and the cuts in central government grants to local authorities will combine to squeeze out still more of the unremunerative but socially essential local services. The Bus and Coach Council estimated that in 1979 the new bus grant amounted to some 20 per cent of external financial assistance to the industry.[19]

By 22 February 1982 the publicly owned National Freight Corporation had become the privately owned National Freight Company. That the business was sold off as a single undertaking and not split up and sold piecemeal was largely due to the initiative of leading managers of the old corporation who raised sufficient funds among themselves and had sufficient support from the staff to persuade the minister to accept the plan of a consortium. The total selling price was £53½m, most of which was provided by a group of major UK banks, but over £4m of equity shares, 82.5 per cent of the equity stake, was provided by the managers and about one third of the 26,000 employees of the old corporation. The bank syndicates subscribed the remaining 17.5 per cent of the equity stake in nonvoting shares. The government transferred £47m of the total purchase price of £53½m to the NFC pension fund. Peter Thompson, the Chairman, was enthusiastic about the change. 'We had a vision', he said, 'We believed, as we do today, that by creating a company controlled and owned mainly by employees, we are launching a new kind of industrial enterprise.'[20] The minister was equally delighted. 'With this sale', David Howell said, 'a major road haulage company is transferred in good running order to the private sector where it belongs.'[21]

In using the words 'where it belongs' Howell was making a sweeping assumption. There had been a substantial publicly owned element in the road haulage industry for 34 years. The NFC was no lame duck. Its profits rose from £4m in 1976 to £13.5m in 1977 and £20.1m in 1978. Roger Moate, Conservative MP for Faversham declared 'its management is first class and its relationship with the work force superb'. No good *transport* reason was offered for making the change in ownership. On the other hand, the case for keeping the successful undertaking under public ownership, if only to act as a yardstick against which to check the efficiency of privately run road haulage businesses, was a strong one.

IV

Before the Transport Act, 1980, was fully operational Norman Fowler was busy seeking out possibilities of transferring the ownership of some of BR's subsidiaries to private investors. He soon discovered in the BR Board's concern to increase investment in Hotels, Seaspeed, and so on, a convenient lever to prise apart some of the Board's important assets. Even as early as 1977, under the Callaghan government, Sir Peter Parker was exploring the possibility of injecting private capital into BR subsidiaries without the Board having to surrender its majority shareholding or abandoning its managerial control. Reasons for seeking this innovation were set forth in an issue of *Railtalk*, the Board's publicity handout: 'The main reason for the policy . . . is that the businesses in question are not able to expand and develop themselves while they remain subject to public sector financial constraints. There is only a very limited amount of money which can be made available through the Treasury and most of this has to be used by the main railway business. The result is that desirable investment in some of the subsidiaries has had to be postponed . . . One consequence will be that the whole of the available investment finance can be directed towards the rail business.'[23]

The Board was forced to think along these lines because it is prevented by the External Financing Limit from obtaining loans or making leasing arrangements to meet current or future needs. The Tories had not included in their general election manifesto any proposals for selling off BR subsidiaries, but once in office they exploited the Board's predicament to the full. The trap in which BR was caught was spotlighted by Julie Hayes: 'The Board's intention of gaining access to private finance to enable the subsidiaries to flourish, while still under the Board, backfired. The government seized upon this opportunity to argue the Board's case that private capital was needed for its subsidiaries, but went further than the Board and argued that it was not possible to inject private capital without wresting control of the subsidiaries from the Board.'[24]

In the background there was strong pressure on Norman Fowler to reduce BR's dependence on the National Loans Fund. Both the Prime Minister and the Treasury were demanding a reduction in government borrowing. The millionaire banker, Philip Shelbourne, was chiefly responsible for drafting plans for stripping some of BR's assets. Fowler's announcement in the House of Commons, on 20 February 1980, that the government was considering the setting up of a holding company came after very little consultation with BR; but pressure was put on its chairman to draw up detailed plans even though he was sceptical of any plans for such an organisation if it meant that profits went to private shareholders rather than the Board.[25] Within a week of Fowler's announcement, Michael Bosworth, Deputy Chairman of BR, wrote to the *Guardian* that the Board had 'no plans to sell off any of its hotels or ferry services' and that it was 'not in the hiving off game'.[26]

A further preliminary statement was made by Fowler to the Commons on 14 July 1980 when he revealed that private capital was to be introduced into Sealink, British Transport Hotels and the non-operational properties of BR. When questioned about these plans he assured the House: 'The proceeds will go to British Rail. We have made that absolutely clear'.[27] However, what did become absolutely clear to members seven months later, in the second reading debate on the Bill, was that although the proceeds of the sale would go to BR, the External Financing Limit would be reduced by a corresponding amount. In July MPs had been led to believe that the proposed sale would give the Board more funds to invest in the railways; in January 1981, it was evident that immediately after the sale it would be no better off, whilst in the long run it would be worse off without the subsidiaries' contribution to group profits.[28]

The Transport Bill which was introduced on 12 December 1980 and passed its second reading in the Commons on 13 January 1981 made arrangements for the selling off of Sealink UK Ltd; BR Hovercraft; British Transport Hotels and the non-operational property of BR. Part II provided for the reconstitution of the wholly publicly owned British Transport Docks Board as a partly privately owned

Associated British Ports. Part III abolished the National Ports Council, which had been set up under the Harbours Act 1964, to advise the government on ports policy, Part IV introduced new measures designed to improve road safety.

In the second reading debate in the Commons Norman Fowler claimed that the proposals in the Bill had 'the full support of the British Railways Board' an assertion which was challenged by opposition MPs. The Rt. Hon. Donald Stewart, Scottish Nationalist MP for the Western Isles, said that few people would believe that Fowler's agreement with Sir Peter Parker 'was anything other than the type of agreement made between Dick Turpin and the people whom he waylaid'.[29] Albert Booth, Labour's front bench spokesman, said that BR Board had consented to the proposed sale of assets on the assumption that it would be allowed to keep the proceeds and that the EFL would be increased to a corresponding extent. This assumption had proved unwarranted since the Secretary of State had made it clear that whatever money was realised by the sale would be *deducted* from the EFL.[30]

In justification of the Bill Fowler pointed out that the subsidiaries had been starved of capital. The introduction of private investment would 'increase the scope and unlock the potential' of these companies. However, if they were to escape public sector constraints the Board would have to surrender control over them. (What he conveniently overlooked was the fact that when the state-owned corporation, British Airways, was converted into a Companies Act company under the Civil Aviation Act in 1980, its EFL was not reduced when a *minority* of its shares were sold to the public, the state retaining a majority holding.) He said that it was the government's intention, once the BR subsidiaries had been hived off, 'to see employees shareholdings schemes established so that those who work in the business would have a commitment and stake in their future success'.[31] Barry Sheerman, Labour MP for Huddersfield, East, saw employee share ownership as ' . . . the old conjuring trick . . . An illusion works on the principle that one focuses one's attention on . . . something perhaps a little titillating and exciting – and at the same time the real trick is being performed slightly out of one's vision . . . The government are setting up the sale of these companies . . . to large institutions . . . At the same time the under-secretary and his colleagues will be pointing to the marvellous idea of wider share ownership. While attention is fixed on wider share ownership, the real investment of the people – long term investment in these public utilities – is being snaffled away.'[32]

John Prescott, Labour MP for Hull, East, warned that BR would be under pressure from government to sell off its assets. When the Board pleaded with the Secretary of State to increase the EFL he would reply 'If it is so bad, sell off those profitable golfing hotels.' That would be the way 'the cat would get skinned'. Because BR was 'desperate for capital' the assets would be sold at a very unfavourable time, in the depths of an economic depression. The taxpayer would lose and the private investor would gain.[33]

It was not possible for Norman Fowler to make any case for the fragmentation of the British Transport Docks Board (BTDB), an organisation which had been set up under the Transport Act, 1962. In fact, in his second reading speech on the Bill he praised its management quite unstintingly. It was a highly successful undertaking. Between 1970 and 1979 its turnover rose from £34m to £134m; profits, before interest, rose from £4.5m to £27m; the return on capital grew from 3.5 per cent to 15.1 per cent and its reserves increased from £8m to £86m. It was entirely self-financing and a pace setter in new technology in the industry. A quarter of the UK's seaborne trade passed through its 19 ports. On 21 July 1980, six months before the Transport Bill came before parliament, Fowler announced that the BTDB would be replaced by a two tier organisation. Investors would be invited to buy shares in a Companies Act holding company which would control a reconstituted docks board (subsequently named Associated British Ports) as if it were a wholly owned subsidiary. The government would take a 51 per cent shareholding in the new organisation which would remain as one unit. What Walter Johnson, Labour MP for Derby South, said of this part of the Bill could scarcely be challenged. The reason why the government was allowing private capital in the undertaking had 'nothing to do with efficiency or profitability. It had to do with private capital being allowed to cream off parts of a profitable public enterprise, and the Conservative ideology of rolling back the public sector.'[34]

Despite the determined opposition of NUR sponsored MPs in Standing Committee E, the Bill was pushed through, the government using the guillotine to cut short discussion. It was enacted on 31 July 1981.

V

Railway involvement in the ownership and running of hotels has a very long history. When the railways were being opened up under private enterprise it was natural that the companies should at one and the same time seek to meet the needs of the travelling public and to profit by them by opening up hotels at important termini and junctions. The Great Western Royal Hotel at Paddington, founded as early as 1854, and the Caledonian and North British Hotels in Edinburgh are well known examples of this type of enterprise. Other railway hotels were of the 'country house' type, such as the Welcombe Hotel at Stratford-on-Avon; the 'golfing' type, such as the Turnberry Hotel in Ayrshire; and the 'racegoers' type such as the Adelphi at Liverpool – though this hotel was also widely used by passengers boarding the transatlantic steamships. When the old railway lines were grouped into four main line companies under the Railways Act, 1921, the propriety of the new companies' retention of the hotels was never questioned by a predominantly Tory parliament. When the Transport Act, 1947, brought railways under public ownership the hotels (together with the catering establishments) were included under the umbrella of the publicly owned British Transport Commission. Even when the Macmillan government abolished the BTC under the Transport Act, 1962, and carried through a major reorganisation of public transport undertakings the 29 former railway hotels were kept together in public ownership in British Transport Hotels (BTH), established in 1963. Throughout the 18 years of its existence BTH made a positive contribution to the finances of BR, though the profits it earned varied from a peak in the boom year 1970 to an all time low in the depression year 1979. Profits as a percentage of turnover in the 1970s were as follows:[35]

1970	8.0	1973	3.6	1976	4.2	1979	0.9
1971	7.9	1974	3.5	1977	5.5		
1972	6.8	1975	4.3	1978	3.3		

Had successive governments taken a more constructive view of the EFL, recognising that funds earmarked, for example, for hotel modernisation, were an investment and not a 'dole', the BTH establishments would have been able to contribute even more to the group finances. The success of the Golden Rail scheme, the fifth largest package tour business in the UK, showed what could be achieved, even with meagre resources.

In an endeavour to keep control of the injection of private capital into its subsidiaries BR established, and owned, BR Investments Ltd. (BRIL), a holding company to which the businesses of BTH, Sealink UK, BR Hovercraft and certain property assets were transferred in November 1980. Subsequent negotiations for the transfer to private ownership of the subsidiaries were conducted through BRIL.

In the negotiations for the disposal of the 29 BTH hotels the government's primary concern was to reduce BR's dependence on the National Loans Fund – the proceeds of the sales would go towards a reduction of the EFL. BR's main objectives were to retain a financial interest in the new companies and to release the hotels in large groups rather than in single establishments. The immediate concern of the trade unions (principally the NUR and TSSA) was to protect the working conditions and living standards of the employees.

On 22 June 1981 the first important transaction was completed when three Scottish hotels, the Gleneagles in Perthshire and the Caledonian and North British in Edinburgh were acquired by a new private sector company, Gleneagles Hotels Ltd., for £13.5m. BR subscribed to one third of the shares and appointed one of the directors but had no effective control over the new establishment. Although, by the terms of the sale all existing conditions of service of the employees were protected, the NUR also invested in some of the shares as some sort of guarantee that these conditions would be kept. Later in an attempt to keep most of the hotels in one organisation and ownership a BTH management consortium, led by BR Hotels group managing director, Peter Land, made a deal with BR on 7 October 1982 for the sale of ten of the hotels for £20.5m. However, since the sum on offer was £3.5m. short of the independent valuation of the properties, the transaction was vetoed by David Howell. Then the consortium tried again with an offer of £38m. for 19 hotels, only to meet with Howell's further veto on the grounds that the package was worth £50m. Faced with this rebuff, BR put 21 hotels up for sale by public tender for completion by 31 March 1983. By 25 February 1983 tenders were accepted for ten of the 21, Mr David Barclay, who acquired the Charing Cross, the Great Western Royal and the Grosvenor for £17m, producing the lion's share of the

£25.8m raised. £7m of the remainder was paid by the Batchshire, a sudsidiary of the US group Sea Containers Corporation, for five of BHT's most distinctive hotels, the Royal Station in York, the Welcombe in Stratford, the Tregenna Castle in St. Ives, the Turnberry in Ayrshire and the Lochalsh in Ross-shire. A week later eight more, less prestigious, hotels were sold to Virani, one of several groups of Asian hotel businesses, for the much smaller sum of £4.6m. At the same time ten year leases of ten London properties, including the Great Eastern Hotel at Liverpool Street and the Great Northern at King's Cross, were bought by executives John Tee and Derek Plant of BTH. On 25 March 1983, the Midland Hotel, Manchester, was purchased by the Greater Manchester Council. Thereafter only two BTH hotels were unaccounted for; the Queens at Leeds and the North British at Glasgow. By the end of March it became apparent that the total proceeds of the sale of hotels (excluding the three prestige Scottish ones sold in June 1981) would fall short of the £38m offer made in the winter of 1982-3 by the BTH consortium. Had that offer been accepted much of the fragmentation of ownership would have been avoided.[36]

The hotel industry is an outstanding case where the operation of market forces does *not* ensure its workers decent conditions of employment.[37] A large part of the labour force is casually employed and non-unionised. In 1979 average gross weekly earnings were lower than any other industry in the country. The exception was to be found in BTH where a union shop agreement became effective from 31 December 1976 after many years in which NUR negotiators struggled to persuade management of its merits. Four years later BTH employees enjoyed substantially better pay, shorter hours, longer holidays and better sick pay arrangements than did those who worked for other hotel companies. BTH had become a trailblazer for improved working conditions in hotel employment. Although by the terms of sale of BTH hotels, existing employees conditions of service were guaranteed, the future had its uncertainties because of the generally high rate of turnover of staff. In Gleneagles Hotels Ltd., for instance, newly recruited staff were not given the same fringe benefits as were enjoyed by those already on the books. The American and Asian owned companies that acquired some of the station hotels were less friendly to the idea of union recognition. The disadvantage experienced by the unions in 1983 was that instead of negotiating conditions of employment with one employer owning 29 hotels they were confronted with up to a dozen of them. Separate negotiations would be required with each.

Just as it was a natural development for the nineteenth-century railway companies to branch out into hotel ownership so was it fully understandable that the companies which served ports should wish to promote steamship undertakings. The Chester and Holyhead and London and South Western railways had their ferry services from the 1840s. The South Eastern Railway provided cross channel steamship services from 1853. These arrangements continued largely undisturbed under the Railways Act 1921, and the Transport Act 1947. The right of the railways to own and run shipping services was not challenged until the Thatcher Government appeared and, under the Transport Act 1981, planned the transfer to private ownership of Sealink, BR's shipping subsidiary. In December 1980 Keith Wickenden, MP, Chairman of European Ferries, one of Sealink's main competitors, announced that his company would bid for a controlling interest in the BR concern. There was an immediate and forceful response from Michael Bosworth, Sealink's Chairman. 'It was an opportunist bid at a time of market depression', he said. 'The whole idea would result in a massive monopoly.' In the event the government thought it wise to refer the bid to the Monopolies and Mergers Commission. On 8 December 1981, John Biffen, Secretary of State for Trade, announced that he was disallowing the takeover since the Commission considered it would create near monopoly conditions. However, there were other reasons which ensured that the privatisation did not take place even though it was authorised in the Acts. For most of its life since 1969 Sealink had been profitable but in 1979-80 it burnt its fingers in a cross channel fare war with its rivals and made losses. It did not look a very tasty morsel to those who at one time had expected to strike a good bargain.

It was a different story with BR Hovercraft formed as a subsidiary of BR in 1966 to run cross channel and coastal services. The profit record of this business was on the whole a good one. At 1979 money values, its revenue increased from £97.2m in 1968 to £173.5m in 1979. On the other hand it made losses in the years 1974-6 inclusive. On 23 October 1981 David Howell gave his approval to a merger between Seaspeed (BR Hovercraft's operating name) and Hoverlloyd, its principal rival. British Rail was allowed to hold a 50 per cent interest in the new organisation, Hoverspeed, formed by the merger of the Swedish and British owned companies. The new company was to be controlled by an independent board of directors and was, for financial purposes, to be outside the public sector.[38]

On 13 June 1980 the *Estate Times* commented that although both Sealink and BTH were reasonably attractive propositions 'it is the Property Board, which made a net profit of nearly £30m, which is most likely to attract interest when it is offered for sale'. The Property Board, which was created by BR in 1969, owes its existence to the substantial rail closures of the Beeching era. The Transport Act, 1962, gave the BRB power 'to dispose (whether absolutely or for a term of years) of any part of the undertaking of the Board or any property which, in their opinion, is not required by them for the purposes of their business'. Over the years the Board has been a valuable financial asset to BR through its sales of spare land and its revenue from station and other sites. In 1980 the total estate of BR amounted to 200,000 acres, 30,000 acres of which was non-operational and valued at £180m. The requirement, under the 1981 Act, that BR should privatise these most valuable assets may be seen as the 'unkindest cut of all' for the Board. It is one thing for the Property Board, in consultation with BR, to decide to capitalise on its landed property at a time it considers advantageous. It is quite another thing for BR to be obliged to sell off its non-operational, and part even of its operational, property in the depths of an economic depression. In demanding this action by BR the government was seriously weakening the Board's future viability. On 14 July 1980 Robin Cook, Labour MP for Edinburgh (Central), asked the Secretary of State to confirm that the Property Board's profits that year were expected to be 76 per cent. 'If hiving that off is not asset stripping', he asked, 'what does the minister understand by asset strip?'[39]

VI

One of the main reasons for the appearance early in 1982 of yet another Transport Bill was the frustration of the government's plans for the bus industry contained in the Transport Act, 1980. It was at that time anticipated that entrepreneurs in the express services would run the NBC off the road. The public sector would be 'rolled back' through the success of private enterprise competition. When Norman Fowler introduced that first Transport Bill of the Thatcher government on 27 November 1979, he admitted that if the new legislation encouraged Freddie Lakers into the bus industry he would 'reckon that part of the Bill an outstanding success'.[40] Many of his colleagues thought British Coachways, the free enterprise consortium, would indeed become the Freddie Laker of the motorways after these were opened to unlicensed express coach services in October 1980. But, alas, the whole plan misfired. Much better equipped to run a national network of express coach services, the National Express division of NBC expanded its services by 50 per cent within a year and, in the process, drove many of its free enterprise competitors off the road. By early 1982 British Coachways, on which such great hopes had been placed, was having to resort to special operational arrangements with the NBC in order to survive in any shape.

When David Howell, Norman Fowler's successor, introduced the second reading of his transport bill on 9 February 1982 he made no mention of Freddie Laker. Two days earlier the Laker empire had collapsed with £270m in outstanding debts. But the minister was at least consistent in his objectives. He said that the first two parts of the Bill 'continued the strategy of reducing the role of the state in the transport sector'. This was being done 'for the most practical and common sense of reasons – the objective of introducing greater efficiency with our transport operations'.[41] Part I of the Bill was designed to 'open up the NBC to private capital'. Part II concerned the routine service of testing heavy goods and public service vehicles which 'could be just as well done by the private sector' as by civil servants. Part III the minister claimed improved and extended the fixed penalty system for road traffic offences.

Not only members of the Opposition but also a number of Conservative MPs were sceptical about the value of the Bill. Albert Booth from the Labour front bench accused the government of 'taking their revenge on the NBC for taking over the role they hoped the private sector would have'.[42] The proposed hiving off of the coaching and holiday activities of NBC could only hasten the already serious decline of the state enterprise as far as its main business – the stage carriage services – was concerned. The profitable parts of the enterprise helped to cross subsidise the unprofitable local services.

Tom Bradley, SDP MP for Leicester East, said that although the minister claimed that he would be helping the NBC by introducing private capital, the real objective was 'to sell lucrative parts of the company to its commercial rivals'. National Express was responsible for only seven per cent of NBC operations but was the major contributor to its profits. If the NBC lost National Express, as the government was proposing, it would be losing its 'profitable arm'. The minister had not been able to destroy the NBC through competition. 'If it cannot be beaten by private enterprise', he says, 'let us cut off its profitable arm.' [43]

David Howell was aware that selling off the profitable National Express and National Holidays parts of NBC presented some difficulties since their earnings went into the general pool. As the accounts were then presented the financial position of the two offshoots could not be separately identified in a way that was needed to attract private speculators and to reconstitute them as Companies Acts companies. In view of the manifestly predatory intentions of the minister, the policy of the NBC in not separating out the accounts can well be understood. In his speech on 9 February 1982, therefore, Howell revealed: 'I have asked the NBC to let me have proposals for accounting for National Express and National Holidays, either jointly or separately, in distinct company accounts. I have asked NBC to do this from the earliest possible date.'

In a sinister sentence, which put a gloss over the harsh reality of Treasury pressure to privatise the most profitable part of the NBC's business, he said: 'I also propose shortly to set a financial target for both businesses which will sustain the momentum to further improvement on what are already promising results.' [44] In less polite language this could be interpreted: 'I am going to tighten the financial screw so that the NBC, like BR, will be obliged to sell off important assets to stay within the EFL.'

Very few MPs had a good word to say of the proposals, contained in Part II of the Bill, to transfer to private enterprise the routine job of testing the roadworthiness of heavy goods vehicles and public service vehicles. Sir David Price, Conservative MP for Eastleigh, who had chaired the Select Committee on Transport in 1981, felt that it was psychic of HMSO to have printed half the Committee's report upside down, for that was how the government had reacted to its recommendations! The key sentence in the report was: 'We do not consider that the Government has yet justified its contention that private operators . . . would carry out annual testing of commercial vehicles better than the current Department of Transport testing stations.' The government had ignored the report.[45] Peter Fry MP, another Conservative member of the Select Committee, could not find any real support from interested parties for the privatisation of testing stations. He felt that the impartiality of the existing arrangements would be placed in jeopardy. He had concluded 'the only person who seemed enthusiastic about the vehicle testing proposals was (his) honourable and learned friend the Under Secretary'.[46] Robert Hughes, Labour MP for Aberdeen North, hit the nail on the head when he said: 'The truth is that the privatisation of heavy goods vehicle testing stations has nothing to do with private industry being able to do the job better than or as well as the existing system. It is simply that the Department has been told that it must shed 900 civil servants.'[47]

The government invited Lloyds to submit an estimate for undertaking the testing and licensing of heavy goods vehicles and public service vehicles. Parliament and the public were kept in the dark for more than a year. Finally the new Secretary of State, Tom King, confessed to the Commons on 29 July 1983 that the proposed transfer would cost the government more than had been anticipated. Testing Lloyds conditions against the government's requirements of 'sound management and good value for money for the taxpayer' he found the privatisation proposals too costly. The transition would have cost the Treasury £3.5 million. He had decided, therefore, to abandon the whole plan. Even so the taxpayer was out of pocket since King revealed that the government had paid Lloyds £500,000 to meet 'approved additional costs incurred in good faith'.

At the time of writing, the arrangements for hiving off the profitable arms of the NBC have not been completed. If these are carried through those who will suffer will be the hundreds of thousands of local bus users whose bus services will disappear – NBC estimate a withdrawal of sixty million miles of services – or will be less frequent or convenient.

VII

A common feature of all three Acts considered above is that they were ideologically motivated. The over-riding aim was to increase opportunities for private profit making in transport and to curtail drastically the role of public enterprise. This objective has been pursued for its own sake, largely irrespective of any considerations of transport policy. The extreme case was the attempt to privatise heavy goods vehicle and public service vehicle testing, a change persisted in despite the opposition of the Road Haulage Association, the Freight Traffic Association, the coach operators and those Tory MPs most knowledgeable about transport.

One of the effects of the legislation has been to distort the pattern of transport services. By its nature the bus is best suited to carry passengers on shorter journeys, a service which the less flexible railway cannot provide. The modern inter-city trains are clearly suited for the longer distance passenger transport. Yet, under pressure from the competition of private enterprise coaches NBC was induced to expand to National Express services, to secure its very survival. To beat off its challenges it switched resources from many country areas – to the extent of no less than eight per cent of its stage carriage mileage – in one year. The areas from which its buses have been withdrawn very often have no alternative public transport. It is certain that this run down of essential services will continue at an accelerated pace if Howell's plans to hive off National Express from the NBC are pushed through to completion.

What has been notable in the government's policies is the complete absence of any concept of integrated services, of bus and train fulfilling the roles for which they are best suited. The character of the legislation – as one hotch-potch of a Bill succeeded another – has reflected this piecemeal approach. The determination to weaken public transport has been the obsessive aim. This is all the more tragic as David Howell, in his most recent book, conceded that public enterprise had an important part to play in the economy. He wrote that it is 'wrong to assume . . . that market economies are enough and that all will settle down in prosperity if entrepreneurial talent is given its head, taxes lowered, and public expenditure constrained.'[48] Since writing those words, however, he has realised what is required of him in a government led by laissez faire extremists, and he has changed his tune.

The flood of legislation coming from the Department of Transport influenced greatly the prospects for success of British Rail and the railway unions whose plans for the 1980s will next be considered.

5
Hopes Dashed: British Rail's Corporate Plan 1980-85

Whenever government ministers have been asked to increase investment in BR they have replied with monotonous consistency that improved productivity must first be displayed on the railway system. Thus, when John Horam, Labour Under Secretary of State for Transport, was asked by the NUR sponsored MP Leslie Spriggs on 24 January 1979 whether he would 'authorise increased investment for British Railways' he replied that this would have to be kept under review 'in the light of business performance'.[1] Likewise, on 21 September 1980 Norman Fowler, the Conservative Secretary of State, passed the responsibility to the Board and its staff by asserting that 'nothing is more important than that the railways should improve their productivity'.[2]

Such replies naturally prompt the question: How efficiently run are British Railways? One way of providing an answer is to make comparison with railway operation in other European states. Such an exercise can only give pointers to differences in performance: it cannot claim to produce very precise results. International comparisons of labour productivity are affected by differences in the organisation of work; the average hours worked; operating conditions, including differences of topography and climate; pricing policy (cheap fares tend to increase the productivity of traffic staff); the climate of industrial relations and the state of the economy in which the railways operate.

We have already seen (in Chapter 3) that capital expenditure in 1977 and the level of government financial support were lower than those of any of the nine other European railway systems whose performance was examined by the Leeds University/BR investigating team. These facts are illustrated in Figs. 3 and 4.

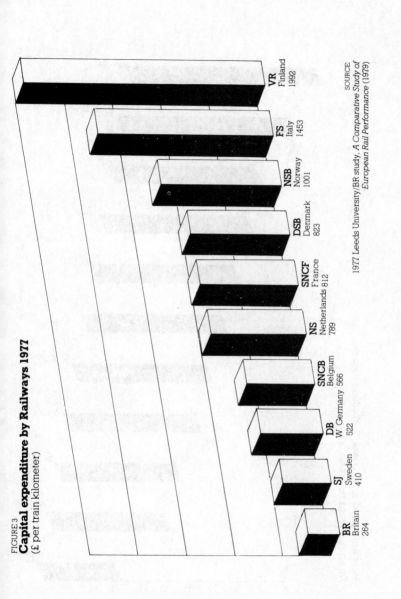

FIGURE 3
Capital expenditure by Railways 1977
(£ per train kilometer)

BR Britain 264	
SJ Sweden 410	
DB W. Germany 522	
SNCB Belgium 566	
NS Netherlands 789	
SNCF France 812	
DSB Denmark 823	
NSB Norway 1001	
FS Italy 1453	
VR Finland 1992	

SOURCE
1977 Leeds University/BR study, *A Comparative Study of European Rail Performance* (1979)

FIGURE 4

Percentage of total costs, including capital, financed from revenue, 1977

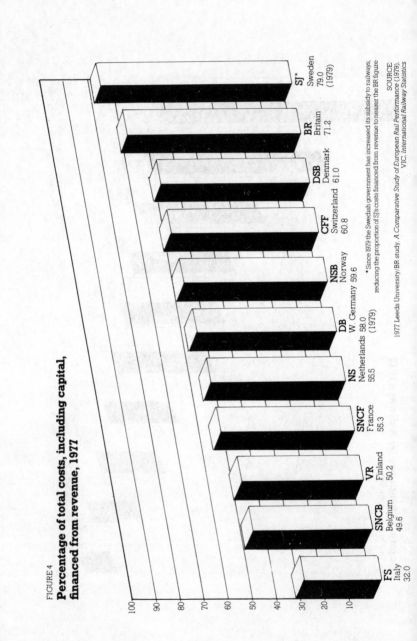

SJ*	Sweden	79.0 (1979)
BR	Britain	71.2
DSB	Denmark	61.0
CFF	Switzerland	60.8
NSB	Norway	59.6
DB	W. Germany	58.0 (1979)
NS	Netherlands	55.5
SNCF	France	55.3
VR	Finland	50.2
SNCB	Belgium	49.6
FS	Italy	32.0

* Since 1979 the Swedish government has increased its subsidy to railways,
reducing the proportion of SJ's costs financed from revenue to nearer the BR figure

SOURCE:
1977 Leeds University/BR study, *A Comparative Study of European Rail Performance* (1979).
VIC. *International Railway Statistics*

When government financial support is expressed as a percentage of Gross Domestic Product (GDP) the low priority given to railways in the UK is apparent:

Table 4
Financial Support as a Percentage of GDP

	1975	1976	1977	1978	1979
BR	0.48	0.40	0.35	0.35	0.35
DB	0.94	0.87	0.95	1.05	1.04
DSB	0.40	0.37	0.33	0.20	0.29
FS	1.36	1.26	1.15	1.16	1.07
NS	0.41	0.49	0.50	0.48	0.48
SNCB	1.45	1.38	1.44	1.39	1.38
SNCF	0.72	0.70	0.76	0.71	0.72
CIE	0.75	0.60	0.46	0.41	0.47

Key: BR British Railways; BD West Germany; DSB Denmark; FS Italy; NS Netherlands; SNCB Belgium; CNCF France; CIE Ireland.

Source: University of Leeds/British Rail, *A Comparative Study of European Rail Performance*, London, British Railways Board, 1979, Table 5.5 p.44. EEC Second and Third Biennial Reports on the Economic and Financial Situation of the Railways Undertakings. UIC, *International Railway Statistics, 1980.*

As can be seen from this table, only Denmark of the eight countries for which information is available, devotes a smaller proportion of its GDP to railways than does the UK.

One widely accepted measure of railway performance is the number of staff employed compared with train kilometres run. Table 5 shows BR's performance compared with that of other European rail systems:

These figures suggest that BR's labour productivity per man was above the average of the twelve countries with which comparison was made, with only the Dutch, Swedish and Swiss railways having a better record. However, if BREL staff employed on BR traction and rolling stock maintenance are included in the estimate, the productivity of BR staff is about the average of the twelve. The productivity of BR's labour force owed a good deal to the fact that the hours worked were longer than on any other of the European railway systems. If the freight and parcels businesses alone are considered, however, all other major European railways systems employed fewer

Table 5
Staff per Million Train Kilometres

	1977 Leeds University/ BR Study	1977	1978	1979	1980
		(UIC International Railway Statistics)			
BR	413.8	404.5	396.1	399.6	391.2
DB	571.5	622.0	584.9	541.5	520.8
DSB	446.1	409.5	397.5	n.a.	n.a.
FS	708.7	743.8	731.7	724.7	719.6
NS	225.8	243.6	242.1	243.6	243.3
NSB	441.2	467.5	465.0	457.6	440.2
SJ	353.3	344.9	336.4	331.2	327.1
SNCB	555.6	618.8	601.1	603.1	629.9
SNCF	477.0	525.0	508.4	492.3	476.4
VR	663.5	560.8	572.1	562.7	544.7
CFF	410.5	394.9	387.5	384.7	381.9
CIE	662.2	718.0	578.3	534.4	547.5

Key: BR British Rail; DB West Germany; DSB Denmark; FS Italy; NS Netherlands; NSB Norway; SJ Sweden; SNCB Belgium; SNCF France; VR Finland; CFF Switzerland; CIE Ireland.

Source: 1977 Leeds University/BR Study, 1977-80, UIC (International Union of Railways) *International Railway Statistics*

staff per million train kilometres than did BR in 1977. The adoption of flexible rostering by guards in 1982 and by most drivers in 1983, and the spread of single manning of locomotives, brought BR's performance closer to the level found on continental railways.

British Rail still suffers from the drawbacks of competitive railway promotion in the nineteenth century with, for example, six London termini serving the South Eastern region. In comparison with continental countries, whose railway development was more carefully planned, BR has a large number of stations for the services provided and a larger number of terminal staff per million train kilometres run than is the case with European railway terminals.[3]

It is a characteristic of BR's passenger business that commuter traffic, with its peaks in the morning and evening rush hours, dominates activity in the great conurbations. This helps to explain why passenger vehicle utilisation, averaged over a 24 hour day is lower in Britain than in any of the other countries.[4] There is less excuse for the situation in freight and parcels services where mean train load, wagons per train and wagon kilometres per wagon on BR are the lowest of any of the railway systems considered. On the other hand, British railway wagons are more nearly filled than they are on any other of the railways.[5] Furthermore, in the ten years to 31 December 1976 BR carried through a major programme of rationalisation of its wagon fleet. It achieved the greatest reduction in the number of its wagons and the greatest improvement in ton-kilometres carried per wagon of any railway.[6]

Bearing in mind that BR has been expected to meet a larger proportion of its operating costs from passenger and freight revenue than any other railway it is scarcely surprising that its fares were the highest of any major European country:

Table 6
Average Receipts per Passenger Kilometre
Current Price Levels at £ Purchasing Power Parities

	1977 Leeds University/ BR Study	1977	1978	1979
		UIC International Railways Statistics)		
BR	2.026	2.013	2.274	2.485
*DB	1.644	(2.458)	(2.773)	(3.105)
DSB	1.355	1.231	1.270	1.619
FS	1.004	1.324	1.499	1.797
NS	1.509	1.230	1.343	1.533
NSB	1.811	1.754	1.839	1.923
SJ	1.922	1.812	1.703	1.669
*SNCB	1.186	(2.822)	(3.432)	(4.290)
SNCF	1.267	1.476	1.664	1.923
VR	1.127	1.009	1.058	1.234
CFF	1.485	1.456	1.496	1.469
CIE	1.477	1.421	1.546	1.758

*Figures in brackets include support payments as receipts – it is not possible to separate out the support element.

Key: See Table 5.

Source:1977: Leeds University/BR Study. 1977-9. UIC *International Railway Statistics.* Director of Strategic Development, BR, *International Comparisons of Railway Performance*, 30 November 1982

As Peter Parker correctly observed in March 1980, BR's high fares are due 'neither to excessive wage levels, nor to poor productivity, but to relatively low support from the taxpayer for railways in Britain'.[7] The low level of financial support afforded BR from public

62

funds also helps to explain Britain's poor performance in passenger vehicle utilisation; for if government backing for the railways was on a more generous scale, fares would be reduced and vehicle occupancy increased. The train staff would also be employed more productively.

The extent to which a country's railways are electrified also affects the productivity of the labour force. Electric locomotives cost less to build, are more reliable, have a longer useful life span and cost less to maintain than do diesels.

Table 7 shows the extent of railway electrification in different countries:

Table 7
Proportion of Track Electrified at the End of 1976

	% of route kms electrified	% of running track kms electrified
BR	20.7	21.1
CFF	99.5	92.8
DB	36.2	45.1
FS	50.4	62.7
NS	59.9	56.4
OBB	49.0	59.3
SNCF	26.0	n.a.
SJ	62.3	62.4
JNR	36.7	51.1
SNCB	30.0	29.9
DSB	5.0	5.3
NSB	57.5	57.3
CIE	0.0	0.0

Key: BR British Rail; CFF Switzerland; DB West Germany; FS Italy; NS Netherlands; OBB Austria; SNCF France; SJ Sweden; JNR Jugoslavia; SNCB Belgium; DSB Denmark; NSB Norway; CIE Ireland.

Source: University of Leeds/British Rail, *A Comparative Study of European Rail Performance*, London, British Railways Board 1979, Appendix 3, Table 3, p.88

It will be seen that all countries here compared, with the exception of Ireland and Denmark, have a larger proportion of rail network electrified than does the UK. Those countries which have a greater proportion of their railway mileage electrified need less labour to provide and maintain locomotive power than do those dependent on steam or diesel traction. Electric traction requires between one half and one third of the maintenance staff input per traction kilometre as does diesel.[8] In addition electric railways generally have a better punctuality record than do those which depend on alternative sources of power. Clearly when the different countries' statistics of staff employed per million train kilometres run are compared, allowance should be made for the different forms of traction employed.

Table 7 shows that nearly 60 per cent of the Dutch railway network (NS) is electrified while Table 5 shows that the same railway's staff productivity is greater than that of any other railway. Of course electrification is only one influence on productivity; but it is an extremely important one. If more than one half, instead of only one fifth of the British railway network was electrified one can be certain that labour productivity could be appreciably improved. To a degree, therefore, the Conservative government put the cart before the horse in demanding improved labour productivity from BR before authorising an electrification programme. If government is serious about wanting more productivity from railway workers it could help to make this possible by giving the 'all clear' to a rolling programme of main line electrification.

In sum, therefore, BR can rightly lay claim to be the most cost effective major railway in Europe.[9] It has the lowest level of government financial support of any major railway and, apart from Ireland and Denmark, has the smallest proportion of track electrified. But despite these drawbacks, it scores well on most measures of labour productivity, having an above average performance in the efficiency of passenger train staff and in the utilisation of wagon capacity. In areas where, until recently, BR staff productivity was low, as in freight train manning, performance has shown marked improvement in the last two years.

II

Although its performance in the 1970s bore favourable comparison with that of other European railway systems BR was concerned to increase its efficiency still further. Until 1981 it produced a *Review* of its plans for improvements in rail services and the enhanced productivity of the workforce. The *Corporate Plan 1981-5*, not only carried a new title but was also the first such document which was not confidential between BR and the Secretary of State for Transport.

The assumptions of the Plan were that BR would be expected to maintain a rail network similar in extent to that of 1975; to aim to run freight, parcels, inter-city passenger trains and the subsidiary activities, such as BT Hotels, on a strictly commercial basis; and to live within an EFL embracing both grants and external borrowing.[10]

The most important assumption made by the Board, however, was that government would allocate increased funds for investment. The limitations of relying primarily on manpower reductions as a means to increased efficiency were stressed: 'It must be emphasised that, important though it is, manpower reduction is not the only source of productivity improvement. Investment, which for the most part means renewal of assets in modern form, leads directly to significant productivity improvement.'[11]

The Board calculated that an investment of £1876 million was needed over the five years 1981-5, an average of £375 million a year, if the other objectives of the plan were to be achieved.[12]

The Secretary of State was warned of the disastrous consequences which would follow a failure to raise investment above the grossly inadequate level of 1980. An increasing number of speed restrictions would have to be imposed and by 1990 some 3,000 out of the existing 22,000 miles of track would have to be closed. By the same date the signalling equipment on 7,000 miles of railway would be more than 50 years old, and in many cases older still. Sir Peter Parker hoped that, even if the government was not prompted to invest more in BR out of a love of railways, it might be persuaded on financial grounds. If the government 'resolutely declined to permit the vital additional investment', he warned, 'it would be impossible to meet the prescribed financial targets in later years'. Whilst it could not be proved or guaranteed that favourable financial results would follow increased investment, it was 'quite certain that they would not follow without such investment'. He challenged the insistence of the ministry and the government that approval of new investment would have to wait until more favourable trading results had emerged. Such an approach was 'likely to put the railways on to a downward spiral of investment decline'. He conceded that 'the nation had, of course, a right to will this consequence, provided that it was a decision consciously taken', but 'it was not a decision that commended itself to the Board'.[13]

The plan's proposals for the development of passenger traffic were based on four important assumptions: that there would be no further deterioration in the country's economic performance; that the level of railway investment would be raised; that the PTEs would be in a position to meet any deficits which arose in their areas and that a major programme of railway electrification would be carried out. It was anticipated that total passenger miles would increase from 19,810 million in 1980 to 20,940 million in 1985. Inter-City passenger miles were expected to increase by 13 per cent and receipts by 25 per cent. It was not anticipated that the London and South East region or the other provincial services would pay their way. The Inter-City traffic forecast was based on the optimistic assumption, soon proved false, that there would be 'quality improvements brought about by investment in the advanced passenger train'.[14]

The Board's long term plan for freight was that it should be a 'robust and healthily profitable business each part of which would be capable of financing replacement of the assets it uses and making sufficient contribution to cover avoidable joint expenses'. It was anticipated that by 1985 freight and parcels traffic would be making substantial profits. The reason for the Board's optimism for the long term was that freight movement offered greater opportunities for labour saving than any other branch of the railway business. In fact expectations were based on predictions of manpower reductions outlined in BR's 'Challenge of the Eighties'. It was recognised that in the shorter run, i.e. the early 1980s, the freight business would not be profitable because of £27 million lost receipts in consequence of the steel strike in the early part of 1981, and the depressed state of the national economy.[15] The source of freight business profit in the longer term would be the implementation of the Speedlink Development Plan, 1980, which provided for the severe rationalisation of marshalling yards and terminal arrangements. Trainload Speedlink traffic would largely displace the more labour-intensive wagon load traffic. The most remarkable change envisaged was the reduction in the number of BR wagons from 125,000 in 1980 to 31,000, entirely airbraked, in 1990. The slimming down of the wagon fleet would be achieved through quicker, computerised, turn round and the larger average capacity load of each unit.[16]

Under the 'intense financial restraints' experienced by the Board at the beginning of the 1980s it was decided to withdraw from all collection and delivery parcels business from the middle of 1981, since this sector was losing £38 million per annum on a turnover of £40 million. The premium parcels business, however, was expected to be a major growth area.

The plan included a programme of electrification of the routes from London to York, Leeds and Bradford, Nottingham and Sheffield, Bristol and South Wales by 1990. Blackpool, Manchester and Liverpool were to be linked to the west coast main line to Glasgow. The Board was counting on the government providing the relatively modest extra sums required to carry out this vital improvement. The additional costs, at average 1980 prices, would be, in £s million:

1981 7   *1982* 16   *1983* 25   *1984* 31   *1985* 33

At the time the Corporate Plan 1981-85 was drafted it was still hoped that the construction of a rail-only Channel Tunnel would be authorised. However, it was considered that even if approval was granted, the financial outlay involved before 1985 would be small. Therefore the tunnel was omitted from consideration in the plan.

BR was fully aware that its success in fulfilling the plans for passenger and freight traffic would depend upon the co-operation of the trade unions and the work force. The number of staff employed on BR was planned to fall from 191,300 in 1980 to 158,500 in 1985, a drop of nearly 33,000 over the five years.

III

Despite BR's attempt, in its *Annual Report and Accounts, 1982*, to put a brave face on things, commercial conditions during the first two years of operation of the *Corporate Plan, 1981-85* made many of the plan's forecasts appear unduly optimistic. Manufacturing production declined by nearly a fifth between 1979-82. Sir Peter Parker called 1982 an 'embattled year', partly because of the economic slump but mainly for the reason that strikes by ASLEF in January, February and July and by the NUR for two days in June virtually closed the railway system for a total of 34 days. The Board estimated that the loss of revenue caused by the strikes was £170 million.[17] With the decline in business activity and the true level of unemployment nearer four million than three, it is not surprising that passenger mileage fell from 19,100 million in 1981 to 17,000 million in 1982. In a recession 'too much transport chases too little traffic'.[18] In consequence, BR carried less freight in 1982 than it did in 1981 − 141.9 million compared with 154.2 million tonnes. In periods of reduced output less fuel is used by industry. The decline in carrying of coal and coke by 6.8 million tonnes, over the year accounted for more than half the decline in total freight carried. In the course of 1980-1 the Board took counter measures in an attempt to offset the fall in revenue resulting from reduced demand in the passenger and freight businesses. Service reductions equal to 2 per cent of train mileage were implemented in October 1980, rising to 5 per cent by June 1981, and cuts in the track renewal, resignalling and vehicle refurbishment programmes brought about a substantial reduction in costs which enabled BR to keep within the EFL in the financial year 1980-1. However, these were one-off economies that could not be repeated indefinitely without seriously damaging the railway's future earning capacity. The Board also gained temporary financial relief through large positive cash flows from privatisation and asset sales in the non-rail businesses in 1980-2. Even so the BR group had an estimated deficit of £154 million in 1982. The 'windfall' earnings from the sale of assets were expected to end in the course of 1983, causing BR to exceed the EFL by £120 million in 1985-6 despite improvements in budgetary control, management economies and a drop in manpower of 38,300 over the five years of the Corporate Plan. In fact the plans for staff reductions were carried out ahead of schedule. In 1981 and 1982 a total of 27,000 railway jobs disappeared, 70 per cent of the number planned for the entire five years.[19] Labour was carrying a large part of the burden of a depressed railway industry.

The prospect of any major progress in electrification receded into the distant future. In his Report for 1982 Sir Peter Parker glossed over the fact of hostility to electrification at No. 10 Downing Street by attributing the delays to the poor state of the economy: 'The recession has forced us to do our sums again on a line by line rather than a network basis', he wrote.[20] There is no doubt that the lack of vision on the part of the government in respect of electrification was one of the principal reasons why the objectives of the Corporate Plan could not be realised.

The government's greatest failure was its refusal to allow BR adequate funds for investment. As a consequence of its financial support being kept at unrealistically low levels the Board was obliged to make a drastic curtailment of its investment programme. Whereas the Corporate Plan provided for an investment of £339 million in 1982 the actual amount invested was only £251 million.[21] In default of adequate investment, the corner stone of improvement, it was inevitable that the objectives of the Corporate Plan would come to be regarded as 'unrealistic' and 'over-optimistic'. It was also inevitable that the railways' role in British transport would be less than economic, social and environmental circumstances demanded.

Hopes Dashed: The Railwaymen's Charter 1979

I

By 1979 there was a groundswell of opinion within the NUR that rail-way labour had contributed handsomely to the improvement of efficiency in railway operations without receiving adequate reward in the shape of improved rates of pay and conditions of service. Members of the railway staff were having to work long hours in order to earn wages comparable with average basic rates in British industry. At the same time managers were keenly aware that because of unsocial hours and unattractive rates of pay it was necessary to offer the inducement of overtime earnings if there was to be any chance at all of retaining staff. Even so, there was a serious drain of labour from the industry. In 1978, in response to pressure from the union, the Board attempted to fill existing vacancies. In the first six months of the year 12,133 staff were recruited, but at the same time no fewer than 11,767 persons left the industry.[1] It was a situation which was unsatisfactory from a number of standpoints. Many rail-way workers were not staying in the industry long enough to become committed to it. Furthermore, if the workforce became resigned to long hours of overtime as the only means of achieving adequate weekly earnings, the unions' attempts to improve basic rates of pay and conditions of service would be undermined.

At the same time BR was under pressure to live within an EFL which was falling in real terms. Deprived of adequate funds for investing in new technologies which could have contributed hand-somely to increased productivity, the Board concentrated its atten-tion on railway labour, which was called upon to bear the brunt of operational economies.

In June 1979 the newly elected Thatcher government reduced the Board's EFL for 1979-80 by £15 million despite the fact that the retail price index was rising rapidly. There was every prospect that unless urgent countervailing measures were taken, BR would fail to stay within the cash limits set by the Government. The Board therefore invited the officers of the railway unions to attend a special meeting at the Great Western Hotel, Paddington, on 23 August to discuss ways of improving productivity. ASLEF declined the invitation; but the representatives of TSSA and the NUR were present. Members of the Board were told that the NUR appreciated management's problems but the union leaders had their problems too. The AGM had ruled that there should be no reduction in the existing railway labour force. They would only consider changes in working practices if they were offered a reduced working week, an improved basic wage and four weeks holiday to all staff. Management replied suggesting that the unions should provide a paper setting out their objectives. This was the origin of the Railwaymen's Charter; for as soon as Sidney Weighell returned to Unity House he instructed the research group to prepare a statement of demands. By 13 September this document had been prepared and had been approved by the NUR executive.[2] A week later, at a meeting of the leaders of the three railway unions, TSSA gave the Charter its full backing but ASLEF pleaded for more time to give it consideration. The NUR's reasons for producing the Charter were given by Sidney Weighell in an address to a conference of signalmen at Chester in September 1980: 'The NUR realised that if we sat back and did nothing, changes were bound to take place – men would go out of the industry, re-organisation and staff cuts would be implemented by management – and at the end of the exercise railwaymen would have gained nothing. It was decided ... that the NUR should take the initiative and draw up a Railwaymen's Charter which spelt out the price of our co-operation.'[3]

The principal demands made in *The Railwaymen's Charter*, as the Unions' price for co-operation in productivity deals, were (a) safeguards of levels of employment; (b) an increase in the railman's basic rate to £60 a week, with commensurate increases for salaried staff and skilled workers; (c) the reduction of working hours from forty to thirty-five per week, a change phased over a period of five years; (d) annual leave to be increased to four weeks; (e) provided it could be accomplished without loss of earnings, the adoption of the continental system of rostering under which each worker is rostered for four or five shifts in any seven days, Sunday being treated as any other day; (f) an added element to compensate for the liability to work irregular and unsocial hours; and (g) the retention of the existing rail network.

One of the main reasons for the demands for a shorter working week and longer holidays was the desire to spread the work load and make it easier to retain on the pay roll staff who would otherwise be made redundant. The aim of increasing basic rates of wages and rewards for working unsocial and irregular hours was to make rail workers' wages more nearly comparable with those paid in outside industry and thus to prevent the kind of large-scale seepage of staff that occurred in 1978.

Before complete agreement of all three railway unions could be reached on the Railwaymen's Charter the negotiations on the pay settlement for 1980-1 were in full swing. On pay bargaining, in contrast to productivity discussions, the unions acted together and, at a meeting of the Railway Staff National Council (RSNC) held on 28 April 1980, secured an increase of twenty per cent on the basic rates, an increase which was superficially impressive, but which was much less so when seen against a rise of the retail price index of 21.8 per cent over the previous twelve months. Included within the pay settlement was the provision that from 1 November 1981 the standard working week would be reduced from forty hours to thirty nine – a first step towards the achievement of the union objective of a thirty-five hour week by 1985.[3]

In the light of the 1980 pay settlement it became necessary to redraft parts of *The Railwaymen's Charter*. The updated version was produced on 11 August 1980 and included the demand for an increase in the minimum basic rate to £72 a week. More precise recommendations were made for compensating railway staff for working the irregular and anti-social hours characteristic of their employment. The extra payment suggested expressed as a percentage of basic rates were as follows:-

1. *Monday to Friday shifts*
    (a) Three shift system (including nights) 30 per cent;
    (b) Three shift system (not rotating over 24 hours) 20 per cent;
    (c) Double day shift (6am to 12 midnight) 15 per cent.

2. *Saturdays and Sundays*

Hours worked to attract a premium of 100 per cent.

3. Irregular hour working – a premium of 5 per cent.[4]

The other major items of the first version of *The Railwaymen's Charter* e.g. the shorter working week and longer holidays, remained unchanged in the revised version. The NUR estimated that the initial cost of all the items in the updated version would be £448 million in respect of those employed on British Rail; for all the Board's staff e.g. including BTH, the BR Property Board and other subsidiaries staff, as well as BR employees, the cost would be £700 million, or eighteen per cent on the cost of the 1980-1 paybill. However, these were said to be *maximum* costs. They were based on the assumption that there would be no productivity increases resulting directly from the changes and that where the working week was reduced or annual leave increased BR would employ sufficient new staff to compensate completely for the shorter hours worked by the existing staff.[5]

Tactically there was much to be said for the three unions taking the initiative with the intention of controlling the pace and character of change on the railway rather than sitting back and waiting for a succession of blows to come from management. But TSSA and ASLEF were slow to respond to the NUR's proposals. When their representatives met those of the NUR at Unity Hosue on 19 August 1980 they were given the updated version of *The Railwaymen's Charter* and they promised to give it serious consideration. But when the executive of the NUR met on 26 September – more than five weeks later – no replies had been received from the other unions. When a letter was received from ASLEF on 2 October Ray Buckton, its General Secretary, reported that his executive found the NUR document unacceptable though they were willing to discuss productivity issues with BR.

Meanwhile the weekly reports coming into Rail House revealed a sharp decline in BR's passenger and freight traffic. The pressure was on to make further economies. On 7 October the Board announced the complete withdrawal from all parcels collection and delivery business which, it was claimed, was losing BR £38 million a year. Ending the service would bring a saving of £13 million by 1982 rising to £30 million in 1983. It was not a wholly unexpected development. The decline in the railway parcels business began in the early 1970s with the growth in the number of supermarkets and discount warehouses.

Later in the decade the sharp increase in the number of juggernaut lorries engaged in the freight business accelerated the trend. As part of the pay deal agreed earlier in 1980 the number of stations operating a collection and delivery service was to be reduced from 200 to forty. Nevertheless the shock of the announcement on 7 October was severe. The rail union executives were given no advance warning of a decision which would cost at least 6,000 jobs. Jock Nicolson, who had devoted most of his working life to this part of the railway business, wrote that the staff concerned were infuriated both by the decision itself and by the manner in which it was announced.[6] In *The Railwaymen's Charter* the first condition for union co-operation with BR in the search for greater efficiency was 'safeguards for levels of employment'. After 7 October many railway workers must have thought – 'so much for the safeguards'.

Because of the sharp deterioration in railway finances, management called an urgent meeting of the BR Council, a body which includes representatives of the Board and of the unions, at Watford on 19 and 20 November 1980. The BR representatives in a document *The Balance Sheet of Change* proposed that the unions should give urgent consideration to the following economies:-

(a) The reduction of the number of marshalling yards and the simplification of their operation;

(b) Speeding up the withdrawal from parcels collection and delivery;

(c) The reduction of passenger train mileage by five per cent;

(d) Administrative streamlining;

(e) Continued co-operation in 'good housekeeping';

(f) A commitment to push consultation procedure at all levels;

(g) The RSNC to meet urgently to review the progress made on 1980 pay deal commitments to increased productivity, particularly with reference to the manning of traction units, the recruitment and training of train crew staff and the open station concept.

Ever since the first version of *The Railwaymen's Charter* was issued the NUR was aware that the financing of the reforms it proposed would require additional financial support from the government. On 2 December 1980, therefore, following the Watford Conference, the NUR executive decided to ask the BRB to associate with the unions in a joint approach to the Minister of Transport. He was to be urged to increase the Board's EFL for 1981-82 from £920 million to £970 million; to renegotiate the terms of the PSO grant to provide increased support for passenger services; to extend government support to BR's freight operations in line with that granted by other European countries; to endorse an electrification rolling programme and rolling programmes for locomotive EMU and wagon building; to approve the development of APT services for the West coast main line and to approve the construction of Jumbo Ferries, Anglian electrification and West of England re-signalling. The NUR promised that if agreement could be reached between the unions, BRB and the government on these schemes it would give a firm commitment to progress to a speedy solution on marshalling yard problems and collection and delivery of parcels.[7]

The next meeting of the British Rail Council expressed broad agreement with this NUR policy and Sir Peter Parker agreed to write to Norman Fowler inviting him to the next meeting of the Council to be arranged as soon as possible. At the meeting with the minister, held on 29 January 1981, the NUR argued that there was need to synchronise commitments by both sides. Sidney Weighell said that 'there were serious doubts whether his union would be able to deliver its side of the bargain if the government's commitment to the future was vague'. In reply the minister appeared to accept the need for investment and for a synchronised approach. He said: 'Many of the problems of the industry were the inheritance of lack of investment over a long period of time. There was need for a sensible bipartisan programme.' Sidney Weighell's concept was that management and unions should march in step; concessions from one side should be matched by concessions from the other side. It also seemed that the minister had conceded the need for more investment and that this implied government making more funds available. Yet over the next eighteen months the unions' confidence in BR and the government completely eroded. How did this happen?

II

The first cause of the breakdown was the failure of the unions to achieve a wage settlement after 1980 consistent with the objectives set out in *The Railwaymen's Charter*. The pay agreement operative from April 1980, despite its apparent generosity, served merely to give railway workers rises which nearly matched the sharp increase in the cost of living. It did nothing to restore comparability with the basic rates in other industries. The average basic rates paid manual workers in British industry rose by 94.4 per cent between 1975 and 1980. The basic wages paid adult railway conciliation staff, excluding higher paid footplatemen, rose by only 45 per cent over the same span of time.[8] Railway workers, to offset the decline in the real value of their basic pay since 1975, were working excessive hours of overtime. In 1979 they worked an average 54½ hour week, 14½ hours of which were overtime. By contrast the average male manual worker in British industry worked only 46 hours each week, of which only 6.3 were overtime.[9]

Negotiations over the unions' pay claim for 1981 were prolonged and took place against what the Board described as 'the very sombre backcloth' of its rapidly deteriorating financial situation. The three unions' application for 'a substantial increase in pay' came before the Railway Staff National Council (RSNC) on 19 March. They stressed that between March 1980 and March 1981 the retail price index had risen by thirteen per cent but that the cost of very important items such as gas, electricity and council house rents had risen more steeply than the general index indicated. When the RSNC met again on 13 April for the Board to give its reply, Cliff Rose, for BR, said that the 'dominant factor' influencing its offer was 'its inability to finance pay increases against the background of a very difficult trading position'. The most that could be afforded was seven per cent and even that was conditional on a satisfactory conclusion of the productivity talks provided for in the 1980 pay settlement. (These concerned the closing of some marshalling yards and the reorganisation of others; the withdrawal from the parcels collection and delivery service and the reduction in the numbers of administrative staff.)[10] Three days later the union representatives told Cliff Rose that his offer was unacceptable. Ray Buckton, for ASLEF, said that in the light of rising prices it was equivalent to 'a reduction of seven per cent in the living standards of railwaymen'. Tom Jenkins, for TSSA, pointed out that the day before, in commending the BRB's *Annual Report and Accounts* for 1980 to the public, Sir Peter Parker had boasted that a saving of 5,000 posts had already been made. Charlie

Turnock, for the NUR, stressed that the offer did not come near to meeting the arguments put forward in support of the claim.[11] On 30 April the executive of the NUR decided unamimously to refer the wage claim to the Railway Staff National Tribunal (RSNT), the arbitration body of the industry which had been set up in 1956.

There was a delay of over eleven weeks while the Board and the unions gave evidence to the RSNT under the chairmanship of Lord McCarthy. Eventually the tribunal's Report Number 75 was published on 16 July 1981. The Award, included in paragraph 191 of the Report, went some way towards meeting the claims of the unions. It recommended that rates of pay for all grades covered in the reference should be raised by eight per cent, backdated to 20 April 1981 – the normal settlement date. A further increase of another three per cent on the rates prevailing on 19 April 1981 should be paid to all grades from 1 August 1981. Thus railway staff were to be offered a total of eleven per cent although for three per cent of this total there would be a delay in payment of more than three months. The granting of the increase in two parts was designed to placate the Board which maintained throughout that it could not afford more than seven per cent if it was to keep within its EFL. From the union's point of view eleven per cent represented a small cut in real wages, since the retail price index on 20 April 1981 – the settlement date for the claim – was twelve per cent above the level of April 1980. It was a far cry from the demand, contained in *The Railwaymen's Charter* that there should be a substantial improvement in real terms in the pay of railway staff. The revised version of the charter demanded a basic £72 a week for those in the grade 'Railman'. Under the McCarthy award the railman's wages were raised from £58.75 to £63.45 on 20 April and to £65.20 on 3 August 1981, well short of the charter claim of the previous year. McCarthy also recommended that the minimum earnings level of railway workers should be raised by fifteen per cent from 20 April 1981. The NUR, in its evidence to the tribunal showed that thousands of railway workers' pay packets were below the DHSS poverty line; the McCarthy recommendation was designed to prevent a worsening of this situation.

The recommendations of the RSNT are not binding on the parties in disputes: but up to this time there was a long established tradition, rarely ignored, that, however unpalatable they might be to one or both of the parties they were accepted with good grace, if for no other reason than a concern to sustain the credibility of the arbitration procedure. Thus when the NUR executive met on 17 July 1981, the day following the publication of RSNT 75, it came to the unanimous decision to accept the award. ASLEF and TSSA came to a similar decision. The next step was for the RSNC to meet and decide on the implementation of the award. Unfortunately, at the next meeting of the RSNC the union leaders were shocked to hear Cliff Rose declare that BR could not implement all of the tribunal's award. It was willing to pay the eight per cent, backdated to 20 April, but it simply did not have the money to pay the additional three per cent – payable in the following months. A case, therefore, had to be made to the government for more financial backing. At earlier meetings of the RSNC, held at Watford on 14 and 15 July 1981, Clifford Rose, for the Board, had warned union representatives that 'the Government had linked productivity with electrification' and that if they were to persuade Margaret Thatcher and Alan Walters to release any more funds for railway investment of any kind there would have to be union co-operation on one man operation of locomotives; the trainman concept; open stations and flexible rostering by train crews.[12] At the meeting on 21 July, after the tribunal award, therefore, the Board's view was that it needed to see 'more detailed progress' on productivity before the three per cent of the 1981 pay award could be handed over. Two days later, when the talks were resumed, the Board's approach had hardened. The word 'agreement' was substituted for the earlier 'more detailed progress'. (The Board were prepared to pay the three per cent at a future date but this must be preceded by agreement on the working practices initiatives. This was absolutely necessary to justify the Board going to the government for assistance.)[13] In vain did NUR and TSSA representatives point out that the unions had already made a substantial contribution to productivity with the number of marshalling yards being reduced from 107 to 74 by 1981. 3000 jobs had been sacrificed in the parcels collection and delivery service. Altogether it was estimated that job losses would total nearly 6,000 in the year, saving the Board some £29 million annually.[14] The two sides met again in the RSNC on 3 August in an attempt to reach agreement. Clifford Rose stressed that the Board needed 'a prospectus to go to the government with confidence'. It needed 'evidence of commitment' to the productivity initiatives listed at Watford in July before it would pay up the three per cent outstanding. The unions complained that evidence of commitment was being required 'before the respective issues had been examined fully'. They had already given evidence of their co-operation in the manpower sacrifices that had been made. They were willing to make a joint approach with the Board to try to persuade the minister to provide more funds.

The following day the NUR executive met at Unity House to consider a report from its negotiating committee recommending a national strike of all NUR members employed by the BRB, BREL, Sealink, Seaspeed and BT Hotels, the strike to begin at 00.01 hours on Monday, 31 August 1981. All but two members of the executive agreed with this recommendation.[15] More than three weeks' notice was given of the intention to strike and this gave ACAS the opportunity to intervene in order to find a compromise which would prevent the shut down of the railway system.

On 18 August 1981 Pat Lowry chaired the expected meeting of the parties at the ACAS headquarters where discussions on the implementation of RSNT Award 75 continued for three days. The union were up against BR's assertion that it could not pay the outstanding three per cent of the pay settlement at the recommended August date until there had been further progress on the productivity proposals. Speaking on behalf of all the rail unions, Sidney Weighell broke the log jam by a compromise proposal that the final three per cent should be paid from the beginning of January 1982, but backdated to 3 August 1981. As a further concession to BR it was agreed that the thirty-nine hour week which was to have been put into operation in November 1981 would be put back to the first week in January 1982. On changes in working practices Sidney Weighell said: 'The trade unions had already given the Board six firm commitments on productivity with dates by which negotiations must be completed and therefore the Board had surely got what it was seeking.' The BR representatives then accepted the unions' counter proposal 'on the understanding that the commitments on productivity would be honoured'.

At the conclusion of the talks ACAS produced two separate documents which were signed by the officers of the unions and the Board: an *Understanding on Pay* and an *Understanding on Productivity*. The pay settlement was in accordance with the unions' compromise, i.e. the outstanding three per cent was to be paid from the first pay period in 1982 but backdated to 3 August 1981 and the thirty-nine hour week was to be introduced on 4 January 1982. It contained a Clause 3 which read: 'The constituent parties of the RSNC accept the commitment set out in para. 190 of RSNT Decisions 75 regarding the continuation of negotiations on productivity issues and commit themselves to continue the progress that has already been made in the areas covered by Clauses 1(i), (ii) and (iii) of the 1980 pay agreement.'

In signing the *Understanding on Productivity* the Board and the unions committed themselves to reaching an agreement on the open station concept, variable rostering of train crews and the single manning of traction units by 31 October 1981; on the trainman concept (providing an avenue of promotion from guard to driver) and the manning of freight trains by 1 January 1982; and for the single manning of passenger trains in commuter areas, starting with the electrified Bedford–St. Pancras line in May 1982. Finally it was 'reaffirmed that specific rewards would be negotiated for those staff whose responsibilities are directly affected under these agreements'.[16]

The day following the signing of the two agreements the executive of the NUR met at Unity House and, with only two dissentients, accepted the agreements reached at ACAS and withdrew its previous strike instruction.[17] On 27 August, with officers of the Board and the three railway unions present, the RSNC agreed Minute 847 that 'the ACAS undertaking of 20 August should be ratified as an agreement on pay for the year commencing 20 April 1981'. Later the same day the parties agreed a separate Minute 848 ratifying the ACAS *Understanding on Productivity* and fixed 2 and 3 September as dates when further discussion on single manning, variable rostering, the open station concept, and so on, should be considered. The independence of the two understandings was confirmed at this meeting of the RSNC; for in the Minute concerning pay (847) there was no mention of the *Understanding on Productivity*, and in the *Understanding on Productivity* (848) there was no mention of rates of pay. However, if there was no hint of the inter-relatedness of the two agreements in the RSNC minutes, in the ACAS document Clause 3 of the *Understanding on Pay* (cited above) did give BR the excuse it was seeking to delay the final settlement of the pay claim.

III

The ACAS agreements of 27 August 1981 may be taken as a convenient milestone from which to look back and assess the impact of *The
Railwaymen's Charter* published two years previously. When compared with the conditions prevailing in the principal European state
railways in 1979 and the standard of living of their employees the
demands presented in the charter were generally modest. The fact
that none of the charter's aims had been achieved after two years
made the prospect for British railway workers all the more depres-
sing.

The charter's first aim was 'safeguards of the levels of employment'. This was something previously lacking. In 1950 the railways
employed 497,000 staff. By the end of 1981 staff numbers had fallen
to 166,000 and yet the passenger mileage figures for 1981 were only
5 per cent below those of thirty years earlier when the number of private motor cars on Britain's roads was only a quarter of the 1981
figure. It was against this background that the unions looked for
greater stability of employment in the closing years of the century,
feeling as they did that great sacrifices had been made in the interests
of efficiency in the Beeching era and after. The loss of jobs was
accelerated rather than checked in the months following the publication of *The Railwaymen's Charter*. TV news announcements
spotlight individual factory closures resulting in the loss of hundreds of jobs and give rise to expressions of deep concern. Yet in the
two years 1979-81 there was a much less publicised loss of 12,000
jobs on British Railways. The NUR estimated that this drastic slimming of staff numbers saved the Board £55 million *annually*. In the
whole of the Board's undertakings the job loss was 17,000 over the
same two years.

Those railway workers who were lucky enough to keep their
employment did not see the fulfilment of the charter's second aim:
the increase in the railman's basic rate to £72 a week. At the end of
1981 the railman was still on a basic rate of only £63.45. He was still
waiting for the extra £1.55 promised from 3 August. It did not seem
to be the case that the shedding of thousands of jobs was intended to
make things better for those who remained. The residue was scarcely
a highly paid elite.

Those who drafted the charter hoped that after five years the working week of railway conciliation staff would be reduced to thirty-five hours. After two years the thirty-nine hour week was still awaiting introduction, though it was to come in 1982. There have been no promises of any further reductions. Nor was there any progress in respect of the increase in the number of days annual paid leave. An objective of five weeks had been stated. It made sense as a small contribution to work sharing; but at the end of 1981 it seemed as far off as ever. The charter stated, unequivocally, the aim of 'the retention of the existing network' of railways. Whilst there was no axing of lines on the scale of the Beeching era, financial pressures from the government on the Board were strong. It was the Thatcher government policy to disavow any intention to introduce major closures: the onus was placed on the Board of the nationalised railways. Between December 1979 and December 1982 they closed 258 miles of track out of a 1979 total of 10,964 miles. It was problematical whether they would be able to keep closures to this relatively modest scale in subsequent years.

The Railwaymen's Charter had nothing directly to say about railway investment. And yet the only prospect for the limited aims of the charter being realised was the presence at Westminster of a government committed to a flourishing railway system. The Prime Minister after May 1979, however, had no positive approach to railways. Her main concern and that of her cabinet was to reduce the government's financial support to BR and to hive off the profitable parts of the Board's undertakings. An Electrification Review carried out jointly by BR and the Department of Transport reported early in 1981 that, in view of the strong case for main line electrification, the government should endorse a rolling programme. The government prevaricated and then asked BR to re-submit its plans using different criteria. Meanwhile the Channel Tunnel project was shelved. With retrenchment in public spending being the outstanding concern in Whitehall *The Railwaymen's Charter* was condemned to gather dust on the shelves. The failure to concede any major part of its demands was a recipe for discontent and disillusionment. This erupted in 1982 as the following chapter will show.

7
The Strikes of 1982
(i) Productivity Issues including Flexible Rostering

I

In the BRB's *Annual Report and Accounts for 1979* Sir Peter Parker made the wholly justifiable claim that the railways were 'amongst those industries with the lowest number of days lost through industrial disputes'.[1] From 1 January 1948, when the railways were nationalised, to the end of the 1970s, there were very few occasions when the entire railway network was closed by strikes. The longest closure was for seventeen days in May and June 1955 when ASLEF brought out its members to support a claim for higher pay for footplatemen. The one day national strike on 3 October 1962 was called in protest against Dr Beeching's closure of railway workshops. Overtime bans and working to rule were applied on other occasions. It remained true, as the Chairman of the Board told the members of the Donovan Commission in 1966, that 'railwaymen generally display a high standard of industrial discipline'.[2]

By contrast, in the one year 1982 more working days were lost through railway strikes than in the entire period from 1948 to 1981. ASLEF strikes closed the railways for seventeen days in January and February and fifteen days in July; two days more were lost through the NUR strike at the end of June. These stoppages were not haphazard ones. They were the culmination of a government of hostility to public enterprise and to railways in particular. A transport department whose main concern should have been to increase the efficiency of railway operation by authorising investment in modern equipment was instead preoccupied in selling off BR's more profitable assets in order to reduce the real value of the PSO.

The strikes which were the outcome of these policies will be considered in this and the following chapter. To avoid confusion in the reader's mind the ASLEF strikes will be considered first, even though the second wave of them came after the two day strike of the NUR from 28 to 29 June. This treatment is justified since ASLEF's quarrel was about productivity while the NUR's concerned low pay.

When Norman Fowler said that 'nothing is more important than that the railways should improve their productivity'[3] he was thinking primarily of job shedding and the change in working practices. In other words, labour was to bear the brunt of the change. In concentrating attention on manpower reductions and changed working practices Fowler conveniently overlooked the more important means of increasing productivity such as investment in new technologies or the introduction of new marketing policies which encourage more traffic and therefore employ labour more efficiently. The productivity of a large number of railway workers is determined by conditions beyond their control. A signalman cannot clear more than the scheduled number of trains passing his box; a booking clerk is more productive when cheap fares attract more customers; he is much less so when fares are prohibitively high; a crossing keeper would not be thanked for opening and shutting the gates to traffic more frequently than the passing of trains justified.

The press helped to nourish the belief that the railways were grossly overmanned and that a reduction in staff numbers was a clear pre-requisite for improved productivity. Thus *The Times* noted 'the quite pathological antipathy on the part of railway unions to concede productivity for higher wages'[4] whilst ignoring the fact that thousands of jobs in marshalling yards, signalling and in the collection and delivery of parcels – to mention only some outstanding examples – had been shed in the interests of improved technology within the short space of two years. When a motor manufacturing firm sacks, say, 500 workers, the news is flashed on the television screens. The loss of many times that number of railway jobs in the course of a year on the railways attracts no such attention. The impression is then created that Leyland and other car firms are modernising methods of production while the BRB manifests an easy going tolerance of over-manning. Nothing can be further from the truth. The reduction in jobs on the railways has been on a massive scale. In 1950 497,000 staff were employed; by 1981 numbers had fallen to 166,000 and yet in 1981 the passenger mile figures were only

FIGURE 5
British Railways: Employee numbers

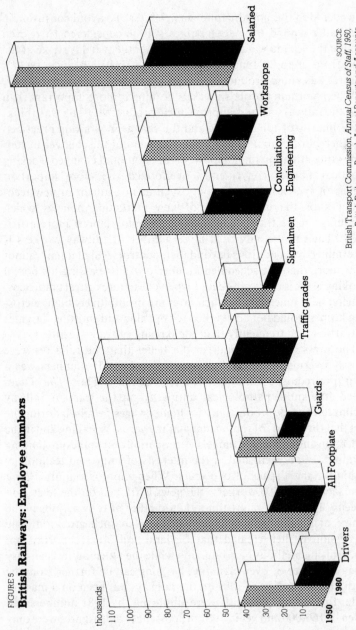

SOURCE
British Transport Commission, *Annual Census of Staff, 1950.*
British Railways Board, *Annual Reports and Accounts*

FIGURE 6
British Railways: reduction in manpower since 1979

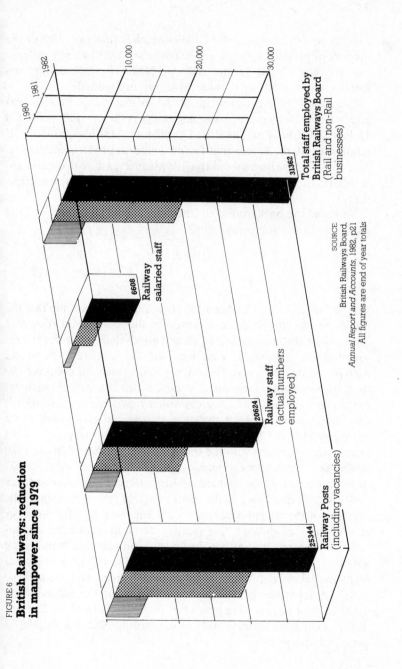

Total staff employed by British Railways Board (Rail and non-Rail businesses) 31362

Railway salaried staff 6608

Railway staff (actual numbers employed) 20624

Railway Posts (including vacancies) 25344

SOURCE
British Railways Board,
Annual Report and Accounts, 1982, p21
All figures are end of year totals

five per cent below the level of 1950 when less than one sixth of the number of private cars were on the roads and railway route mileage was eleven per cent greater than in 1981. The fall in numbers employed in the different grades is shown in Figure 5.

From May 1979 the pressure on BR to shed yet more jobs was intensified. The increased pace of sackings is shown in Figure 6. On 13 July 1982 Cliff Rose, BR Board member responsible for industrial relations, told the unions that further evidence of job shedding was needed so that the Board would have 'a prospectus to go to the government with confidence'[5] and ask for the funding for railway electrification.

This was the background to the bitter industrial disputes of the winter and early summer of 1982.

II

The pay settlement of 28 April 1980 contained a declaration that the unions would co-operate in schemes for the rapid scaling down of the work of the marshalling yards and goods depots and for the re-organisation (i.e. staff reductions) of the control offices and accounting departments. The unions also agreed 'to continue the discussions/negotiations already begun on changes in national agreements and working practices with a view to early completion'. The programme designed to achieve these objectives was to be agreed by 31 May 1981.[6] By the end of 1981 substantial progress had been made in dealing with the specific items mentioned in the 1980 pay award. The number of marshalling yards was reduced from 107 to 74, a change which enabled BR in its *Report and Accounts* for 1981 to state that 'despite the continuing climate of recession' the finances of the freight department had improved by fifty three per cent in the year through 'the running down of outmoded wagon-load services and the rationalisation of terminals and marshalling yards'.[7] The same report noted the completion of the 'withdrawal from the loss-making part of the general parcels sector', a move which undoubtedly contributed handsomely to the reduction by 7,662 in the numbers of railway staff that year.[8] The big reductions in the number of salaried staff took place in 1982 when 6,608 of these jobs disappeared.[9]

In the *Understanding on Productivity* agreed at ACAS on 20 August 1981, the 'changes in national agreements and working practices' which the Board was seeking in order to improve its financial position and impress the Secretary of State for Transport, were principally six in number. They included (1) the flexible rostering of guards and footplatemen; (2) the single manning of passenger trains; (3) the removal of guards from freight trains; (4) the single manning of train engines; (5) the introduction of the trainman concept; and (6) open stations. The financial savings the Board anticipated from the introduction of flexible rostering were £0.4 million in 1982; £1.7 million in 1983; £3.2 million in 1984; and £3.8 million in 1985,[10] giving an aggregate of £9.1 million spread over the *four* years, or little more than one per cent of the government's PSO grant of £887.2 million for the one year 1982. It is clear that the savings the Board expected to achieve from the change would affect its balance of profit and loss only very marginally. More substantial savings could be expected from the single manning of trains; but the Board considered flexible rostering to be important 'not so much in itself but as one of a succession of steps to a more automated railway'.[11]

In the twelve months following the signing of the ACAS *Understanding on Productivity* the Board and the unions made considerable progress in dealing with most of the items the Board had singled out for changes in working practices, though the achievement of a number of agreements attracted far less publicity than did the disagreements between ASLEF and the Board on the issue of flexible rostering.

Given the financial pressures on the Board, its concern to expedite the single manning of both passenger and freight trains can well be understood. Train crews accounted for twenty-one per cent of the Board's staff and absorbed £270 million, or twelve per cent, of total costs annually.[12] The guards, who would be displaced under single manning, belonged to the NUR. The case for their retention on freight trains was that they could help the driver in the case of a breakdown. On other trains they could act as one means of communication with passengers, informing them of the train's progress and, especially late at night, protecting them from assault. They could also protect the carriages from the activities of vandals. The NUR countered the Board's single manning proposals with the open station plan under which the job of issuing tickets would be taken away from the smaller stations and transferred to the guard. In this way stations would come to resemble bus stops and guards would assume duties as travelling ticket collectors.

Smoothest progress was made in experimenting with open stations. On 21 May 1981, i.e. three months *before* the ACAS *Understanding on Productivity*, the NUR executive agreed, with only two dissentients, to the proposal that detailed plans should be considered at Sectional Council level.[13] When union representatives met the Board on 3 September, however, it was clear that regional management had taken longer than had been anticipated in preparing proposals. Despite these delays, on 9 October the NUR executive agreed unanimously to the adoption of a six months' experiment, starting in November 1981, and affecting fifty-one stations in the Scottish region on the routes from Inverness to Aberdeen, Dunkeld, and Kyle of Lochalsh, Wick and Thurso.[14] The agreement was later extended to cover the route from Aberdeen to Dunbar. On 12 November it gave its blessing to a further experiment, starting on 4 January 1982, on the Western Region on lines west of Weston-super-Mare.[15] In each case it was made a condition of the union's endorsement that there would be no loss of jobs, that average earnings were protected and that there would be regular reports from the Sectional Councils of the regions concerned to the national executive.

On the subject of the single manning of passenger trains the ACAS report of 20 August 1981 had stated: 'Without any preconceived conditions on either side, discussions shall take place on the prototype system of the Bedford-St. Pancras services.' The first indication the Board gave to the NUR that it intended to introduce one man operation on the Bedford-St. Pancras line was given in a letter dated 13 May 1981. Some elaboration of the proposal was given in a further letter to the union a fortnight later. On 11 June Sidney Weighell wrote an unequivocal reply: 'I would confirm that under no circumstances is this union able to discuss one man operation of trains.'[16] One reason for this unusually strong opposition was that members of the union resented what they saw as the 'steam roller' tactics of the Board which had already ordered carriages specially designed for OMO – there was no place for the guard. Unity House was being presented with a fait accompli. Furthermore the case for employing a guard on a train for revenue and passenger protection was a strong one. If the highly efficient Swiss Federal Railways found the employment of conductor guards worth while, why should not this be the case on BR? It was known that BR had decided to spend £150 million on track overhaul, new signalling (the replacement of thirty-three old boxes by one new one), radio equipment for locomotive to signalbox communications and closed circuit TV, long before the union was contacted to discuss the manning of trains. In the NUR it was felt that the Bedford-St. Pancras line was almost certainly being regarded at Rail House (BR's headquarters) as the harbinger of the more general introduction of OMO on BR. It was all the more important therefore to get right, from the start, the arrangements for the new type of service.

After discussions at the RSJC (Traffic) and RSJC (Loco) the NUR's proposals were summed up in a letter to the Board on 15 February 1982. It was suggested that 'in presenting the new, modern, service to the public . . . the Board should grasp the opportunity to extend the operation of the Open Station Concept to this service'. The union was willing to 'redefine the role of the guard so as to lay greater emphasis on revenue protection and customer service'.[17] The guards involved would be redesignated train superintendents and be given a rate of pay of £93.05 a week on the understanding that they would 'play a major role in revenue protection and customer servicing'. As a result of negotiations conducted in the RSJC (Traffic) and RSJC (Loco) in December 1982, it was agreed that drivers working Driver only Operated (DOO) trains on the electrified Bedford-St. Pancras line should be given an additional allowance of £6 per turn to compensate them for their increased responsibilities. Since the signalmen on the line were to be responsible for maintaining radio communication with the drivers they were to be given an extra £2 per turn. The Board agreed to the NUR's suggestion that guards should be retained for revenue protection and customer service, but for an experimental period of six months only, following which there would be a reassessment of their employment.[18]

Although this compromise settlement made possible the opening up of the new Bedford-St. Pancras service in October 1983 there were shortcomings in what was being provided. When the coaches were ordered the Board was so concerned to make financial economies by dispensing with the services of the guard that no van was provided to accommodate bicycles. BR's fear was that the van might become the guard's van. For the same reason no provision was made for the accommodation of mail bags which had to be carried in part of a passenger compartment. Clearly the claims of financial economy took precedence over considerations of customer safety and convenience.

That the Board was very keen to introduce DOO on freight trains at the earliest opportunity was revealed in the ACAS *Understanding on Productivity* which read (in part) –

> There shall be an immediate joint examination with a view to establishing, to the satisfaction of the parties, circumstances in which some freight trains could be operated without guards. Two or three pilot schemes shall, if possible, be ready for introduction by 1 January 1982.

The financial gains to be anticipated from DOO freight trains were greater than would be likely to accrue from any other single reform of working practices. That is why the agreement made between BR, the NUR and ASLEF in December 1981 to conduct trials on three routes: Port Talbot-Llanwern (iron ore), Immingham-Scunthorpe (iron ore) and Willesden-Garston (Freightliner) was so important. The trial schemes were on the basis of one round trip in each of these services per day. Each train could be accompanied by observers from BR, NUR and ASLEF if so desired. The extra compensation given to drivers was the same as that agreed for the Bedford-St. Pancras line – £6 a turn.[19]

Another area in which the Board hoped to be able to achieve substantial economies – £13 million was the figure quoted – was in easing the conditions of single manning of locomotives. Two important post-war agreements, reached on 18 December 1955 and 28 October 1965 introduced, and then greatly extended, single manning. Under the 1955 agreement passenger train locomotives were to be single manned wherever the driver's trip did not exceed 200 miles or his tour of duty six hours. For freight trains permitted distances for single manning were shorter. The 1965 agreement extended single manning distances on both passenger and freight trains.[20] ASLEF was reluctant to make major concessions on locomotive manning and in a memorandum to the Board proposed only minor amendments to the earlier agreements. The changes the Board were proposing would result in a greater loss of drivers' jobs, and hence of ASLEF membership than could be expected from the introduction of flexible rostering. Thus virtually no progress was made in negotiations on this item in 1982.

There was little progress either in promoting the 'trainman concept'. For more than a century the line of promotion to driver had been clear, but restricted. The aspiring express driver would start his railway career as an engine cleaner and proceed by (often prolonged) stages to the various grades of fireman and engine driver. Revolutionary changes in railway technology made many of the old grade distinctions less meaningful. Under the trainman concept these rigid lines of demarcation would be removed and promotion onto the footplate would be possible from other grades in the service.

In sum, the railway workers made a substantial contribution to increased productivity in 1981. There was co-operation in the streamlining of the freight business and extensive experiments had been agreed in the introduction of open stations and in DOO of freight trains. The NUR had produced a constructive alternative to DOO on the Bedford-St. Pancras line. Above all, nearly 12,000 jobs had been lost on the altar of improved efficiency. On the issue of flexible rostering of footplate staff there was no progress. It was the failure to make headway in this area which was the immediate cause of the closing down of the railway system for thirty-two days (out of the thirty-four lost to strikes) in 1982.

III

Within the close knit community of ASLEF members in 1982 the agreement the union reached with Sir Albert Stanley, President of the Board of Trade in Lloyd George's coalition government on 6 December 1918, providing for the introduction of the eight hour day from 1 February 1919, was seen as one of the greatest achievements in the union's more than century long history. Included in the first official history of the union, S.R. Raynes's, *Engines and Men* (1921), is a photograph of one of the letters sent from Stanley to Jack Bromley, ASLEF's general secretary. It is arguable that the industrial muscle represented by the 416,000 members of the NUR was at least as important as the final negotiating efforts of ASLEF in achieving the substantial reduction in working hours. The craft union's activists are not impressed by such an interpretation; the eight hour day – the great victory of their predecessors – was seen as sacrosanct.

Of course it would be a mistake to imagine that after 1 February 1919 no footplateman worked more than eight hours in a shift. The main points of the agreement with Stanley were that each footplateman was guaranteed at least eight hours pay a day, whether or not there was eight hours work to be done, and that overtime rates were payable to him if any shift exceeded eight hours in length. At a meeting of the RSJC (Loco) on 25 February 1982 the ASLEF representative conceded that 'the management now (i.e. already) had the right to roster between seven and nine hours and the ability to roster over nine hours by agreement'. What concerned management in the environment of the financial pressures of 1981-2 was that the 1919 agreement for the eight hour day 'precluded the opportunity to maximise the productive work done by drivers'. In a shift involving a 2½ hour driving duty each way, for example, total useful working time would be 6½ hours, made up of five hours driving, thirty minutes for a physical needs break and another thirty minutes for booking on and off duty, studying instructions, and so on. The remaining 1½ hours could not be profitably utilised. However, a seven hour shift would reduce the unproductive time to only half an hour while a nine hour shift would enable another driving turn to be worked.[21]

A further reason for the demand for flexible rostering was a clause in the 1980 pay agreement which read:

> The Board accepts a commitment to reduce the standard working week of staff covered by the RSNC from the present levels of forty hours for conciliation staff by the equivalent of one hour from 1 November 1981 providing this is done within the context of measures which will minimise the cost effects.[22]

The trouble was that while eight hours divided into forty easily enough, dividing them into thirty nine presented more problems. Initially the Board proposed that the working day should be curtailed by twelve minutes. The NUR considered that such a change would prove largely meaningless. It proposed instead that staff should be entitled to an extra free day once in eight weeks. The Board fell in with this suggestion, but insisted that to comply with the requirement to 'minimise the cost effects' of the shorter hours, flexible rostering of guards and footplatemen would need to be introduced.

In the six separate meetings which were held in the RSNC (Loco) between 2 September and 30 November 1981 when a 'failure to agree' was recorded, BR representatives maintained that flexible rostering was both feasible and beneficial to the staff. Comparisons were made with other European countries where flexible rostering had been found perfectly practicable. In West Germany drivers shifts varied from four to twelve hours and could begin at any time round the clock. In France the variations in working hours were far greater than was being proposed by BR.

What was conveniently forgotten when comparison was made with the working conditions of French footplatemen was that their basic rate of pay was £180 a week, more than half as much again as the basic rate of the BR driver, while standard hours of work were only 35 to 39 per week.[23] Agreement with ASLEF on a relaxation of the terms of the agreement of 6 December 1918 may not have been so unlikely as BR and the government were suggesting. What *was* unlikely was any agreement within the severe financial restraints being imposed on BR as a result of Thatcherite monetarism. In its written evidence to RSNT in May 1982 ASLEF stated: 'The question of flexible rostering may perhaps be looked at in a different light if they were accorded pay and conditions of employment similar to those enjoyed by footplate staff in the countries cited.'[24]

The sad fact was that this suggestion was never taken up. In 1975 drivers were fourth in the pay comparability league; in 1981 they were thirty-fourth. It is not suggested that relativities should be immutable. But it is conceivable that had BR felt able to offer even half of the twenty-nine per cent ASLEF said was needed to restore their position in the comparability league, the union would have been willing to conduct serious negotiations instead of playing for time as it did in the last quarter of 1981. The cost to BR would have been far less than the £168 million lost in consequence of the strikes of 1982.[25]

Flexible rostering affected the working conditions of guards who belonged to the NUR, as well as of drivers, most of whom belonged to ASLEF. In the absence of trade union unity or even a close working federation, the two unions made their own decisions on how best to serve the interests of their members. The NUR approach was that the achievement of the eight hour day was an important stage, but certainly not the final one, in the union's continuing campaign to shorten the hours of work and spread job opportunities in the industry. The agreement on the thirty-nine hour week was seen as an opportunity by means of patient negotiation, to improve the working conditions of the membership. Thus, in the nine meetings of the RSNC (Traffic) which took place between 3 September and 16 December 1981, Russell Tuck, Senior Assistant General Secretary, did some hard bargaining with the Board's representatives. BR's first proposal was that rosters should vary between four and twelve hours daily. By 29 October Russell Tuck had persuaded the Board to limit the range of shifts to between six and ten hours. By 16 November it was from seven to ten, and in the final agreement a month later it was between seven and nine. Other points conceded by the Board included the grouping of rest days, more long weekends off work, the reduction in the number of unsocial booking-on times and the inviolate right to take allocated free days. Three days before Christmas 1981 the NUR executive, by a two to one majority, approved the arrangements which had been negotiated for the flexible rostering of guards.[26]

The NUR representatives in RSJC (Loco) accepted in principle the proposals for the flexible rostering of footplate staff, maintaining that the same kind of advantages which had been secured for guards would be available. However, the failure of ASLEF to modify its opposition to any deviation from the eight hour day agreement made progress in the negotiations impossible. TSSA also co-operated fully in securing for its members the maximum benefits obtainable under flexible rostering.[27]

By the third week in December 1981 the Board had come to the conclusion that it was time to take a strong line over flexible rostering which Sir Peter Parker regarded as 'a very important symbolic piece of efficiency'.[28] In a letter sent to all the trade union general secretaries the Board's Director of Industrial Relations wrote of 'a specific resistance to change ... within the RSJC (Loco) section' which had made the Board decide not to introduce the shorter working week on 4 January 1982 and not to make payment to the footplate grades of the three per cent outstanding from the 1981 pay settlement.[29] The unanimous opinion of the NUR executive was that the Board was 'totally wrong in their action'. They instructed Sidney

Weighell to see Sir Peter Parker with the object of having the Board's decision reversed. Meanwhile ASLEF instructed its members to work to rule from 4 January 1982 and to stop work completely on 13 and 14 January.

The executives of all three rail unions considered that the Board had acted improperly in withholding the final payment of the 1981 pay award. Negotiations on the 1981 pay settlement were exceptionally long and difficult. Since agreement could not be reached in the RSNC, the dispute was referred to the RSNT, which, in its decision number 75 issued on 16 July 1981, ruled that an eight per cent increase in pay should be given, back-dated to 20 April and that a further three per cent should become payable from 1 August. The Tribunal split the pay award into two parts to meet BR's plea of financial stringency. The three unions accepted the award, but at a meeting of the RSNC on 21 July Cliff Rose, for the Board, said that BR would pay the three per cent only when there was more agreement on the productivity issues. A strike at this stage was averted only through the intervention of ACAS, which on 20 August produced its two famous, separate, agreements on pay and productivity. It was under the first of these agreements that the union had with reluctance, agreed to the delay, until 4 January 1982, in paying the outstanding three per cent of the 1981 pay award. When it is remembered that the normal payment date is in April and that the Board had failed to implement in full a Tribunal Award which, in any case, did not match the rise in the cost of living – the total award was eleven per cent over the year: prices had risen by twelve per cent – the anger of the unions after two postponements of payment can well be understood. In reply to the Board's assertion that under the ACAS *Understanding on Pay* the unions had committed themselves to continue progress on the productivity negotiations, ASLEF referred to the Board's Circular No. 121 of September 1981 which informed staff of arrangements for the payment of the three per cent from January 1982. This circular was issued long before any union had agreed to flexible rostering. It was clear that at the time of its issuance the Board was treating the *Understanding on Pay* as something separate from the *Understanding on Productivity*. That this was the Board's view at the time is shown by its reaction to an *Observer* comment that it was planning to withhold the three per cent if progress on productivity was slow. The Board's spokesman immediately repudiated this suggestion. He told the BBC that 'pay and productivity remain separate issues and there was no intention ...of using the three per cent punitively'.[30] It was financial pressures which changed, and hardened, the Board's stance by December 1981.

Since ASLEF considered that there was little point in calling a meeting of the RSJC, the general secretaries of both TSSA and the NUR took the initiative in arranging an ad hoc meeting between all three rail unions and the Board on 11 January. The unions were agreed that it was wrong of BR to withhold the outstanding 3 per cent of the 1981 pay award and stressed that if the money was paid the strike would be averted. However, the Board refused to pay up until ASLEF had agreed to proposals for flexible rostering. The NUR representatives pointed out that their union had agreed to a scheme for flexible rostering and said that it was particularly unfair to withhold the money from NUR drivers. After there had been a number of adjournments to the meeting the Board promised to meet the NUR's demand. On the main issue there was deadlock and the strike went ahead two days later.[31]

IV

On 13 January, the day the series of ASLEF strikes began, Sir Peter Parker, who until then had a reputation as a conciliator, was quoted as saying: 'This is the Grand National of Change and this is really the first big fence. There is no going back on that.'[32] Behind him were those members of the Board generally regarded as taking a tougher approach to the unions: Bob Reid, the Chief Executive, and James Urquart. ASLEF had the backing of the NUR and TSSA which instructed their members not to cross picket lines and of the TUC which accepted the train drivers' case that the two understandings reached at ACAS on 20 August 1981 were separate and that there was no justification for BR withholding the outstanding wage award. The press was generally hostile to ASLEF's action, but few went to the lengths of the leader writer of the *Daily Mail* who described the action of the train drivers as 'cynical, greedy and utterly without moral or material justification'.[33]

Despite a mixture of stern warnings and blandishments from the

Board and the press there was an impressive response from the drivers to the ASLEF executive's call for a series of one day strikes. On the third day of the strikes, of 20,000 footplate staff employed by BR, less than 300 took out trains. The 500 mile long traffic jams in Greater London provided confirmatory evidence of the completeness of the shutdown. A variety of reasons persuaded footplatemen to sacrifice their pay in the eighteen days of strikes of the winter. (The union decided not to offer any of its members strike benefit.) The introduction of flexible rostering would result in the loss of 800-850 jobs in the short run and a total of 4,000 in the longer term.[34] Although the Board insisted that the job losses could be met through natural wastage, the prospect for the union of losing nearly a quarter of the members it had on BR was a forbidding one. The typical driver's working life was already a very 'unsocial' one. He could be called upon to start a shift at any time in the early hours of the morning and something like a quarter of his gross earnings – about £32.60 a week – came from overtime and premium payments gained from working on Saturdays and Sundays.[35] Footplatemen did not like what they knew about flexible rostering in the German Federal Republic where drivers' shifts could last anything from five to twelve hours and could begin at any time in the day or night.[36] The union office was telling members that BR's proposals were 'unworkable' and 'would cause chaos'.[37] It was widely rumoured that the adoption of the new proposals would result in a big loss of earnings. BR failed to indicate in time how much extra money, if any, would be available to members of staff who worked flexible rosters.

From the earliest days of the strikes the leaders of the NUR and TSSA were in touch with Pat Lowry, Chairman of ACAS, with a view to arranging a committee of inquiry which might result in some agreement which would bring the industrial action to an end. After delays, due to the failure of the other parties concerned to persuade ASLEF to participate, the three man Committee of Inquiry, chaired by Lord McCarthy, heard evidence from 9 to 11 February inclusive. The report, which was published on 16 February, advised ASLEF to instruct its members to return to work and advised BR to pay the overdue three per cent increase of the 1981 pay award. ASLEF was also advised to confirm its continued commitment to the ACAS Understanding on Productivity, particularly with respect to variable rostering. On the day following the publication of the ACAS report,

Pat Lowry brought together the representatives of BR, the three railway unions and Len Murray, Secretary of the TUC. The three unions agreed to accept the report as printed and BR agreed to pay the three per cent wage increase, back dated to 3 August 1981. ASLEF ordered the resumption of work from 0.01 hours on 19 February.

Geoffrey Goodman, the veteran industrial relations correspondent of the *Daily Mirror*, considered that although no formal letter was sent to Sir Peter Parker from any member of the government urging him to pay the three per cent due to the footplatemen, it was clear that senior cabinet ministers, including Premier Margaret Thatcher, were against pushing the dispute into a major confrontation with the unions.[37] Tebbit and Howell were advising the Premier that it was 'the wrong issue at the wrong time for a showdown with the unions'.[38]

The Committee of Inquiry had recommended that if no agreement on the flexible rostering issue could be reached within a month, i.e. by 19 March, the dispute should be referred to the RSNT. The expected happened. Discussions in the RSJC (Loco) on 25 February and in the RSNC on 1 March led nowhere and a failure to agree was recorded.

So the scene was set for the RSNT to consider what Lord McCarthy described as 'the most difficult reference' he had had to deal with since he became its chairman.[39] The Tribunal heard evidence from the trade unions and the Board on 15 and 16 March and then went on a tour of some of the leading locomotive depots, including those in York, Glasgow and Bristol, to discover at first hand the drivers' views. Representatives of the unions and of BR accompanied the members of the tribunal. The key appointment was undoubtedly that of Bill Fordham, a veteran guard who came from March in Cambridgeshire and was a member of the NUR executive. He was extremely conscientious and a dedicated member of his union. What he did not know about the working conditions of guards and about flexible rostering was not worth knowing. The NUR had accepted flexible rostering for guards in December 1981 and in a number of depots men of this grade had already experienced some weeks of its operation. At each depot visited Bill Fordham was at Lord McCarthy's side to give chapter and verse answers to each of the ASLEF member's objections. At York they answered the objection that implementation of the scheme would reduce footplatemen's earnings by requesting the yardmaster to produce his books for recent weeks. The entries showed that staff gained financially from flexible rostering. At the North British Hotel in Glasgow the visiting party and the local representatives sat round a large table until two o'clock one morning dealing with the footplatemen's doubts and questions.

When the findings of RSNT 77 were published on 7 May 1982 the members of the tribunal reported their finding in the depots, 'real and widespread resistance to the Board's proposals for flexible rostering which ASLEF's submission to the tribunal reflected with accuracy and force'. Nevertheless, the tribunal considered that 'the legitimate fears of ASLEF could be met'[40] and the Board's proposals for flexible rostering should be adopted since they would result in a more effective use of the driver's time 'without causing an unreasonable variation in the length of each working day or week'. They would make possible for drivers 'additional free days, a reduction of booking on and off at unsocial hours and an inviolate right to rest days off'.[41] The Tribunal recommended that, at LDC level, thirteen different safeguards concerning working conditions should be observed. These sprang directly from the objections the tribunal had heard expressed in the depots, and included a requirement that a majority of the turns should not exceed eight hours duration; there should be no increase in the number of turns signed on and off at unsocial hours and drivers should be ensured full advance information of turns of duty in the programme cycle of eight weeks.

Despite Lord McCarthy's meticulous and sustained efforts to meet the objections of ASLEF, that union's executive was unconvinced of the merits of the tribunal's findings. On 13 May 1982 Ray Buckton wrote to Sir Peter Parker rejecting RSNT 77 as 'a totally unacceptable award'. Although the exercise must have looked hopeless, negotiations were resumed in the RSNC on 28 May when Clifford Rose declared that if there was no agreement on flexible rosters at national level the Board would introduce them locally. Hopes of a settlement were raised at a further meeting of the RSNC on 17 June when Ray Buckton said that ASLEF had always been willing to look at the question of flexible rostering but they were convinced this was only achievable through existing agreements. The Board, for its part, expressed a willingness to conduct a joint experiment, with its plan for new rosters being tried out in the Scottish region and ASLEF's proposals being tested in another part of the country. At a further meeting of the RSNC on 22 June Buckton at first reported that ASLEF could not agree to the Board's proposals; but later in the meeting he said the union might agree to trials in two areas providing there was no imposing of the rosters from London and provided its assembly of delegates had the power of veto. On 23 June BR spelt out, in a letter to ASLEF, its proposals for simultaneous experiments. Two days later the Board sent a further letter in which it indicated that if ASLEF accepted the proposals it would cancel the order to managers to introduce its own plan for flexible rosters from 5 July. If it did not receive a reply by 30 June the order to the managers would stand. The ASLEF executive reply was that after giving consideration to BRB's letter it had decided to instruct the union's members to withdraw their labour from midnight on Sunday 4 July 1982 until further notice.

Geoffrey Goodman's view was that there could have been a settlement on the night of Wednesday 30 June, but that Sir Peter Parker had become 'a prisoner of government policy on the railways'. This policy 'demanded blood from the unions before any further investment could be injected into the system'.[42] Certainly that day Sir Peter Parker had a long session with David Howell during which they agreed that the strike should be fought to a finish.[43] Ray Buckton's proposal, made the following evening, that ASLEF would call off the strike in return for BR's withdrawing the rosters, cut no ice with either the Board or with David Howell. Consequently the strike began as planned. This time it was continuous; there were no half measures.[43]

More drivers worked during ASLEF's July strike than had defied the picket lines in January and February. It is impossible to say whether this was mainly due to members feeling the financial pinch and wishing to avoid getting further into debt or to the effects of the quite unprecedented steps taken by the Board to break the strike. By 15 July the number of men reporting for duty was 835.[44] However, at no time were there more than five per cent of the footplate staff at work. The railway system remained effectively closed and BR was losing £8.5 million a day.

The first tactic adopted by the Board to try to crush the strike was the despatch of a personal letter from Sir Peter Parker to each ASLEF member at his home address. The chairman warned: 'If this strike goes ahead thousands of jobs will go. Perhaps yours'. The letter concluded: 'Convince your union leaders to see sense. Your strike will drive customers away and wreck this great industry. Let us work together for a good future.'[45] The Board next considered conducting a secret ballot of ASLEF members in the hope that it would reveal rank and file opposition to the union executive's decision to call the strike. The plan was abandoned when the Electoral Reform Society pointed out that it would take between two and three weeks to complete.[46] Probably the most successful tactic adopted by BR was the free phone service undertaken with the help of British Telecom. After dialling 100 and asking for 'Freephone Alpha' the husky voice of a woman gave the enquiring driver details of how his earnings and pension would be affected if he was on strike. More than 10,000 enquiries were received.[47] Local managers informed footplate staff that if they were deprived of their union membership as a result of their continuing work during the strike, they would not be dismissed from the service. In other words the closed shop agreement between BR and the unions which came into operation on 1 August 1975 would no longer be enforced.[48] The action of the Board which underlined how deep was the crisis in the industry's industrial relations, and how urgent it was to reach a settlement, was its announcement on Wednesday 14 July that, if the strike was not called off, it would close the entire system from midnight on Tuesday 20 July and dismiss all the striking train drivers who did not accept flexible rostering.[49]

These developments prompted Len Murray to meet the leaders of the rail unions on 15 July and to urge Ray Buckton to get back into negotiations and call off the strike. Meanwhile Sidney Weighell wrote to David Howell, Secretary of State for Transport – 'You should be discharging your responsibilities more aptly if you were to cease your inaction and make a positive effort to find a solution to the current rail dispute'. However, it was consistent with government policy to be content with the run-down of the publicly owned railway industry and the weakening of trade union power, and so the minister did not follow Sid Weighell's suggestion.

It was the Finance and General Purposes Committee of the TUC which retrieved the situation for the railway workers and their unions. It summoned the leaders of the three railway unions to Congress House, the TUC headquarters. Negotiations began at 10 am on Friday 16 July and ended almost exactly a day later. The committee heard, in turn, the case separately presented by the NUR and TSSA in favour of flexible rostering and the ending of the strike. It then listened to Ray Buckton defend ASLEF's stand and appeal for the support of the trade union movement. At question time, with all railway union representatives present, the following exchanges took place:

Alan Sapper:	Would you accept movement away from the eight hour day during experiments?
Ray Buckton:	Yes.
Alan Sapper:	The reason you could not agree to RSNT 77 was the decision of the Annual Assembly of Delegates?
Ray Buckton:	You've got it.
Sidney Weighell:	Our document dispels all the fears ASLEF have.
Ray Buckton:	Yes, but we would be sacked if we went against the AAD decision.[50]

The TUC committee and the railway union leaders then left the discussions to go to another part of Congress House. The Committee reached the unanimous decision to ask BR to withdraw flexible rostering from the seventy-one depots where it had already been introduced in exchange for ASLEF calling off its strike. Its members drove down to the ACAS headquarters to meet the BR representatives who had booked in at the nearby Charing Cross Hotel. After hours of discussion, interlaced with sandwiches supplied by the New Scotland Yard canteen, the TUC committee concluded that the Board was determined not to cancel the rosters already posted though it was prepared to describe them as 'provisional'. At 7.15 am it concluded that nothing further was to be gained from discussions with the BR representatives and it rejoined the railway unionists who had been waiting overnight at Congress House. The committee in its statement, unanimously agreed, expressed deep concern 'about the effects of the current stoppages on British Railways, its workers and the country as a whole' and recommended:

1. BR should withdraw its threat to sack strikers and close the rail networks, treat as provisional the flexible rosters already posted at seventy-one depots and introduce no further new rosters before August 2.

2. Acting on the advice of the Finance and General Purposes Committee, ASLEF will immediately terminate the strike and instruct their members to return to work and recall their annual delegate conference within 7-10 days hereof, and recommend the conference to authorise the EC of ASLEF to enter into negotiations and conclude an agreement for footplate staff on the basis of the recommendations and safeguards contained in RSNT decision 77.

3. These negotiations should begin immediately after the ASLEF conference and will be completed in six days.[51]

The ASLEF executive considered refusing the TUC's advice but realised this could breach the TUC's rules and lead to the union's suspension. It therefore came to the unanimous decision to approve the TUC's proposal. Thereafter it was 'plain sailing'.[52] A day-long conference of ASLEF on 27 July accepted flexible rostering though with strong reservations.[53] Meetings of the RSNC were held on 22, 23 and 26 July and 2 August culminating in the signing of a *Draft Agreement for the Variable Programming and Rostering Hours for Footplate Staff* by representatives of BR and all three railway unions.[54]

V

The intervention of the TUC on 16-17 July 1982 was a rescue operation, not a betrayal. Contrary to popular belief, BR is by no means in a monopoly position in British transport. The ASLEF strike, which fuelled the Thatcher government's anti-rail and anti-union prejudices, did serious damage to the railway industry. The cabinet was, no doubt, unperturbed to learn that Ford's traffic to Ireland, hitherto going most of its way by rail to Holyhead, was diverted into ship from Dagenham during the strike. The traffic in Heinz products was switched from rail to road. Passenger traffic slumped. BR's Director of Finance and Planning estimated the losses attributable to the strikes in 1982 at £168 million.[55] The view at Rail House is that the strikes damaged, perhaps irreparably, any prospect of government funding of major electrification schemes or other vital investment projects. It is arguable, of course, that, strike or no strike, the Thatcher government would not have sponsored large schemes for railway improvement. What is incontrovertible is that the strikes did not improve the chances for their adoption.

The character of industrial relations on the railway changed for the worse as a result of ASLEF's action. In place of a tradition of consultation and negotiated agreements, strong-arm tactics of confrontation, sometimes borrowed from American industrial relations practice, were adopted by the Board. The by-passing of the unions and direct appeal to the staff by letter and telephone undermined the negotiating machinery carefully built up over the years. The future of the closed shop was threatened by the Board's letter promising non-striking drivers the retention of their jobs even if they lost union membership.

Ultimate blame for the record number of days lost through strikes on the railways in 1982 rests with the Thatcher government. It could have prevented the strikes if it had made an unequivocal statement at an early date that the publicly owned railways had a major role to play in British transport and that adequate funding would be provided for the fulfilment of that role. In the late summer of 1983 locomotive depots were accepting flexible rostering at an accelerating rate as news got around that a minimum of £6 a week extra was available to drivers working the new rosters.[56] Had such money been widely announced as available eighteen months earlier the tragedy of the summer of 1982 could have been averted.

Although the Thatcher government must accept ultimate responsibility there was no excuse for ASLEF playing into its hands. In July 1982 the craft union was striking against the adoption of proposals which, on balance, stood to improve drivers' working conditions. The concessions which the NUR had wrung from the Board, including six additional free days in the year; the opportunity of grouping rest days; the reduction in the number of 'unsocial' booking-on times and the inviolate right to free days, made the flexible rostering agreement of August 1982 one of the best in Europe from the railway workers' point of view. It was for this reason that left-wing members of the TUC, such as Alan Sapper, who entered Congress House on the morning of 16 July expecting to back the ASLEF case and were cheered by the small crowd outside the building, changed their minds when they listened to the facts as presented by TSSA and the NUR. The decision of the Finance and General Purposes Committee, composed of a mixture of right-wing, moderate and left-wing members, was unanimous.

The Strikes of 1982
(ii) Workshop Closures and Low Pay

I

Although the dispute over flexible rostering attracted more press coverage than any other railway matter in the first half of 1982 it was by no means the only issue which aroused strong feelings among railway workers. In May the NUR came to the brink of a strike over projected workshop closures. At the end of June all the union's members were called out on strike to back a claim for an improvement of the 1982 pay offer. In the event only two working days were lost; but the issues at stake were of the utmost importance for the future of the industry.

In 'normal' times the fortunes of British Rail Engineering Ltd (BREL) closely mirrored those of its parent organisation BR, from which it gained ninety-eight per cent of its orders. When freight traffic is heavy, locomotives, wagons and carriages are more intensively used, need repair more frequently and need replacement sooner. In times of economic depression the use of locomotives, wagons and carriages declines and workshop activity slackens. In the early 1980s, however, things were far from normal. An exceptionally severe economic slump, aggravated by the government's monetarist policies, a sharp curtailment of funds available for investment and the impact of radical changes in technology combined to bring about a major crisis in BREL.

The threat to the job security of the 34,500 men and women employed by BREL at the beginning of 1982 did not arise from the absence of need for new locomotives and rolling stock. Year after year, in his introduction to BR's *Annual Report and Accounts*, Sir Peter Parker drew attention to the urgent need for the replacement

of obsolete equipment. In 1979 he wrote: 'Without increasing investment, standards will continue to drop at an ever accelerating rate
and profitable freight traffic – £10 to £15 million of it in 1979 –
turned away. Only 16 locomotives were built in 1979 out of a total
fleet of 2,000 which need replacement.'

A similar warning was issued in 1980. In 1981 he emphasised the
point again – '66 per cent of our fleet of electric and diesel multiple
unit trains – the work horses of the commuter and rural services – is
between 20 and 30 years old. The age of our trains is one aspect of
the problem, the one which the customer can see and feel for himself.'

It was because these needs could not be met from the finance provided by the government that orders received by the workshops
slumped so severely. As has been shown in chapter three, BR's
investment in the railways fell from £290 million in 1979 to £242 million in 1982. In *real* terms this represented a decline of forty-three
per cent. By 1983 BR's investment was barely a quarter of that of
SNCF's investment in French railways and only one-sixth of DBB's
investment in the railways of West Germany.[1]

The consequences for the wagon building programme of the
government's financial squeeze of BR were devastating. To fulfil the
replacement requirements repeatedly emphasised by Sir Peter
Parker, an average of 1,424 wagons a year needed to be built, the
target fleet for 1986 being 42,000 wagons. Building from 1979-81
matched these requirements. After this it fell dramatically short:

Year	1979	1980	1981	1982	1983	1984 (projected)[2]
Number of wagons	1,483	1,375	1,416	833	120	6
		Average 1,424				

BR's drastic slimming down of the wagon fleet from 165,000 units
in 1977 to 72,918 in 1982; the increased capacity of the remaining
wagons; the substitution of air brakes for vacuum brakes, making
possible the faster movement of freight and, above all, the introduction of TOPS, the computerisation of the control of wagon movements to eliminate unnecessary journeys, played an important part
in reducing the need for new wagons and for the repair of damaged
ones. Freight ton-miles carried on BR fell by sixteen per cent between
1977 and 1982; but the number of wagons in use fell by a staggering

fifty-six per cent. Contributing to this impressive rationalisation of freight movement was BR's decision to withdraw from most wagon load traffic and concentrate on the more economic train load business.

Another development which affected the volume of business undertaken by BREL was the growth in the number of privately owned wagons, the majority of which have been built by private wagon construction companies rather than by BREL. That the work went to private industry rather than the state owned concern was due to a government policy of 'privatisation by the back door'. Discriminatory fiscal policies favoured privately owned companies and disadvantaged BREL. The private wagon builders gained from the 100 per cent capital allowances which they can offset against corporation tax. Private company customers of the wagon manufacturers often prefer to lease the vehicles rather than buy them outright. The savings which the wagon manufacturers make from the capital allowances are passed, in part, to the leasing customers in the form of lower repayment terms. BREL is disadvantaged in that it cannot claim these tax allowances. The private companies have the support of wealthy banks to finance the construction of wagons. BREL, by contrast, confronts a government determined to reduce its financial support to public sector industries and intent on giving maximum encouragement to the private sector.

These are not the only advantages enjoyed by the wagon manufacturing companies. Under Section 8 of the Railways Act, 1974, companies planning to move freight by rail can apply for a grant to cover fifty per cent, and, in some cases, sixty per cent, of the cost of sidings, loading equipment and wagons. In clause eleven of the Transport Act, 1978, some ambiguities concerning the availability of Section 8 grants for wagon construction were removed. BR and BREL, however, are specifically excluded from benefiting from these concessions. In the light of these facts it is scarcely surprising that there has been a rapid growth of the private owner wagon fleet. In 1980 it represented thirteen per cent of the UK railway freight fleet. It has been predicted that, unless BREL is given the power to construct wagons for direct leasing to private owners so as to compete with the private wagon manufacturer on more equal terms, over half the wagons running on the rail network will be privately owned by 1990.[3] The significance of these trends for the future of

BREL workshops, such as those at Shildon and Horwich, can well be appreciated.

With the growth of wagon manufacture in third world countries the prospects for increasing the scale of export orders are decreasing; but where goodwill has been built up through the fulfilment of orders in the past, as in the case of Nigeria, the outlook is brighter. The over-valuation of the pound in relation to foreign currencies during most of Margaret Thatcher's first term of office tied BREL's hands behind its back when it came to competition with other wagon manufacturing countries for foreign orders.

Despite all these developments affecting adversely BREL's order books, it is still reasonable to expect that, with a projected wagon fleet of 42,000 units by 1986, a building programme of 1,424 wagons annually is valid. Were it not for the government's financial straitjacket making the execution of such a programme impossible, there would be sufficient orders to keep threatened workshops in business. But since the strait-jacket was maintained and the government's hostility to the publicly owned railway industry continued the crisis in the workshops deepened.

II

At a meeting of the Rail Shopmen's Informal Liaison Committee on 22 April 1982 BREL management confronted the union representatives with some drastic proposals for workshop closures and manpower redundancies. Basing their recommendations on the estimated requirements of BR for locomotives, carriages and wagons for the period up to 1986, they stated that it would be necessary to close the workshop at Shildon completely, to close the Horwich works, except for the foundry and spring shop, and to close a part of the Swindon works by December 1983. If these plans were carried out there would be 2,285 redundancies at Shildon, 1,381 at Horwich, and 1,300 at Swindon. The addition of 367 redundancies at two Derby workshops would bring to 5,333 the total number of staff facing the loss of their livelihoods.[4]

In April 1982 the NUR had over 13,000 members working for BREL and a further 18,000 members who were employed in BR's own workshops and maintenance depots. The Confederation of Shipbuilding and Engineering Unions (CSEU) recruited a majority of the skilled craftsmen in BREL's workshops whilst the TSSA organised most of the clerical and supervisory grades. But it was the NUR which took the lead in mobilising opposition to the closures and in submitting constructive alternatives to BREL management. The reaction of the union's executive to BREL's proposals was unequivocal. At its meeting held on 29 April it carried unanimously the following resolution: 'That we inform BREL that this union is totally opposed to its policy for railway workshops, which include the proposals to close Horwich and Shildon, and the run down of Swindon. It they proceed with this policy it will be met with the full industrial strength of the union which will include strike and other forms of actions.'[5]

The decision was not taken lightly. The executive had in mind the appalling social consequences of the proposed closures as well as the impact on the railway industry. Shildon, a town of South West Durham with some 12,000 inhabitants, was closely associated with the early development of railways in England. At the entrance to the workshops a brass plaque proudly proclaims the fact that the first British passenger train to be hauled by a steam locomotive left Shildon on the Stockton and Darlington Railway on 27 September 1825. In April 1982 the workshops employed 2,600 persons, more than half the total number of gainfully employed people in the town and eighty-six per cent of the male manufacturing jobs. Apprentices had been trained there for 150 years and many families in the town had provided labour for the works for four generations. The prospects for men and women finding alternative employment in the area were bleak. Unemployment in the Bishop Aukland area, of which Shildon is a part, was already at a level of nearly twenty per cent and an average of fifty-four persons were chasing each new vacancy. It was calculated that, should the closure take place, unemployment in Shildon would rise to at least forty-five per cent.[6]

Horwich, in the Bolton 'travel to work' area, was also in a district of heavy unemployment before the closure of the works was announced. 15.7 per cent of the work force was unemployed. The addition of those sacked from the works would bring the rate of unemployment up to 20.7 per cent.[7] David Young, Labour MP for Bolton, East, summed up the tragedy which faced the town when he said: 'We are talking not about accountancy figures but about individual tragedies of people who are sacked, whose skills are lost, and who have nowhere to go. We are looking at the death of a community, and the responsibility lies at the door of the government.'[8]

At Temple Mills, in the borough of Waltham Forest, unemployment – at ten per cent in the immediate locality – was not so heavy, but the closure and loss of 296 jobs would affect the situation in nearby Newham and Hackney where the unemployment rates were around eighteen per cent.[9]

If it had been the case that the capital equipment of the workshops was obsolete and the skills of the work force outmoded, closures might have been regarded as a sad necessity. The contrary was the case. The Under Secretary of State for Transport, Reginald Eyre, winding up a Commons' debate on the railway workshops, conceded: 'The problem is not that BREL's workshops are out of date or inefficient'[10] and his boss, David Howell, the Secretary of State, in opening the debate from the government benches, said 'The men at Shildon have superb skills. They can make any type of wagon and they have done so. The finish and the accuracy are excellent.' The irony of the situation was that industrial relations and productivity at Shildon were considered so exemplary that its shop stewards were sent to other workshops to explain how flexibility and cost cutting helped competition.[11]

In both Horwich and Shildon there was a community-wide resistance to the closures. At Shildon the campaign was led by the Works Joint Shop Stewards Committee and by the local MP, Derek Foster. Bolton Council joined with the Horwich shop stewards in publicising the case for the retention of the works and mobilising deputations to parliament. These protests had the effect of bringing about a stay of execution. On 7 June 1982 the BR Board informed the unions that because there was now some prospect for export orders for the BREL workshops and because of the uncertainty about the future until the Serpell Committee reported on the future role of the industry, it had decided to defer the projected closures. A consideration for the Board was that ASLEF still had not accepted flexible rostering and it would be best to avoid a strike of the NUR, TSSA and the CSEU before the productivity issue was settled. In any case the closure plan was not abandoned, only shelved, as the events of 1983 were to demonstrate.

III

In every year from 1976 to 1982, with the exception of 1978, railway workers received pay rises which were below, sometimes substantially below, the rise in the retail price index. In 1980, with the price index rising by 21.8 per cent from April 1979, a pay rise of twenty per cent, the result of combined efforts on the part of the three railway trade unions, was considered one of the best for many years; but it still left the staff marginally worse off than they had been a year earlier. In 1981, with the price index in April thirteen per cent above the level of April 1980, the award eventually squeezed from BR management was eleven per cent. However, this was only made available in two stages: eight per cent was payable on 20 April; the remaining three per cent was not to be available until January 1982, though back dated to 3 August 1981. Even then the Board delayed handing over this balance until mid-February 1982. The result of the constant lagging behind both the rise in the retail price index and the level of pay settlements in other industries was that whereas the average rise in basic rates of pay in industry as a whole between 1975 and 1980 inclusive was 94.4 per cent, the rise for railway workers was only forty five per cent. In an endeavour to make up for their low basic rates railway staff worked long hours of overtime. In 1979, for example, railway staff overtime averaged 14½ hours a week compared with a national average of six hours. BR manual workers therefore worked more than twice as many hours overtime as the average manual worker for a total wage that was £3 less than the average.[12] In 1980 the earnings of many thousands of railway staff fell below the level which the Department of Social Security considered entitled a two child family to receive family income supplement. The BR minimum earnings level was £66.66 and the level below which family income supplement was payable was £74.[13]

These are among the reasons why the AGM of the NUR in July 1981 carried unanimously a resolution instructing the executive to negotiate 'a substantial wage increase'.[14]

In the course of February 1982 all three railway unions submitted claims to BR for improved rates of pay, a shorter working week and longer holidays, and these were discussed at a meeting on the RSNC on 11 March. It was not until 28 May that, at another meeting of the Council, the Board submitted its reply and the union representatives spoke in amplification of their reasons for the claim. The Board's offer was of five per cent, payable from 6 September, instead of the usual April anniversary date. This meant an effective rate of increase of only just over three per cent over the year. There were no concessions on working hours or increased annual leave. The NUR case was that by April 1982 railway workers would need a rise of between 29.7 per cent and 39.3 per cent, depending on the grade of employee concerned, to bring their pay up to the level of April 1975 in real terms. The TSSA representatives stressed that since April 1980 the Board had saved at least £66.5 million through the shedding of nearly 16,000 jobs but 'none of these savings had been used to improve rates of pay and conditions of service'. Further meetings of the Council were held on 22 and 25 June, but the deadlock continued.

Meanwhile on 9 June the NUR executive, by nineteen votes to six, rejected the 'derisory offer' of the Board and decided to call upon all its members employed on BR, BREL, Sealink and Travellers Fare to withdraw their labour from 00.01 hours on 28 June. The co-operation of the other railway unions and the other two partners of the Triple Alliance (the miners and the steel workers) was to be sought.[15] The minority on the executive favoured pursuing the claim further through the RSNT, urging the Board to adopt the April 1982 anniversary date for the introduction of the new pay structure.

The Times' comment on 10 June – the day following the executive's decision – that 'The executive committee of the NUR decided on strike action against the advice of Mr. Sidney Weighell' was misleading. Since 19 May the twenty-six members of the executive had been in possession of a three-page typed document drafted by Sidney Weighell setting out alternative forms of industrial action it would be possible to adopt to put pressure on the Board. The first alternative was 'An all out strike of members employed by BR and all its subsidiaries.' The second was 'a total ban on overtime, rest day and Sunday working for all BR staff and its subsidiaries' and the third was 'a series of guerrilla actions' aimed at causing the 'maximum disruption with the minimum loss of earnings'. The particular proposal favoured by the General Secretary was to organise half day strikes of signalmen stopping the movement of passenger, but not freight, trains. He saw the merit of such action was that 'the most vulnerable sector of the business, freight, would be allowed to continue, thus protecting our members against job losses'. The action would 'create maximum chaos, but under our control'. Although the executive voted for an all out strike rather than for the selective action he had advocated, Sidney Weighell wrote in the *Transport Review*, the NUR newspaper, that 'every member of the NUR must be ready to fight if our modest demands are so ignorantly denied'.[16]

The strike began on 28 June 1983, the day the AGM of the NUR opened at Plymouth. By the rules of the union, from nine o'clock that morning the direction of the strike passed from the executive committee to the seventy-seven delegates elected to the AGM. Before them was a resolution, moved by representatives from Birmingham and York 'to suspend strike action and instruct ... members to resume duty at 00.01 Wednesday 30 June'. The reason for the recommendation was embodied in earlier words of the resolution: 'that having regard to all the circumstances and the strength of the union's claim' the General Secretary was instructed to refer the union's case to the RSNT. The significance of the phase 'having regard to all the circumstances' was brought out in the course of the debate which followed. It was clear that the response to the strike call was patchy. Delegates from York and Birmingham, who moved and seconded the resolution favouring a return to work, said that their members were either 'dubious' or definitely against strike action. They thought the union's executive should first of all explore every avenue for a better settlement. Men who came from Nottingham, Newcastle (Staffs), Holyhead, the workshops at Derby, Carlisle, Cheltenham, Ashford and Truro all reported branch members reluctant to strike at that stage and confident that the union had a good case to take to arbitration. They argued that if, after resort to the RSNT, the award was still inadequate, a special general meeting could resume the strike call. After all, they said, the proposal was to *suspend* strike action, not to revoke it.

Tony Donaghy, a guard from St. Pancras, who moved the amendment supporting the executive's decision to call a strike, stressed that, by long tradition, the union's policy was that 'wages and productivity were separate and apart', and should remain so. The three per cent on offer was an 'insult'. As a guard he did not want signalmen to fight his battles; they were 'all in this union together'. Gordon Coles, from South Wales, reported strong support for the strike not only among railway workers but from steel workers and coal miners as well. Caroline Stephens, a leading railwoman from Battersea, overcame the 'feeling of powerlessness' she experienced in the branches in her district by energetic canvassing. She sat down with carriage cleaners and explained the situation to them, after which they supported her 'totally'. At a very well attended meeting of station staff she again hammered away at the issues; Then someone said, 'Do you support the EC decision Caroline?' When she replied 'Yes', they said, 'Well, there is no question is there?'

Sidney Weighell, speaking from the platform, largely confined himself to a summary of recent events; but when asked for 'his own personal view' replied: 'The only difference between the executive and myself was about the sort of industrial action. That is all. There was no division about the need for it because we were driven into a corner and had no way out.'

He claimed that BR's shedding of 15,000 jobs in two years had saved £100 million; but these gains from improved productivity had, by and large, not been passed on to the work force.

However, when it came to the vote it was clear that a majority of the delegates had been mandated to vote for the resolution for calling off the strike. This was carried by forty-seven votes to thirty after the amendment supporting the EC decision, was defeated by the same margin.[17]

It should not be concluded that the delegates, or the men and women they represented, were satisfied with BR's pay offer. In the AGM debate Brian Whipp from Brighton quoted some words of Nye Bevan: 'In the minds of the Tories unemployment is the continuous lock out by which wages are kept low and hours of labour long'. There is no doubt that the pay of many railway workers was low. A delegate from Southampton said that he had seen the pay slip of a fellow railwayman of his town. The man's take home pay was £49 for a forty hour week. The *Guardian* reported that Mick Boulton, who worked at the beautifully kept station at Kemble in Gloucestershire, considered himself lucky when he took home more than £50 a week 'because there was no scope for overtime'.[18] These cases were not isolated ones: thousands of others were in similar circumstances.

In some of the districts, such as the South West and the North East, the 'continuous lock out' of unemployment made staff fearful for their jobs. In other areas, as in the north east of Scotland there was fear that a strike would tip the balance in favour of line closures. A more general fear was generated by the letter sent by Sir Peter Parker before the strike to everyone on BR's payroll. It had been drafted by Mr. Tommy Thompson, head of Opinion Research and Communications, which is a consultancy service for right-wing businessmen. The firm also carries out secret staff surveys for management. Sir Peter's letter, addressed 'Dear Member of Staff', and headed 'YOUR JOB AND YOUR FUTURE AT RISK', contained the following paragraph: 'So what happens if your union calls you out on strike, or orders some form of industrial action which wrecks the railway? The answer, I am afraid, is no pay increase, no job to come back to for many, no prospect of investment in electrification.' The total cost of the preparation and dispatch of the letter was £90,000.[19]

A further reason for the incompleteness of the stoppage called by the NUR was the decision of ASLEF members to work normally. An ASLEF spokesman told *The Times* 'It is the NUR's game, not ours.'[20] However, the ASLEF executive advised its members not to carry out duties normally done by NUR members.

Immediately after the return to work accusations were made that the leaders of the union and the staff at head office were not sufficiently energetic in briefing the rank and file on the issue at stake. These accusations will not stand up to critical examination. The members of the executive decided to limit their payment to strike pay plus out of pocket expenses for the duration of the strike. They travelled the length and breadth of the country addressing branch meetings and (railway) district councils. The General Secretary sent a letter to each member of the union urging support for the strike. From head office, seven branch circulars were issued giving strike instructions, an account of the events which led up to the dispute with BR, and so on. A special issue of *NUR News* explained the NUR case and the issue of the union's newspaper, *Transport Review*, for 18 June gave the arguments for the strike.

It is necessary to look for longer term explanations of why up to 30,000 railway workers either reported for duty or were off sick during the two days of the strike. Low pay and unsocial working hours led to an exceptionally high rate of turnover of staff, many thousands of whom had not worked on the railways long enough for them to have developed any long-term commitment to the industry or to their union. Worries about meeting the rent or, sometimes, mortgage payments and other domestic expenses were more prominent in the thinking of the poorly paid traffic grades than they were with the generally better paid footplatemen. The last nation-wide strike of NUR members was a one-day protest against Beeching cuts on 3 October 1962, nearly twenty years earlier and long before the majority of those whose names were in the union books in June 1982 had joined the work force. By contrast, ASLEF members had been more frequently called out and had built up a fund of experience on how to conduct industrial disputes and a tradition of loyalty to a strike call.

IV

The resolution which was carried at the AGM of the NUR on 28 June instructed the General Secretary 'to refer the NUR case to the RSNT'. This was promptly done. Lord McCarthy, the chairman of the tribunal, also received an appeal to adjudicate on TSSA's claim for a substantial improvement in salaries and conditions of service.[21] In the meantime the Board re-emphasised its determination to tighten the purse strings until more productivity concessions were gained at the expense of the traffic grades. On 6 July Sir Peter Parker wrote to the general secretaries of the rail unions informing them that the pay offer of five per cent from 6 September, conditional on all productivity improvements listed in the ACAS agreement of 20 August 1981 being carried out, was withdrawn because of the NUR strike of 28-30 June and the ASLEF strike which had begun on 5 July.

The tribunal began hearing evidence from the unions and the Board on 3 August. It is indictive of the developing crisis within the railway industry that it was the twenty-fifth meeting of the RSNT within seven years. Before that the previous twenty-five hearings had been spread over eighteen years.[22] In its 123-page submission to the tribunal the NUR referred to the Board's publication *Opportunity for Change*, issued in response to the Labour government's *Transport Policy* Green Paper in 1976. The Board had stressed that the development of the railway system was conditional on the provision of a sound financial framework. This was for two reasons: there was a need to increase investment to achieve the required increase in productivity; and it was recognised that union co-operation on internal change could only be achieved 'if the government and the Board can point to a substantial, positive and ongoing role for the railways'. When Norman Fowler met the members of the British Rail Council on 29 January 1981 he conceded that 'many of the problems of the industry were the inheritance of lack of investment over a long period of time'. On 17 December that year his successor as Secretary of State for Transport, David Howell, underlined the point. He said he was 'in favour of a flourishing well-invested industry'. However, according to the NUR statement, the minister did not match his words with actions. There was 'no evidence that the government had taken any steps to provide the finance'. Both TSSA and the NUR were agreed that if railway workers were to obtain a just settlement the Board would have to approach the government for extra financial support. In its submission TSSA wrote: 'The tribunal has the task of putting down on paper exactly what they feel in naming an award . . . The question of the money does follow and obviously, the Railway Board will have to go to the government for it.' The NUR's demand was: 'When you award an increase, as we want you to do, we want you to state that the finance must come from government.'

This the tribunal was not prepared to do. BR had pointed out that its losses in 1982 in consequence of the strikes and the industrial depression would amount to £240 million and that a pay increase to match the rise in the cost of living was not on the cards. In its report the tribunal showed that it was impressed with the Board's argument: 'The Board says "money is scarce". We think this is all too true.' In deciding how it should rule on the unions' claim, it did not think they 'would be justified in assuming the loss of revenue would be recoverable from the government'. There were thus 'severe limits' to what they could recommend. The RSNT Award No. 78 was for an increase of six per cent from 6 September, but accompanied by the rider that the next pay award should operate from the customary April starting date. The members of the tribunal were clearly impressed with the unions' contribution to improved productivity. They pointed out that 'without co-operation from the unions it would not have been possible to cut the labour force over the last thirty years by over seventy per cent without similar reductions in services – most notably on the passenger side'. The award did contain a few crumbs of comfort to the staff. It recommended 'that the parties should get together with a view to agreeing an additional day's holiday from 1983'. The tribunal accepted the unions' case that the Board had been slow in making payments for specific contributions to productivity. It urged that 'When links are established between pay and productivity they should be clear and unambiguous' and that 'payments linked to specific changes should be estimated, agreed and paid at the earliest possible date'. No doubt these recommendations were made not only because the members of the tribunal accepted the justice of the unions' case but also because they would help to make the awards as a whole more palatable to railway workers.

At the AGM in Plymouth on 28 June 1982 an overhead lineman from Wigan, N. Guy, had warned: 'If we . . . vote to send these men back to work not only are we destroying the strength that is the unity . . . there will be absolutely no point in calling a SGM because the minute you send these men back to work you will not get them out again.'[23]

He judged rightly. If fear of job losses and line closures stalked in the background at the AGM debate in Plymouth on 28 June it dominated the SGM in Birmingham on 13 October. The official figures for the number of unemployed had increased by a quarter of a million in that interim; the real increase was nearer half a million. Sidney Weighell, who had seen his hopes of retaining office as General Secretary dashed that October morning, returned to the fray in the afternoon to strengthen those fears. In a characteristically forthright and eloquent speech urging delegates to accept the award, he pointed to the window of the conference hall and said: 'There are four million out of work out there. There are 30,000 private lorries parked against walls waiting to carry freight traffic. That is the world you live in. I went down to North Wales, down the Barmouth coast. They are frightened to death to stop in case the line never, ever, opens again. These are the stark realities.'[24]

Some delegates who had voted for the continuance of the strike in June were for the acceptance of the tribunal's award in October. Even those who had argued for the rejection of the six per cent, conceded that there was little stomach for a fight in the branches. So an amendment from the Lancaster Rail branch 'to accept the findings of RSNT Decision 78 and proceed with negotiations on pay, grading and promotional structures for traffic grades including guards' was carried by the safe margin of forty-four to thirty-three.[25]

V

One of the reasons the Board gave on 7 June 1982 for shelving plans for workshop closures was that the Serpell Committee had been appointed and that it would be wise to await its report before deciding on the fate of Horwich, Shildon and Temple Mills. In the event the report was far less favourable to BR than the members of the Board had hoped would be the case. It favoured more of an arms length relationship between BR and BREL and urged consideration of privatisation of the business. The report appeared when the staff at Rail House were busy preparing the Board's *Corporate Plan 1983-88*. That document, which was published in August 1983 shows evidence of top management's concern to forestall more drastic intervention by the Department of Transport. It noted that workshop staff had been reduced in numbers by 9,800 in the years 1981-83 and forecast further job losses of 1,700 by 1988.[26] The NUR executive saw the *Corporate Plan's* objectives for BREL as 'Serpell by stealth'.

Meanwhile, on 22 March 1983, an allotted opposition day in the Commons, Albert Booth, Labour front bench spokesman on transport, moved: 'That this House, being opposed to the reduction in capacity of British Rail Engineering Limited which would arise from the proposed closure of Shildon, Horwich and Temple Mills railway workshops, is concerned at the devastating unemployment which would result, and therefore calls upon the Government to reject entirely the Serpell strategy for British Rail Engineering Ltd and to develop a comprehensive programme for the modernisation and expansion of freight and passenger services.'

Although six Labour members spoke in the short debate and a large majority of the parliamentary party supported the resolution in the division lobbies, the performance of the Liberal and Social Democratic Party members was abysmal. There was no Liberal speaker and only one SDP speaker – Mike Thomas. As the under Secretary of State for Transport, Reginald Eyre, rose to reply from the government benches, Arthur Lewis, MP for Newham North

West, intervened saying: 'Will the Hon. Gentleman put on record that during the whole of the debate, not one Liberal Member has been in attendance and that the Hon. Member for Newcastle on Tyne, East (Mr. Thomas) has been the only Social Democratic party member present.'[27]

Not surprisingly the resolution was defeated by the large margin of 280 votes to 209 with only a handful of SDP and Liberal MPs entering the division lobbies.

In the summer of 1983 the NUR made strenuous efforts to save the workshops under threat of closure. Jimmy Knapp, the General Secretary, met the Secretary of State for Transport on 28 July but found him unwilling to intervene in the matter. On the following day the union's executive endorsed a report of its Shops sub-committee recommending BREL members at Shildon, Horwich and Temple Mills to ignore redundancy notices until advised by the union: BREL members in other workshops were to black any work diverted from the three shops under threat of closure and the transfer of documents to other workshops was to be prevented. Many other detailed measures were proposed.

However, bad news came in the autumn. At a meeting of the BREL Joint Consultative Committee on 4 October the NUR representatives were advised that an expected order from the Congo had not materialised and that BRB was determined to complete the programme for a fully air-braked freight network by June 1984. There would have to be a rapid rundown of the Shildon work force. There would be some work breaking up wagons and in wagon repairs, but that the 864 staff which would still be employed at 30 June 1984 would have to go after that date. Concessions were made in response to union pressure on the amount of notice to be given and the redundancy payments available, but, in sum, the news was that it was to be a slow death at Shildon, Horwich (with the exceptions of the foundry sheet and spring shops) Temple Mills and Ashford rather than the quicker extinction which seemed likely in the spring of 1982.[29] On Monday 10 October the NUR executive accepted that the best possible conditions obtainable in the circumstances had been achieved. It was realised that only by the replacement of the Thatcher government by one pledged to a secure future for the railway industry would the prospects of the railway workshops be improved.

9
The Serpell Report

I

One of the most unenviable aspects of the work of the BR Board is coping with a lack of clear government leadership in transport policy. At no time was this uncertainty in leadership more pronounced than in the years of the Thatcher administration from 1979. Under Sir Peter Parker's chairmanship the Board made repeated attempts to obtain unequivocal policy guidelines from the Department of Transport. Hopes were raised when the Monopolies and Mergers Commission was asked to investigate the London and South East commuter services and when it reported in October 1980 that there was a need for clear strategic objectives for the railway. Disappointment followed. The government failed to take the opportunity, provided by the report, for removing the uncertainty about BR's future. On 24 February 1981 BR enlisted the support of the railway trade unions, the AUEW, the TGWU, the British Road Federation, the Freight Transport Association, the National Freight Company and the Road Haulage Association in submitting an appeal to Norman Fowler for more investment in transport. Combined road and rail investment had fallen from 1.2 per cent of GDP in 1970 to 0.63 per cent in 1981. Decisions on the allocation of financial resources, they claimed, 'should be taken with an appreciation of the essential difference between wealth creating investments in areas like transport infrastructure, which only central Government can make, and spending money on services and consumption'.[1] A month later BR tried again with the publication of *Rail Policy*, a more detailed statement of the Board's plans for the 1980s. It was claimed that a 'crucial decision' had to be taken soon about BR's future; either the government could 'take the path of progress by re-equipment and modernisation' or that of 'decline through a gradual but deliberate rundown of the system'. But however much these appeals may have carried some conviction with Fowler, it is evident that Mrs. Thatcher's closest advisers were unimpressed. In default of a more positive response from government, the 'deliberate run-down of the system', about which BR was so apprehensive, was allowed to continue.

The initiative for setting up the Serpell enquiry came from BR. In its *Rail Policy* statement of 25 March 1981 the Board asked the Secretary of State for a 'form of Contract for the Social Railway' which would give it 'a clear sense of direction and a workable financing framework'. What brought matters to a head was the publication on 28 April 1982 of BR's financial results which revealed a net group loss of £37 millions. When David Howell announced the publication of the Serpell Report in the Commons on 20 January 1983 he confirmed that the Committee of enquiry had been appointed on 5 May 1982 'after the BRB had proposed a review'.[2]

After canvassing 'several prominent public figures'[3] to chair the investigation, the government eventually chose the 72 year old Sir David Serpell who had been a permanent secretary at the Ministry of Transport and the Department of the Environment. Since 1977 he had been a part time member of the BR Board and had signed BR's *Rail Policy* statement in March 1981 which included the declaration: 'There is no serious doubt in anyone's mind that a railway network of major proportions is necessary to the efficient operation of the country'.[4] Of the three other members of the committee, Alfred Goldstein was senior partner of R. Travers Morgan, consulting engineers, a firm specialising in road and bridge schemes. It is highly likely that this appointment was directly due to the recommendation of the Prime Minister's economic advisor, Alan Walters, who served with Goldstein on the Roskill Commission of Inquiry into the Third London Airport and who said of his friend: 'I suppose you could say he's a genius. He has a superb brain.'[5] Leslie Bond, the third member of the committee, was personal director of the Rank organisation. His achievement in reducing the company's work-force by 17 per cent would not have gone unnoticed by those who were of the firm opinion that the biggest single cause of BR's financial difficulties was 'overmanning'. James Butler, the fourth member of the committee, was a partner of Peat, Marwich Mitchell, a firm of accountants and management consultants which in 1981 was paid a fee in excess of a million pounds for auditing the Rank Organisation's accounts.[6] Before the appointment of the committee Butler had been briefed by BR and the Department of Transport to investigate BR's 1982 budgets and to suggest ways of improving its finances. This work was subsequently merged with the investigations of the committee.

The terms of reference of the Serpell inquiry were: 'To examine the finances of the railway and associated operations in the light of all the relevant considerations, and to report on options for alternative policies, and their related objectives, designed to secure improved financial results in an efficiently run railway in Great Britain over the next 20 years.'

With his characteristic ebullient optimism Sir Peter Parker welcomed the appointment of the committee. He saw it as 'a decisive step towards a new Railway Act which will, we believe, seek to bring railway objectives and finances more closely in line and provide a sound long term base on which to restore pride in a modern rail system.'

The Chairman of BR still appeared to believe that the Thatcher government was keen to see a prosperous, publicly owned railway industry. He might have given a less enthusiastic welcome to the appointment of the committee had he anticipated it would be given new guidelines in the course of its deliberations. In September 1982 David Howell wrote to Sir David Serpell, the chairman of the committee, directing him to give priority to suggestions for cutting railway operational costs over the next five years.[7]

If this was the minister's main objective, why did he not ensure that it was given due prominence in the committee's terms of reference? Appearances suggest that he was instructed from number 10 Downing Street to focus the enquiry more narrowly on the possibilities for immediate financial savings in railway operation. Certainly the consequences of the new directive were important. The all-party Transport Committee of the House of Commons found that Serpell and his three colleagues 'concentrated very heavily on the prospects for a short-term improvement in BR's finances'.[8] In Sir Peter Parker's view the committee had 'got involved in a level of work that really had not been intended at the start'. Instead of an inquiry into the long-term role of railways in British transport and the appropriate methods of funding BR, the investigation had degenerated into a 'management audit'.[9] The transport MPs were of the opinion that this shift of emphasis was 'not very helpful ... in determining the long term future of the railways'.[10]

II

Evidence was presented to the committee by 66 individuals and 106 organisations including such well-known bodies as the NBC, CBI, TUC, GLC the National Coal Board and the three major railway unions, as well as much smaller concerns such as the Corfe Parish Council and the Devon group of Transport 2000. In writing the report, the Chairman and Messrs. Bond and Butler leant over backwards, particularly when drafting Chapter 6, dealing with railway engineering, to accommodate the more extreme views of Alfred Goldstein so that the report of the committee might seem to be unanimous. Imagine their surprise, therefore, when, during the afternoon of 9 December, Goldstein informed his colleagues that he felt unable to add his signature to the document and that he would be submitting a minority report.

It appears that following his return to England from a trip abroad, Alan Walters was shown a copy of the draft and, after a quick glance through it, said to Goldstein, 'But, surely, you cannot sign this' – or words to that effect – and that Goldstein then agreed to write his minority report, an exercise which took him 11 days.[11] On 20 December 1982, in their covering letter to David Howell, Sir David Serpell and Messrs. Bond and Butler confessed that they did not know what Goldstein's observations would be.

III

Few committee reports have received such hostile notices as appeared in the daily and weekly newspapers following the publication of *Railway Finances*, the report of the Serpell Committee, on 20 January 1983. The *Financial Times* found it 'an unhelpful report, and probably misleading in important respects'. The *Daily Telegraph* complained that 'instead of looking at radical ways to make the existing route structure work efficiently, the committee has, primarily, gone for the easy solution of closures'. *The Times*'s transport correspondent deplored 'the negative view of the railways' taken by the committee. The leading article in the same paper found it a serious omission that there were no comparisons with other countries 'many of which consider railways worth subsidising at a far higher rate than we do'. *The Sunday Telegraph*'s comment was that the committee's research was 'shoddy and unproven'. The headline to the *Guardian*'s leader read 'A really rotten report.' The *Daily Mirror* found 'the several solutions in the report 'all ludicrous', while *The Standard*'s succinct assessment was, 'As cures go, it's a killer.' [12]

Sir Peter Parker found it much harder than usual to respond with his characteristic optimism. He is reported to have said that the report was 'as cosy as a razor blade'. More soberly, in the BRB's printed commentary, *The Review of Railway Finances*, published in January 1983, the report was declared to be 'a disappointing document', mainly for the reason that 'the gap between obligations and resources remains unsolved'.

In Parliament as well as in the press, the committee's choice of consultants and the high fees paid for their services were subjected to severe criticism. Lord Marsh, who spoke from experience, both as a former Minister of Transport and as a former Chairman of BR, thought it improper that '50 per cent of an independent inquiry came from the very firms actually providing the advice and submitting the invoice at the end of it'. He thought the total fees paid to the two firms of consultants – £627,000 – 'outrageous in relation to any conceivable work which could have been involved'.[13] There was a case for the committee employing consultants to advise on financial and engineering aspects of the inquiry; the criticism was that the firms chosen, Peat, Marwick, Mitchell and Co., and the engineering consultants, Travers, Morgan and Partners, had not been subjected to competitive tendering. No other estimates for the work to be done were sought by the Department of Transport. When challenged on this point in the Commons on 20 January 1983, David Howell claimed that he had followed the correct procedures in making the appointments. Ken Sharp, head of the government's accountancy service, did not agree. In a letter to the Chairman of the Institute of

Chartered Accounts, written on 18 November 1982, he indicated that 'written presentation from a number of competing firms would normally be involved' in such circumstances. The standard procedures, which had been drafted with the approval of the Treasury, required the drawing up of a 'short list of perhaps three candidates for further assessment' after a government department had received written applications. Furthermore, a candidate firm would be 'ruled out, without detailed consideration, if there was a clash of interests that would result from its appointment.' It was 'wholly contrary to government policy that any sort of inner circle' of 'acceptable' firms should be established.[14]

The case against the appointment of Travers Morgan and Partners was that Alfred Goldstein, a member of the Serpell Committee, was a senior partner of the firm and likely to benefit from the fees of £370,000 it was paid for its advice. Similarly, the objection to Peat, Marwick, Mitchell and Co., was that James Butler, serving with Goldstein on the committee, was senior partner of the firm which received £182,000 of government money so liberally disbursed.

Why was there no competitive tendering for these lucrative appointments? Although, in the Commons, Howell defended the record of R. Travers Morgan, declaring it 'a very substantial and respectable firm',[15] his Department had not shown it much confidence in the past. In 1980, when, with two other firms, it tendered for a study of the design and evaluation of trunk and local road schemes, its application was rejected as 'a rather pedestrian proposal' while the experience of the firm was considered too widely spread for the study required.[16] The current edition of *Jane's World Railways* included details, spreading over 33 pages, of railway consultants worldwide.[17] It would have been perfectly possible to have selected other firms from these pages. Explaining his actions to the members of the Commons' Transport Committee, David Howell said: 'I saw it as entirely desirable and right that Mr. Goldstein, whose services I wished to use, was already backed up by R. Travers Morgan, of which he was senior partner. This was a step that I deliberately and clearly took in order to achieve the linkage and support services that were going to be needed on the engineering side.'[18]

Would it be so wide of the mark to suggest that Alan Walters made such a strong recommendation for his 'genius' friend Goldstein to be appointed to the committee and for his consultancy firm

R. Travers Morgan to be employed, that normal procedures of competitive tendering were bypassed?

IV

Railway Finances appeared almost exactly twenty years after the publication of another famous report – *The Reshaping of British Railways* (The Beeching Report, 1963). The earlier enquiry was much criticised for its blinkered approach. The performance of the railways was examined in isolation from other forms of transport, so that the impact of line, station and depot closures on the road transport industry was largely ignored. The one important lesson that should have been learned after Beeching is that no means of transport is 'an island entire of itself', it is 'part of the main' of the nation's entire transport system. Had the members of the Serpell Committee taken this much needed, more comprehensive, view, they could have defended it by reminding critics that their terms of reference were to examine the railway's finances 'in the light of all relevant considerations'. However, Howell's September letter narrowed the focus of their attention and in the introduction to their report they stressed that their review was 'concerned with the railway finances, not transport policy.'[19]

Since Britain's European neighbours have also had to decide how big a part railways should play in their transport systems, there was an obvious case for comparing, at least in outline, their government policies with those of the UK to discover whether there were any lessons to be learned. The Serpell Committee failed to do this. When asked why the team had completely ignored such comparisons, Alfred Goldstein replied: 'In the six months we had, that was not an area that I think could be productively entered into.'[20] It was not that he and his colleagues were unaware of the facts; BR, the NUR and many other organisations plied them with information. It was rather that the conclusions which would have been prompted by such comparisons would have challenged preconceived notions about the 'obsolescence' of railways. In his Minority Report Goldstein wrote: 'Though each form of transport has throughout history created cultural and social change ... each has been overtaken, in some or all respects, by successors.'[21] To have recorded that it was

French government policy to invest four times as much money in SNCF in 1983 as the British government was investing in BR; that French railways were winning traffic from the internal air lines and were being provided with 182 *additional* kilometres of track, would have upset the theory that the 'outmoded' railways had had their day.[22]

The Serpell Report was divided into two main parts. Part I being entitled 'Examination of the Finances of the Railway' and Part II 'Longer Term Options'. Throughout, the main aim was to reduce the level of government support for the railways. Hence the first part of the report occupies twice as many pages as the second. Economies amounting to £220 million spread over the years to 1992 were suggested. BR claimed that before Serpell was appointed it already had plans for savings amounting to £147 millions.

To cut the cost of operating the passenger railway the committee proposed the reduction of service frequencies; but, obsessed with looking at only one side of the balance, they made no estimate of how much revenue would be lost through passengers deserting BR once the standard of rail services declined.[23] The suggestion that season ticket holders, particularly in the South Eastern region should be charged more 'economic' rates was based on the assumption that customers in this area constitute a 'captive market'.[24] The history of the last decade, during which each new increase in fares was followed by more commuters finding alternative means of travel, shows how shaky that assumption is. The BR view is that if commuter fares were raised to meet the full money cost of providing services they would have to be 'doubled at least' and that the social impact of such a change – e.g. the increased road congestion – would be 'enormous'.[25] Few would disagree with the committee's complaint that in 1982 BR had such a variety of 'saver' fares that the potential customer was often 'confused'. On the other hand the suggestion that the discounts on offer were too large and should be regarded as only a 'temporary expedient' was challenged by Robin Cook, the Labour MP, who said it would put the price of rail travel beyond the pocket of large sections of the population.[26]

The committee advanced proposals for a 30 per cent cost saving on the maintenance of track which, it claimed, would help to lower freight and passenger charges. However, the Conservative MP Robert Adley, described as 'nothing less than grotesque' the suggestion that 'some experiments should be carried out, particularly on minor lines, to establish the lowest level of maintenance consistent with maintaining safety'.[27] No indication is given in the report on how such experiments would be conducted. Was the idea progressively to lower safety standards until an accident indicated that the 'lowest level' had been passed? The MP was right. There is no halfway house on safety. The system is either as safe as it can be made or not.

The policy advocated for railway signalling was, surprisingly enough, one of 'make do and mend' rather than modernisation. 'Replacement is justified', they believed, 'only when old equipment becomes so unreliable as to be unable to cater for the timetabled service.'[28] This is an example of the committee's blinkered, cost oriented, approach. No account is taken of passengers' frustration at the late arrival of trains due to 'signal failure' or that, when this happens, some who travelled by train will switch to the coach, thus losing BR future revenue.

The dangers inherent in the Serpell policy for the railway signalling system are exemplified in what happened when the 21.40 London Victoria-Littlehampton electric multiple unit train ran into the back of the 21.50 Victoria-Brighton emu between Hassocks and Preston Park on 19 December 1978, killing the driver of the 21.40 train and another railwayman and injuring seven passengers. According to Major C.F. Rose, Inspecting Officer, the collision was due to the failure of a colour light signal which should have shown red. If the Serpell policy of replacing equipment 'only when it becomes so unreliable as to be unable to cater for the timetabled service' was to be adopted many more accidents like that of 19 December 1978 could be anticipated.

Chapter 6 of the report, concerned with engineering questions, caused most anger among senior BR managers. When the members of the Monopolies and Mergers Commission investigated the railways of the South East they thought it useful to have frequent talks with senior BR engineers at all stages of their enquiry. The procedure adopted by the consultants R. Travers Morgan, working for the Serpell inquiry, was very different, as described by Ian Campbell of the BR Board: 'The people they put on to it were very competent intellectually. The man who did the civil engineering was a very good bridge designer; he had no experience in railway management, no experience of any management. The man they put on to mechanical engineering was an economist with no experience of railway work at all ... We opened out books to them, we invited them in ... They went away, brooded on it, did not come back to us and say, 'This is the sort of thing we think'; they went on in their own beliefs, prejudices maybe, and published on that basis. They have not produced in their report a single recommendation of substance which did not emanate from our own directors.'[29]

The members of the Serpell Committee were unimpressed by BR's claim that, owing to shortage of funds, there were serious arrears in the maintenance of the track and that on over 300 miles of the permanentway there were speed restrictions. The situation, they reported, 'was for the most part operationally acceptable'.[30] They found it deplorable that for renewals of the track BR bought all its steel rails from the British Steel Corporation and that they depended on only two suppliers for concrete sleepers. They believed cheaper rails might be purchased abroad.[31] It was a suggestion which did not find favour with Bill Sirs of the Iron and Steel Trades Confederation, who said that British Steel's Workington plant produced excellent steel which was in demand all over the world.[32]

The consultants had a valid criticism when they pointed out that lack of standardisation of locomotive design had increased both initial and lifetime costs.[33] On the other hand their proposal that BR should think of buying 'vehicles available from outside suppliers' was ill considered and damaging to British Rail Engineering Ltd (BREL), BR's workshops subsidiary. These 'off the cuff' recommendations regarding rails, locomotives and rolling stock were made without pausing to consider the costs of their implementation in the form of redundancy payments; the probable closure of British Steel plants and the loss of export orders as well as the domestic ones. (An export business in railway engineering products depends on a prosperous domestic market, as overseas purchasers like to see in operation the items of equipment they contemplate buying.) If the British government adopted a more positive attitude towards railway development, as most European governments do, new orders for export of railway equipment are likely to arise. As it was, in the 1970s BREL earned valuable contracts from Nigeria, Hong Kong, Kenya, Bangladesh and elsewhere before the financial squeeze stunted Britain's own railway development and hence reduced the likelihood of export orders. Even so export orders worth £50 million were achieved in 1982. If this achievement is to be maintained, however, a substantial increase of investment in BR is essential. In the Lords' debate on Serpell the Bishop of Durham found it 'disgraceful' that 'heavily subsidised overseas manufactures could corner the market in wagons, offering them for sale in the British market at less than the cost of steel required in Britain to build them'. He spoke with the knowledge that BREL's Shildon wagon works, which is in the heart of his diocese, was due for closure.[34]

In Chapter 7 of the report the committee took a pessimistic view of BREL's future. It would never receive sufficient demand for locomotives for it to be able to achieve 'economic production'. Purchases from abroad would always be cheaper. The fact that BR purchased all its rolling stock from BREL and that 'only one per cent of BREL's purchases of materials in 1981 were from manufacturers outside the UK' was deplored.[35] Apparently Mrs. Thatcher's plea to 'Buy British' had no influence with the committee. Three alternative proposals were put forward for BREL's future: BR could dispose of its share capital in BREL direct to the government; BREL could be privatised, with the existing structure to be split into at least two groups to be owned by manufacturing consortia; or BREL could cease to operate independently, with its facilities reabsorbed into BR. If the last option was chosen, however BR should be forbidden to contract for private 'outside' orders. The fallacy in the Serpell Committee's approach was in attributing BREL's troubles to the form of its organisational link with BR. The fundamental problem was the failure of successive governments to give a clear and positive lead to BR and to afford it adequate financial support. Positive advantages have arisen from BR's association with BREL. Both organisations have benefited from common research and development facilities. It is doubtful whether a private company, or companies, would be so attuned to the special needs of BR. If BREL was closed down, or sold off to the private sector, it would be a waste of taxpayers' money placed in a valuable national investment.

In somewhat summary fashion the committee blasted most of BR's hopes, expressed in *Rail Policy* (1981) for more substantial investment in the rail infrastructure and in equipment. It claimed to have tested a 'high investment' option for the railways but concluded 'that the improvement that would be secured in operating results would not be sufficient to justify the increased investment'.[36] After hearing evidence given by the members of the Serpell Committee, the Secretary of State and Sir Peter Parker, the Commons all party Transport Committee came to a very different conclusion. It concluded that 'investment in the system will need to be increased in the fairly near future in order to prevent a severe deterioration in service quality . . . cumulative effects of investment cut-backs could be extremely serious'.[37]

On electrification the committee's comments were cursory in the extreme. In justification it was pointed out that the Secretary of State had advised that the joint BR/Department of Transport Report on Main Line Electrification had appeared as recently as December 1980 and that there was therefore no necessity for repeating the exercise. However, the members of the committee found space, within a seven line paragraph on the subject, to have a swipe at BR's enthusiasm for main line electrification. They wrote, 'We do not consider that the Board will be able to meet all the conditions laid down by the government for approval of an electrification programme'.[38] This must be considered the prize 'wet blanket' comment of a generally very negative report. The Commons' Transport Committee certainly thought that it was high time the government stopped its shilly-shallying on the subject. Included in its 'main conclusions' was the statement that 'the time has now come . . . for an early decision on the Board's proposal for the electrification of the East Coast Main Line and a clear statement of the government's attitude towards a continuing programme of electrification'.[39]

On page 61 of the report brief consideration is given to the claim that railways ought to be supported because they are energy efficient. This important claim is dismissed in the space of nine lines with a concluding comment that there 'is no case on energy grounds for subsidising railways in the next 20 years'.[40] This statement is based on the assumption that the short-term costs of fossil fuels (oil) adequately reflect their longer-term value. It ignores the fact that railways can draw their energy from a variety of primary energy sources. As BR has rightly stressed: 'Investing in and supporting railways on energy grounds is an insurance policy for the future.'[41]

The Serpell Report dealt equally summarily with the argument that it is worthwhile to maintain a railway system in order to avoid road congestion in the great conurbations. It conceded the argument with regard to Greater London; but for the rest it considered the events of the rail strikes in 1982 showed that 'only a little more congestion' was created in provincial conurbations.[42] It gave no consideration to the fact that, especially in the UK, land is an increasingly scarce resource and that road transport is notoriously more land hungry than railways.

The pitfalls created by the failure of the engineering consultants to refer their work, after the initial stages, to BR management, before the committee prepared the final draft of the report, is most clearly shown in Part II entitled, 'Longer Term Options'. It was this section which prompted comments in the press such as 'shoddy' or 'hatchet job'. Based on computer models designed by R. Travers Morgan, the committee submitted views on how the railways might look in 1992, depending on the amount of financial assistance the government was prepared to give. The options were illustrated by maps which showed the reductions in the rail network which would follow each assumed reduction in the PSO grant. There is considerable evidence of the botched character of the consultants' work. Two options (C2, p.75 and D, p.79) terminate the Highland line at a tiny hamlet Crianlarich, which only has a station because it is on the route to the more important centres of Oban, Mallaig and Fort William. In Option C3 the railway ends at Exeter, well short of two of the most important traffic centres in the West of England, Torbay and Plymouth. The assumption is made that passengers from Cornwall and Western Devon would start their journey by bus or coach and then transfer to rail at Exeter. It is a view which Richard Hope, editor of *Railway Gazette International*, found 'quite incredible'. He considered BR would be lucky to attract as much as 30 per cent of such traffic.[43] With option A, limited to 1,600 route miles, the consultants claimed that passenger traffic would lose £32 millions, but that this would be more than offset by a profit on freight operation of £66 millions, leaving a net gain of £34 millions. The method by which the consultants reached this conclusion has been described as 'nothing short of outrageous'. A glance at the network map reveals that most of the coalfields and cement works are not linked to the surviving skeleton railway. The consultants were not to be put off by this slight difficulty. They made the wholly unconvincing assumption that the loss of freight receipts would be limited to the revenue which could be directly attributed to the missing rail link. No allowance was made

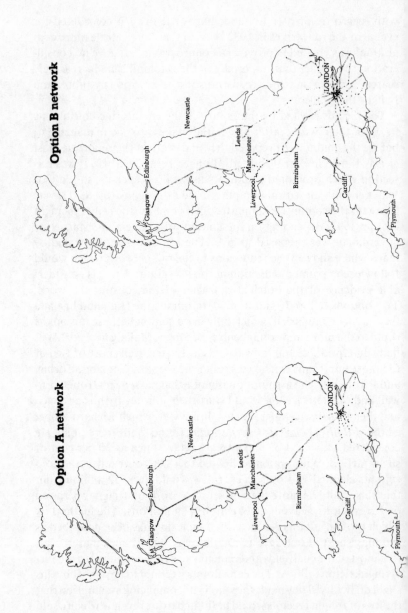

Option A network

Glasgow
Edinburgh
Newcastle
Leeds
Manchester
Liverpool
Birmingham
Cardiff
Plymouth
LONDON

Option B network

Glasgow
Edinburgh
Newcastle
Leeds
Manchester
Liverpool
Birmingham
Cardiff
Plymouth
LONDON

Option C2 network

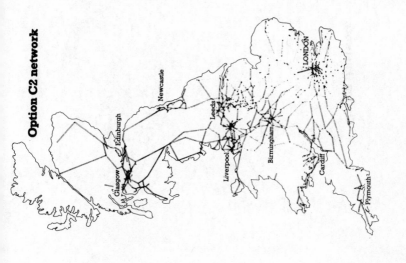

Option C1 network

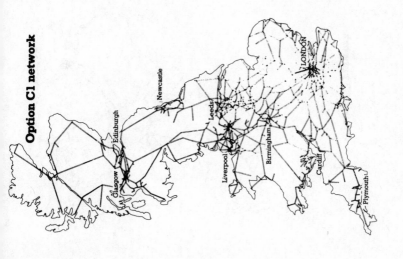

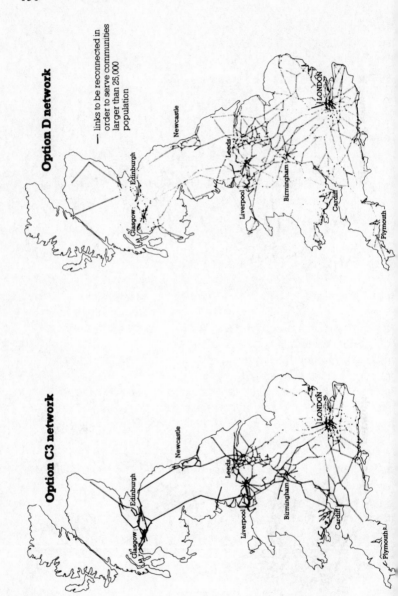

Option C3 network

Option D network

— links to be reconnected in
order to serve communities
larger than 25,000
population

Newcastle

Edinburgh

Glasgow

Leeds

Liverpool

Birmingham

Cardiff

LONDON

Plymouth

for any loss of revenue elsewhere on the network. As Richard Hope so aptly observed: 'The feeder lines may have gone, but revenue is still being credited to the trunk lines from ghostly trains of coal and cement.'[44]

In the Commons, Robin Maxwell-Hyslop, Conservative MP for Tiverton, clearly had doubts about the quality of the consultants' work. He asked David Howell: 'Why the important passenger flow diagram in the supplementary volume does not show the route between London and Exeter as an Inter-City route – which it is, but shows the route as far as Salisbury as 'London and the South East', when Salisbury has nothing to do with the South East? Will he explain why the brown-coloured code for freight does not appear anywhere and why some of the lines are coloured black although there is no black colour code?' The Secretary of State could offer no satisfactory explanation.[45]

One of the most important conclusions reached by the committee in Part II of its report was that 'the high investment option would not show a satisfactory return'.[46] It was an assessment potentially very damaging to BR's future and to the whole railway industry in Britain. To reach the conclusion they did the consultants were guilty of a remarkable feat of legerdemain with the mathematical model used. The model 'High Investment Option H' assumed extra investment of £1,600 millions in the five areas of continuous welded rail, radio signalling, new rolling stock, train cleaning equipment and station building and equipment. Despite investment conjectured as rising by 67 per cent above the level of 1982 the decline in the number of staff was computed to be only 0.4 per cent and the increase of revenue only 1.1 per cent. The staff reduction anticipated was far below the 9 per cent actually realised in 1981-2 inclusive, and the estimate of increased revenue was very conservative. In the three years 1979-81 passenger receipts rose by 27 per cent. The assumptions so far in the argument were bad enough, but the next stage was worse. Instead of comparing the High Investment Option 'H' with what they called 'Base Option R1' (which represented the position which they thought would be reached if current policies continued), they chose to make the comparison with a 'High Efficiency Option R2' in which, with a ten per cent reduction in staff, there would be a £160 million cut in the railway deficit. This was taking the, untenable, position that high investment and high efficiency were mutually exclusive. Had they, instead, compared the High Investment Option H with the Base Option R1 – which would have been the realistic exercise – the cut in the deficit would have been £179 million a year – a substantial sum. As it was, the comparison of Options H and R2 resulted in a cut in deficit of only £19 million, suggesting that high investment was 'a hopeless waste of resources'. A study of the consultants' method of working led Richard Hope to doubt 'whether such an extraordinary and implausible result could have been arrived at by misadventure'.[47]

In commending the Serpell Report to MPs David Howell declared that it offered 'further large scope for improvements in efficiency'.[48] By 'efficiency' he and the members of the committee understood 'cost efficiency' i.e. moving passengers and freight at the lowest possible money cost. The passenger, however, sees 'efficiency' in terms of the speed, comfort, puntuality and cleanliness of trains, the dedication of staff and the attractiveness of fares. These considerations did not enter into the calculations of the committee because most of them are unsuitable for processing through a computer. They nevertheless have a real importance in the railway business.[49] Sir Peter Parker was keenly aware of them. He told the Commons' Transport Committee: 'It seems to me that financial objectives are simply inadequate and will lead to continual harassment for another generation unless we say things to one another about the importance of quality standards and what they should be: we should be nailed on such questions as frequency, accessibility and reliability. Standards and performance quality should be part of the deal.'[50]

A fundamental disquiet which the Commons' Transport Committee felt about the Serpell Report was expressed by Sir David Price, Conservative MP for Eastleigh, when he deplored 'the extraordinarily negative attitude' the Serpell Committee had taken when considering the options. 'It was', he said, 'rather, are we likely to lose? not how do we expand?'[51]

All members of the Commons' Transport Committee – Conservative, SDP and Labour alike – wanted a radical change of attitude on the part of the government. They demanded: '(1) revised financial and operational objectives for the main railway business; (2) Agreement on the level of investment required for the renewal of infrastructure and replacement of rolling stock over at least the next five years, and a commitment to ensure that the financial targets imposed on the railways will provide sufficient room for the achievement of this level of investment; and (3) An early decision on the Board's proposal for the electrification of the East Coast Main Line and a clear statement of the government's attitude towards a continuing programme of electrification.' The concluding words of their report read: 'We believe, therefore, that a comprehensive statement on rail policy is now required and that the Secretary of State should give urgent consideration to the production of a White Paper on this issue. A clear statement of the government's continued commitment to the railways would do much to recreate a climate of confidence among British Rail's staff, customers and suppliers.'[52] Sir Peter Parker could not have wished for more than this.

V

The Serpell report received such a hostile reception in the press and in parliament that there is a danger of assuming that its findings will be ignored by any government wishing to retain a measure of public support. The *Daily Mirror* comment at the time of its appearance was: 'The best thing the government can do with the Serpell report on the future of the railways is to forget it. Fortunately that is exactly what it looks like doing.'[53] The *Daily Mirror*'s assumption may certainly be questioned. David Howell told the Commons that the report gave his department 'a basis for decisions and for action'. Although he reassured Sir Hector Monroe, Conservative MP for Dumfries (who was concerned that under the Options A and B networks Scotland would lose all its railways north of the Glasgow-Edinburgh line) that 'the extreme options were not acceptable', he refused to specify which blueprints were ruled out, and at another moment during the same afternoon declared: 'The options deserve study and we should not close our minds to any changes in the structure and pattern of our railway system.'[54] He later told Richard Hope that he was considering plans for the privatisation of the railway lines of Wales, Scotland and South East England, though these would be feasible only if government subsidies were continued. He asserted that the new chairman of BR who would be appointed in September 'would have a very clear picture of the government's view before he took over'.[55] When he met representative members of the NUR on 14 February 1983 he tried to reassure them by saying that 'the part railways would play would be decided in the public forum rather than through a private enquiry like Serpell'.[56] However, when he was giving evidence to the Commons' Transport Committee on 9 March, it became clear that, despite the earlier soothing words about 'the public forum', a decision had already been taken to implement what the government saw as the most important part of the report – immediate reductions in the cost of BR's operations. When questioned by Harry Cowans, MP, Howell conceded that 'the cost savings by 1986 that Serpell identified I have asked BR to see whether they can secure'. There was a sharp contrast between the precision of Howell's statements on BR's cost cutting and his vagueness and evasiveness on the positive recommendations of the Transport Committee. When pressed again by Harry Cowans he agreed that plans for increasing the level of railway investment were 'worth examining'.[57] Such evidence shows that the *Sunday Telegraph* was perceptive in pointing to 'the reluctance of Mr. Howell to challenge the hostility to railways in Downing Street'.[58] This is indeed the crux of the matter. Whoever may be nominally in charge at Marsham Street (the Transport Department's headquarters), so long as Margaret Thatcher and Alan Walters are directing affairs from Downing Street, the Serpell report will be taken seriously. After all, they appointed the committee, knowing full well the anti-rail bias of some of its most influential members.

VI

In case it should be said that 'there is no alternative' it is worth examining proposals made by another consultant firm, Transport and Environment Studies (TEST). From April 1983 this firm began work on a report commissioned by Transport 2000. Using the main assumptions on which Serpell was based, they examined an alternative high investment strategy which they called Option T. The new option embodied a major electrification programme similar to the one endorsed by the joint Department of Transport/British Rail enquiry team; operational improvements such as the faster introduction of continuous welded rail, radio signalling and rolling stock replacement; service improvements, including station refurbishing and better information services and new freight investment, such as the acquisition of new wagons and the opening up of new distribution depots. With capital investment £243 million less than in Serpell's Option R1, the anticipated railway deficit in 1992 is £64 million less than that under Serpell's Option H. TEST is no upstart organisaton. It was founded in 1972 and has undertaken consultancy work for the World Bank, OECD, the Transport and Road Research Laboratory, London Transport and many other organisations.[59]

It is interesting, finally to contrast the Serpell approach in Great Britain with the way in which the Swedish government faced similar problems confronting Swedish State Railways (SJ). 55 per cent of SJ's 11,700 kilometre rail network carries only eight per cent of the traffic, is not commercially profitable and has been treated as a social service. With economic depression hitting both passenger and freight carryings, SJ was in crisis. But the kind of clinical approach of Serpell was politically unthinkable in Sweden. Therefore, for the financial year 1983-4 the government cut SJ's debt burden by one third; increased the 'social service' grant to the uneconomic part of the network by 50 per cent and undertook to finance a large part of the cost of the rail infrastructure. SJ was thus able to invest in 6,000 new freight wagons from its own resources besides introducing substantial improvements in its train ferries. There was no talk of cutting the rail network or raising commuter fares.[60]

10
Urban Transport: London and the PTAs

I

The importance attached to London Transport is shown by the fact that it receives forty per cent of total national financial support for local transport, even though it contains only fifteen per cent of the UK's population.[1] Since London is the commercial and administrative capital of Britain any deficiencies in its transport system affect the health of the national economy and society. This is the case for giving it priority of treatment in a chapter on urban transport.

Herbert Morrison, who was largely responsible for bringing most of London's transport undertakings under the public ownership of the London Passenger Transport Board on 1 July 1933, subsequently wrote that Londoners became proud of 'our buses and tubes'.[2] Although he recognised by 1960 that some of this goodwill had been lost, it was possible for a later Minister of Transport, Barbara Castle, to boast in 1968 that, by comparison with most transport undertakings in large cities abroad, London had a worthy record in the reasonableness of its fares and in its ability to finance capital investment out of revenue.[3] Such proud claims could no longer be sustained in the 1970s when the real cost of travel in London increased dramatically – only in Helsinki of European capital cities were fares per mile higher – and the quality of service deteriorated. By 1982 the House of Commons all party Transport Committee was deeply concerned about the decline of the service and reported that 'London's entire public transport system is in need of a face lift'.[4] It warned that unless radical improvements were introduced as a matter of urgency, London would become increasingly unattractive to commerce and increasingly unattractive as a place of residence and as a centre for work, entertainment and tourism.[5]

The fall in passenger mileage, sharp rise in fares and mounting revenue shortfall of London Transport are shown in Table 8.

This shows BR fares and LT bus and tube fares rising more steeply than the cost of living, with consequent decline in bus and tube train patronage and worsening of LT's financial position.

The sad story of declining passenger usage of LT buses and trains is explained partly by the demographic changes of the second half of the twentieth century. Between 1951 and 1979 the population of Greater London (the GLC area) fell from over eight million to under seven million, or by 12.5 per cent, while Inner London numbers fell from 3.3 million to 2.4 million, or by 27 per cent. However, these population movements did not provide successive governments, the GLC and LT with an adequate excuse for falling business performance, for those ex-Londoners who had moved to the outer suburbs or even to towns such as Reading and Brighton often needed to use public transport on the last stage of their journey to work. Moreover the 1970s saw a huge increase in the number of foreign tourists visiting the capital; numbers grew from 6 million in 1972 to 7.8 million in 1977. The large majority of these visitors had need to use London Transport's services.[6]

The most important reason for the growing crisis in the public transport services of the capital was the increase in use of privately owned motor vehicles and the failure of the authorities to deal with the consequent problem of congestion. Between 1972 and 1979 there was an overall growth of 13.4 per cent in the total volume of traffic using London's roads.[7] The number of car users entering central London during the morning peak rose from 125,000 in 1961 to 183,000 in 1980.[8] Opportunities for increasing road space within the GLC area without incurring inordinate expense are strictly limited because of the nature of London's development. From Roman times onwards roads have been built radiating outwards from the centre to dozens of small towns and villages on the periphery, and a huge area was already closely built up before the age of the motor car. Between 1965 and 1980 only twelve miles of new motorways and trunk roads were built in the GLC area.[9] The consequence for the second half of the twentieth century has been traffic congestion of an increasing intensity. The incursion of privately owned motor

Table 8

Service, traffic, and fare trends on London Transport 1970-1980

Year	Train m. 000,000	Bus m. 000,000	Pass traffic m. 000,000	Av. bus fare (Index)	Av. tube fare (Index)	Av. BR fare (Index)	Retail price Index	Revenue surplus (+) or shortfall (−) (£000)
1970	30	199	6,155	100	100	100	100	+ 3,668
1971	31	198	6,112	109	115	117	109	+ 0,660
1972	30	190	6,177	122	130	131	117	+ 2,604
1973	30	182	6,204	122	139	144	128	− 8,161
1974	27	175	6,271	122	139	157	148	− 52,850
1975	30	178	6,006	149	185	213	184	− 116,349
1976	30	182	5,686	216	269	278	215	− 113,597
1977	30	179	5,616	257	321	331	249	− 99,297
1978	30	172	5,619	293	366	384	270	− 96,165
1979	29	165	5,464	332	421	419	306	− 142,077
1980	30	173	5,236	456	565	513	361	− 149,044

Source: House of Commons, Transport Committee 5th Report, *Transport in London*, 1982 Vol. 3, p.165.

vehicles on to the highways seriously impeded the movement of buses. In the seventies average traffic speeds declined from 12.9 to 12.1 mph in the morning peak; from 12.6 to 11.6 mph in the day time off-peak hours and from 12.7 to 12.2 mph in the evening peak.[10] Sir Peter Masefield, at that time Chairman of London Transport, told the Commons' Transport Committee in February 1982: 'Our scheduled speed in road traffic is going down steadily from year to year because the road traffic congestion is getting worse.' Since each bus cost £2 a mile to run, the operation of the services was increasingly uneconomic.[11] Congestion on some of the main routes is particularly damaging to the reliability of the bus services. Dr Quarmby, a senior member of the London Transport Executive, told the Transport Committee on 18 February 1981: 'On average, twice a week the Edgware Road somewhere between Marble Arch and the North Circular jams solid and that will affect the operation of 300 buses. While the person in the private car will get through the jam and then forget it, a bus that is delayed here will affect the waiting time of passengers all the way down the rest of the road and they will not know what has happened.' He noted, by contrast, that if LT could schedule Monday to Friday services at the speeds achieved on Saturday mornings it would save £40 million a year and give a better service.[12]

The problem of congestion would have been eased if governments had acted to ensure the punishment of those who park their vehicles illegally. An estimated 350,000 parking offenses are commmitted in Greater London each day, 17,000 of these being within the boundaries of the City of Westminster. Although high ranking officers of the Metropolitan Police have repeatedly stressed that at least 4,000 traffic wardens are needed to cope with the problem, the size of the force was only just over 1,200 in 1981, having declined from a maximum strength of 2,100 in 1973 as a result of public expenditure cuts in 1977-8 and since June 1979. It is also true that the Home Office, which carries ultimate responsibility for traffic law enforcement, has failed to make any assessment of the 'costs to society of the low level of compliance which now exists'.[13] The Metropolitan Police reported that in 1980 1,900,000 fixed penalty notices were issued. It looks a large figure until it is remembered that Scotland Yard estimates that it represents only two per cent of the total number of offences. When it is also remembered that only about half the fixed penalty notices issued actually result in the payment of the fine it becomes clear that ninety-nine per cent of illegal parking remains unpenalised. Alan Greengross, former (Conservative) leader of the GLC Planning Committee found the situation quite indefensible: 'It seems to me to be lunatic to have a massive investment in a road infrastructure which is then used in the centre of London and other places as a form of free parking facility, and to build and maintain a road and have half its capacity taken up by someone parking his car while he buys a packet of cigarettes. To save five or ten million pounds on enforcement measures and to lose hundreds of millions on mobility does seem to be the economics of the madhouse.'[14]

As road congestion reduced the reliability of the buses so more Londoners abandoned public transport for their motor cars. When the inevitable drop in passenger revenue followed, LT raised fares in a vain endeavour to balance the books. There were five fare increases between June 1978 and September 1980. The higher fares in turn frightened off still more customers, especially those travelling short distances; and so continued the downward spiral of ever decreasing patronage and ever mounting financial deficits.

It was the poor quality and unreliability of the service of buses and underground trains which drove many people to seek alternative means of transport. The discomfort of travel on the underground and the unpredictable timing of the buses were in part the result of inadequate investment and maintenance and the unsocial hours and relatively poor pay of many of the staff. Between 1975 and 1981 the real value of the subsidy to LT from central government funds and the rates was declining. It is true that in money terms the subsidy rose from £93 million in 1975 to £149 million in 1981; but to maintain real values through years of rapid inflation it should have been £203 million in the later year. In consequence, by the end of the seventies, LT was saddled with thirty-four lifts which were over seventy-five years old, sixty-three escalators over forty years old, some tube stock over forty years old and a significant proportion of plant and machinery over thirty years old.[15] If LT commuters experienced delays and inconvenience through broken-down lifts and escalators and crammed-tight passenger carriages, BT commuters often fared no better. Sir Peter Parker reported 'constant under-investment in physical facilities and the inability to make proper provision for the future', with the result that rolling stock had not been replaced or refurbished when required, speed restrictions had been imposed and reliability and punctuality had deteriorated.[16] In June 1981 the NUR drew attention to the effect on the quality of LT and BR services which resulted from the poor conditions of service of railway employees. Low pay and unsocial hours were responsible for staff shortages and high turnover problems. The train cancellations which were necessary as a result, severely damaged the quality of service.[17]

While Parliament and County Hall were starving both BR and LT of the necessary capital and revenue support to enable public transport to offer a more attractive service to passengers, governments and municipal authorities abroad were providing more generously for the needs of travellers. While Britain still clung to the objective of commercial viability, they acted on the different philosophy that a prosperous public transport infrastructure was vital for the economic and social well-being of the people. Mr Jeff Allen, LT's Finance Director (Railways), in a study of 27 major municipal transport undertakings in Europe, Asia and America, found that the mean average 'farebox ratio' (ie. the proportion of total operating costs covered by regular fare paying passengers) fell from sixty-one per cent in 1975 to fifty-four per cent in 1979. The mean average for British conurbations fell from seventy-three to sixty-seven per cent. London Transport achieved a farebox ratio of sixty-one in 1975, but this had increased to seventy-five per cent in 1979.[18] This means that while the average contribution of fare paying passengers on most European and North American urban transport systems had fallen between 1975 and 1979, passengers on LT had significantly increased their contribution to operating costs. The recent situation in twelve of the leading conurbations is summarised in Table 9.

Sir Peter Masefield found the contrast between transport policies in London and New York particularly striking. He found it 'extraordinary' that in New York 'that home of private enterprise' only twenty-eight per cent of public transport expenditure came from passenger fares whereas in London passengers contributed to the tune of seventy-six per cent.[19] He also noted that in the ten years to 1982 the equivalent of £1.8 thousand million had been spent on capital improvements for Paris's RATP — more than three times the amount received by LT over the same span of time.[20]

The Tory administration of Sir Horace Cutler at County Hall

Table 9

Financial support for urban public transport operators: International comparisons

	Farebox Ratio		Total Grant proportion of Total Expenditure	
	1980 %	1981 %	1980 %	1981 %
London Transport	78	69	29	36
Paris RATP	44	45	49	52
Tokyo TRTA	143	n/a	18	n/a
Chicago CTA	42	63	60	52
Toronto	72	72	36	36
Brussels	30	27	60	66
Milan	23	22	76	83
Stockholm	32	31	66	66
Copenhagen	58	68	60	53
Munich	60	60	40	35
Vienna	50	n/a	64	n/a
Zurich	63	57	13	18

Definitions: Farebox ratio – Proportion of fare income paid by travelling public to expenditure incurred on operating, maintaining and administering the undertaking. This definition *excludes* interest payments, depreciation and renewal, provisions and concessions payments made by the authorities for the aged and the handicapped.

Total grant – Total grants paid by authorities as a proportion of total 'cash' expenditure ie. Revenue expenditure plus capital expenditure less depreciation and renewal provisions included in Revenue Account.

Source: House of Commons, Transport Committee Fifth Report, *Transport in London*, Vol 1 p.xlvi.

between 1977 and 1981 continued the bankrupt policies that had so damaged LT in the past. The response to a decline in bus passenger mileage of seven per cent was an increase in fares of seventy-seven per cent.[21] Before the introduction of the new GLC's Fares Fair policy in October 1981 LT was expecting its share of the total passenger market to fall from thirty per cent to about twenty-five per cent by 1990.[22] Passenger disillusionment was intensified when buses scheduled to run did not appear. In 1981 201 million bus miles were scheduled but in the first half of the year only 168 million miles were operated.[23]

II

The London Labour Party gave a great deal of thought to the preparation of policies on which to fight the GLC elections of May 1981. The regional executive committee of the party set up working parties to give consideration to the major policy issues coming before the electorate. The reports from these groups were brought together and printed as *Discussion Papers on Labour's GLC Election Policy*, (1980, pp.157). After affiliated organisations had been invited to suggest amendments, the policy was decided at a special meeting of the Greater London Regional Council of the party held in Camden Town Hall on 17 and 18 October 1980. The programme for transport included the proposal to cut LT fares by twenty-five per cent, action which it was estimated would cost the average London ratepayer an extra 25p a week. It included much else besides – to deal with the questions of road congestion, water transport, capital investment, and so on; but it was the proposal to reduce fares which caught the public imagination and helped Labour to win the election, despite the fact that the manifesto made clear that rates would rise to pay for the proposed changes. The election manifesto, based on the decisions of the October meeting, was agreed by *all* Labour candidates, including, for example, Anne Sofer who soon after the election joined the SDP, and Andrew McIntosh, leader of the Labour opposition group at County Hall before May 1981, as well as Ken Livingstone who was chosen by the Labour group to succeed McIntosh after the election.

After the Law Lords had outlawed the Fares Fair policy on 17 December 1981 there was a sustained campaign in the press and from the Tory benches in the Commons to depict the new transport policy as a kind of conspiracy engineered by Ken Livingstone and his 'Marxist' friends. The London *Standard* said that the Law Lords' decision 'was an indictment of the GLC leadership alone . . . for acting rashly and unconstitutionally without stopping to think of the consequences'.[24] In the Commons Mr. Neubert, Tory MP for Romford, bewailed the situation across the Thames where 'one of the great capital cities of the world (was) being used as an opportunity for a Marxist experiment by Mr Livingstone and his colleagues'.[25] However, it must be emphasised that the policy of cheaper fares was not the peculiar brainchild of Ken Livingstone; it was the collective decision of the London Labour Party.[26] And if subsidising fares to the extent of forty-six per cent made Ken Livingstone a dangerous Marxist, how do we categorise Mayor Koch of New York whose City Fathers subsidised public transport to the extent of over seventy per cent?

In the GLC election of May 1981 the Labour Party gained a clear majority of seats and immediately took steps to implement its election promises. Careful preparation was needed before the new transport policies could be put into operation, but the new Fares Fair policy was introduced throughout the GLC area on 5 October 1981. Because of the introduction of a comprehensive zonal system (following the Cutler administration's sponsoring of an 'outer zone') the average reduction in fares was greater than that promised in the election manifesto – thirty-two per cent instead of twenty-five per cent. There were now four bus zones, one each for the City, West End and Inner and Outer London. A maximum fare of 20p was established for rides within a single zone; crossing two zones cost a maximum of 30p while for any ride across three or four zones the maximum was 40p. The 'short hop' fare for journeys up to three quarters of a mile in Inner London and one mile elsewhere was halved from 20p to 10p. Weekly, monthly and annual bus passes were correpondingly reduced in price and there were special bargains such as the maximum Sunday fare of 20p throughout the whole GLC area. The transformation of underground charges was less complete, graduated fares still applying through most of Greater London; nevertheless, the scale of charges was reduced by at least twenty-five per cent.

The response of the public to Fares Fair was generally enthusiastic. The *Standard* reported that – 'Londoners queued in their thousands at bus garages and ticket offices to get hold of the new cheaprate bus passes and underground season tickets. Demand for bus passes was so intense that supplies ran out at offices all over London.'[27]

As a result of Fares Fair there was a thirteen per cent increase in bus travel and a seven per cent increase in underground travel. Private transport use declined by an estimated two per cent. At last a governing party at County Hall had reversed the seemingly relentless decline in public transport use in the capital.[28]

Following the introduction of Fares Fair, London ratepayers were

presented with a supplementary rate demand averaging £1.30 a week
– substantially more than they had been led to believe would be payable. The total extra bill that Ken Livingstone's GLC was called upon
to meet in 1981 was £230 million. Only £61 million of this was directly
due to Fares Fair; although to this should be added another £8 million
incurred through increasing bus mileage by 6.5 million miles and
underground train mileage by 300,000 miles. The remaining £161
million of the bill was made up of a transport account deficit of £48
million inherited from the Cutler regime – Sir Horace was reluctant
to increase fares just before the election – and a penalty of £111 million for 'overspending' imposed on the GLC by Michael Heseltine,
Secretary of State for the Environment. Dave Wetzel, Chairman of
the GLC Transport Committee from May 1981, claimed that, but for
the penalties, the added rate burden would have been 70p a week
(rather than the £1.30 made necessary as a result of government
policy) and that with a 'normal' type of Conservative Government,
of the kind led, say, by Harold Macmillan or Ted Heath, seventy per
cent of the cost would have been met by central government grant
leaving the added burden to the ratepayer only 21p a week.[29]

A glance at the London underground map reveals that most Londoners living south of the Thames have no easy access to LT train
services, though the area is criss-crossed by a dense network of BR
rail and LT bus routes. Commuters who used BR train services were
keenly aware of their gaining no financial advantage from the Fares
Fair policy (at least for that part of their journey). In fact their rail
fares were raised by BR in November 1981. This situation need not
have arisen. The GLC, all too well aware of the discrepancies
between rail and underground fares, appealed to Norman Fowler,
Secretary of State for Transport, to authorise the subsidisation of
BR commuter fares to match the reductions in force on LT since 5
October. Fowler quickly scotched the suggestion. If Dave Wetzel,
Transport Committee Chairman, tried to subsidise BR commuters,
he would deduct a pound from the Government's grant to the GLC
for every pound paid out to reduce rail fares. Brian Reading, Bromley Council Chairman, and his friend and council colleague, Dennis
Barkway, both keen Conservatives, were aware of Wetzel's efforts
but knew that most Bromley residents had not heard of them, but
were, on the other hand, resentful that they were being called upon
to pay a supplementary rate to make journeys cheaper for Londoners

living north of the Thames and for visitors to the capital. (In fact most of the Fares Fair subsidies went to the buses. South Londoners were inclined to say they gained nothing from the new policy. This was not true. A 'short hop' trip on the bus before 5 October cost them 20p: after that date it was 10p.) The two councillors decided the omens were favourable for Bromley Council to make an appeal to the courts. At first it looked as if they had miscalculated. Two Divisional Court judges, Lord Justice Dunn and Mr Justice Phillips, gave their case short shrift. 'Matters of this kind', they ruled, 'are for the appropriate authority and eventually for the electors, and not for the Court to determine.' The Appeal Court, however, overturned the lower courts verdict and Lord Denning gave its reasons for finding in favour of Bromley. Finally, on 15 December 1981, the five Law Lords turned down the GLC's application to reverse the Appeal Court's Verdict. The Fares Fair policy was declared illegal.

The *Financial Times* took a poor view of the Lords' decision. It considered 'Their lordships unanimous contention that an "economic" public transport system is one which aims to ensure that costs are covered by passenger revenues would not survive the red pencil of an A level economics examiner who is aware of elementary economic concepts such as "external benefits" and "economies of scale".[30] Margaret Thatcher, however, had no doubts. At the first opportunity, at question time in the Commons on the day following the Lords' decision, she welcomed 'the clear and unambiguous judgement from the House of Lords' and congratulated Bromley for having 'clarified the position for London's ratepayers'.[31] Her Secretary of State for Transport, David Howell, declared that the crisis was 'entirely the fault of the GLC who had managed in seven months of folly to create financial chaos'.[32] When Sir Peter Masefield and Ken Livingstone saw him on 18 December to try to persuade him to pass an emergency law with alternative methods of financing LT, he refused to act.[33] His argument was that he was 'not prepared to let the GLC go back to its unbalanced policies which placed such huge burdens on the ratepayers'. Nigel Spearing, Labour MP for Newham South, suggested that if he wanted a balanced policy for ratepayers he should ask the Secretary of State for the Environment (Michael Heseltine) to remove his penalties which contributed most to the sums needed from the supplementary rates. Howell made no promise to do this.[34] His main suggestion to the Commons, repeated three times, was that if the GLC found itself 'incapable of sorting out its difficulties' it should come and see him.[35] *The Sunday Times* was unimpressed by David Howell's performance. It found it 'hard to conceive a more pinched, less imaginative ministerial response'.[36]

III

Howell's attempt to put the entire blame on the GLC can be understood. It helped to obscure the chaotic situation resulting from the Law Lords' decision. For their judgements were far from being 'clear and unambiguous' as the Prime Minister had asserted. Their unanimous decision that the Fares Fair policy was illegal was based on the Transport (London) Act, 1969, which established GLC control of the general direction of London's transport policies and set up the London Transport Executive as its executive agent. The five lords were in agreement that, under this Act, the GLC had two major responsibilities. Under Section 1 it was to promote 'integrated, efficient and economic transport facilities in Greater London'. But the council also had a 'fiduciary responsibility' of ensuring that ratepayers were not unduly burdened as a result of extravagant expenditure by the LTE. The Lords considered that, particularly after Heseltine's fines had added to the GLC's debts, the council had neglected its fiduciary responsibility 'in pushing ahead regardless with its manifesto policy'. Although the Lords agreed that the LTE was to live within its 'revenues', they were split on their understanding of what might be included under that term. Lords Brandon and Wilberforce supported Bromley's claim that LT should 'balance its books' with fare revenue alone; Lords Scarman and Diplock believed that it was legal for the GLC to make grants to the LTE, even for the purpose of reducing fares, provided the interests of the ratepayers had not been violated. (They thought in this case they had been.) Lord Keeth of Kinkel's judgement may be seen as giving qualified support for the interpretation made by Lords Scarman and Diplock.[37] Thus on the *principle* of the GLC giving grants to the LTE we may say that two and a half lords considered the practice legal and two regarded it as illegal.

It is the practice of the Law Lords, when considering judgement on appeal, to pay close attention to relevant legal precedents and even closer attention to the wording of statutes whose interpretation is under question, but judges are not allowed to read *Hansard* to probe the intentions of ministers introducing legislation.[38] In this case the five who heard the GLC appeal considered *Prescott vs Birmingham Corporation*, 1955, Chap. 210, in which the corporation's action in introducing free bus passes for pensioners was declared illegal, (though by 1981 the practice was widespread), but did not consult *Hansard* for 17 December 1968 when Richard Marsh, Minister of Transport, introduced the second reading of the Transport (London) Bill and explained its purposes. The minister said: 'The main powers that the council (GLC) will have, apart from the power to appoint, will be to pay grant to the Executive (LTE) for any purpose it thinks fit and to issue directions to the Executive. This gives the council the right to prescribe the policy lines to be followed and take financial responsibility for its decisions. This is very important because if the council wishes the Executive to do something that will cause it to fall short of its financial targets, it will itself take financial responsibility for it. The council might wish, for example, the Executive to run a series of services at a loss for social or planning reasons. It might wish to keep fares down at a time when costs are rising and there is no scope for economies. It is free to do so. But it has to bear the cost.'[39]

Margaret Thatcher was then opposition spokeswoman on transport. She followed Dick Marsh by giving a general blessing to the Bill – 'I do not think anyone will quarrel with the main purpose and the method of achieving it.' She made no objection to the GLC being given powers to grant subsidies from the rates. Michael Heseltine began his winding up speech from the opposition front bench by saying: 'It will be generally agreed that the one coherent theme running through these deliberations is that the principle of trying to centre these transport functions on the GLC is accepted and welcomed on all sides.'[40] At that time the Conservatives ruled at County Hall, and Thatcher and Heseltine viewed with equanimity the transfer to them of great powers over transport policy. Fifteen years later the Tories' antipathy to the Livingstone administration was a byword and the Cabinet was working out plans for the GLC's abolition and the establishment of a new quango to run London's transport.

In the aftermath of the Law Lords' judgement there was a striking contrast between the speed with which the government sponsored and passed through all its stages in Parliament by 2 March 1982 the Travel Concessions (London) Bill, which authorised the GLC to continue subsidising the LT bus and train passes for retirement pensioners, with its refusal to legislate to give the council power to continue its cheap fares policy. The advantages these tactics brought to Margaret Thatcher were that she was shown as the pensioners' friend, while the extravagant 'folly' of the 'Marxists' in control at County Hall continued to be exposed as the general public waited for their fares to be doubled. The irony of the situation was that the Law Lords had made much of the distinction between a GLC grant given to cover a LT deficit unavoidably incurred following strenuous efforts to balance the books, and a grant doled out in fulfilment of a deliberate social policy. The former situation they considered legitimate. At least two of the Law Lords judged the other kind of situation impermissible under the 1969 Act. Lord Scarman, in his judgement had written, '. . . though it envisages budgeting for a deficit it permits it not as an object of social or transport policy, but as a course of action which it may not be practicable or possible to avoid'. Nevertheless, within three months of the Law Lords' decision the government was rushing through a Bill which allowed the GLC to spend nearly £59 million of ratepayers' money on a grant for pensioners' bus and LT underground passes which was of a purely social service character and in total only £2 million short of the cost of the Fares Fair policy.[41]

III

By 22 March 1982, the earliest date by which the administrative arrangements could be completed, the Fares Fair policy came to an end and new, higher, fares, generally double those previously charged, were introduced. The social and environmental consequences of the change were disturbing. London Transport's revenue statistics show that there was a fall of sixteen per cent in bus journeys and of over thirteen per cent in underground journeys (excluding OAP travel). Immediately following the fares increase there was a five per cent rise in peak period car traffic throughout London

156

which, with increased car occupancy, resulted in a rise of six per cent in journeys by car. Pedal cycle travel increased by fifty per cent. Not surprisingly, then, the earliest road casualty figures showed the biggest increase was in injuries to cyclists, though there were also alarming increases in the number of motor cyclists injured. A report made to the GLC Transport Committee on 28 April 1983 stated that over the preceding year there were 3,700 extra road casualties in the GLC area. The cost of the higher fares policy in additional petrol, car operating costs and extra travel time was estimated at £39 million a year – some two-thirds of the cost of Fares Fair – though, of course, many London ratepayers gained more from the cheaper fares than they paid out (initially) in higher rates. It is difficult to measure the environmental costs of more congested, noisier roads and the heavier pollution of the atmosphere.[42]

The first impression gained by Sir Peter Masefield, the GLC and the trade unions, following the Law Lords' decision, was that new legislation was needed before it would be possible to restore even that level of grant support from the GLC to LT that had prevailed during the Cutler administration at County Hall between 1977 and 1981. Sir Peter wrote a letter to the *Financial Times* on 17 December 1981 stating that he would be 'pressing for legislation to be enacted as quickly as possible to make lawful the ability of London Transport to be supported by subsidy as it had been since 1973'. The NUR's research department notes for the union's officers stated that, as things stood on 21 December 1981, 'LT must follow a policy of attempting to ensure fares cover all costs'.

Before long, however, it became evident that the government's interpretation of the Law Lords' ruling was becoming more flexible. Thus when the Solicitor General was questioned in the Commons on the legality of pensioners' bus passes he replied cautiously: 'Do not ask me questions like that: it is extremely difficult;' but within an hour the Under Secretary of State for Transport assured another questioner that the survival of the free fares system was 'not in doubt'.[43] Then, on 2 February 1982 David Howell wrote to Ken Livingstone enclosing guidelines from Sir Michael Havers, the Attorney General, on the interpretation that might be placed on the Law Lords' judgement: '"Fiduciary duty" requires that the authority must do its best to reduce the burden fairly on the ratepayers. It does not require that the authority must relieve the ratepayer of all the burden. A fair balance must be struck.'[44] Neither the Law Lords nor the Attorney General gave any indication to the GLC or LT of what would be regarded as 'a fair balance'. During the four years of the Cutler administration at County Hall the GLC had subsidised LT to the tune of over £250 million and the legitimacy of these payments had not been challenged.[45] Sir Peter Masefield and the GLC therefore came to the conclusion that the only way to discover where the 'fair balance' lay was by trial and error. They proceeded to draw up a draft budget for 1982-3 and awaited the outcome.

In the meantime the trade unions combined forces in a programme of action to enlist public support and to try to persuade the government to change its mind and to legislate to make possible a continuation of the Fares Fair policy. On 4 January 1982 a meeting of the representatives of the trade union involved in organising LT workers agreed on a programme of publicity, public meetings, joint representations with LT to the Secretary of State for Transport and a one-day strike, all designed to draw attention to the case for continuing the lower fares.[46] On 10 March, the date of the one-day strike of LT workers, the RAC reported that the streets of London were choked; approach roads to the capital were crammed with cars and the evening rush hour lasted until late at night – eight hours after it had started.[43] On the following afternoon there was a lobby of MPs. A further lobby took place on 23 April, the day on which Douglas Jay MP introduced his (unsuccessful) ten minute rule resolution to re-establish the lower fares policy. The joint statement from the GLC, LT and the trade unions, which was presented to David Howell on 25 May, pointed out that the 'enforced doubling of fares' which was 'out of step with established practice in all major cities on the continent and in North America' would 'seriously harm the well being of London'. It urged that 'funds from central government should be combined with those from ratepayers to provide support for public services on a scale and at a price adequately to meet the needs of London'. Gradually the press began to show more sympathy for LT's situation. In a leading article *The Times* commented: 'If the law does not allow systematic subsidy it must be changed.'[48] But David Howell was determined to prevent the GLC reviving its Fares Fair policy. He was not to be deflected from his purpose by any of the agitation.

In the winter of 1982-3, therefore, the GLC and LT worked together to produce a *Balanced Plan* for the next five years of transport policy. It fell far short of what the GLC had hoped to achieve, but was a compromise forced on the GLC and the LTE by the government's financial restraints and by the political hostility to the Labour-controlled council. The approach was based on the council's obligations, made clear in sections 1 and 2 of the Transport (London) Act, 1969, to promote 'integrated, efficient and economic transport facilities for Greater London' and to take account of the transport requirements of the Greater London Development Plan. Fares were to be reduced by an average of twenty-five per cent (but rising subsequently on a par with inflation), and they were to be greatly simplified by a system of Travelcards valid for journeys on both bus and underground. The simplified zonal system for bus fares which had survived the Law Lords' ruling was extended to include underground train services (except to the most distant destinations, such as Heathrow). It was hoped to improve bus reliability by improved manning and by increasing the number of bus lanes. From 1971 to 1975 the introduction of bus lanes and traffic engineering, such as the increase in the number of one-way streets, had, for that quinquennium, increased marginally the speed of traffic, until the growth in the number of vehicle registrations nullified the improvement. Under the *Balanced Plan* it was hoped that a new era of improvement would come about.[49]

The GLC had taken legal advice before Fares Fair was introduced and had been assured that the lower fare plan was legal under the 1969 Act. This time it determined to make doubly sure. When the LTE doubted whether the *Balanced Plan* would be accepted in law the GLC appealed to the High Court. On 27 January 1983 the three judges were unanimous that the plan, involving a twenty-five per cent reduction in fares and a £100 million increase in transport subsidy, was a valid exercise of the GLC's powers under the 1969 Transport (London) Act.[50] The new fares package, described by LT as 'Just the Ticket', came into operation on 22 May 1983 and was very popular with Londoners. The rise in the number of journeys on tubes and buses was double that which had been anticipated.[51]

Meanwhile the damaging effects of the government's severe financial restraints were partially offset by greater co-operation between BR and LT to improve transport facilities in the Greater London area. Hitherto one of the disincentives to cross-London travel by public transport was the necessity of re-booking for Underground or bus travel after arriving at a BR terminal. By February 1982, however, cross-London ticket bookings were possible at 420 stations so that customers were able to travel straight through to their final destinations. There was also co-operation in the preparation of timetables and the joint training of BR and LT staff for information services.[52] But these were only palliatives, though appreciated by the travelling public. The big obstacle to better co-ordination of services remained in the different sources of grant support, BR looking directly to the Department of Transport and LT to the GLC. This meant that before Fares Fair was introduced in October 1981 BR fares on routes running parallel to the Underground were lower than those charged by LT. After Fares Fair the position was reversed and much custom was transferred from BR to LT services. When LT was obliged to double its fares from 22 March 1982, the position was reversed again. It was very difficult to improve transport co-ordination in these circumstances. It required government subsidisation of fares charged by the two organisations in such a way that see-sawing of the kind experienced in 1981-2 was avoided.

IV

The GLC and LT were denied any lengthy period of stability to further exploit the advantages of the zonal system and extend the co-operation with BR which had made impressive progress since 1980. On 5 November 1982 the government published simultaneously its White Paper on transport policy and its Transport Bill. In so doing it departed from precedent. Normally, sufficient time is allowed to elapse between the publication of the two documents to allow informed discussion to take place. On this occasion the government gave every indication that it was not anxious to give its proposals much of an airing; MPs were debating the second reading of the Bill only ten days after the appearance of the White Paper.

The Transport Act, which became law on 28 March 1983, concerned the future of the Passenger Transport Executives (PTEs) in England and Wales and the London Transport Executive. Under the Act, each of the executives was obliged to prepare annually a three-year rolling programme for the development of transport services in its region. The Secretary of State for Transport would review these plans and set guidelines on the level of subsidy considered reasonable. David Howell, in introducing the second reading of the Bill to the Commons, claimed that it would remove the uncertainties which had arisen about the permissible level of rate support for public transport. The PTEs and the LTE were not *obliged* to keep within the financial limits the minister laid down. However, it was not long before Howell published the figures shown in Table 10.

Table 10

Authority	Subsidy £ million		Increase/Decrease
	1983-84	*1982-83*	*1983-84 over 1982-83*
Greater London	220	188	+ 32
Greater Manchester	46	45.9	+ .1
Merseyside	40	50.6	− 10.6
South Yorkshire	40	57.4	− 17.4
Tyne & Wear	18	20.6	− 2.6
West Yorkshire	44	46	− 2

Source: HMSO, *Public Transport Subsidy in Cities*, Cmnd 8735, November 1982. TGWU *Guidelines on Transport Bill* 11 November 1982.

(The increase granted to London is accounted for by the paying back of some of the government's transport grant withdrawn as a penalty for the introduction of the Fares Fair policy.)

Although no executive was obliged to keep within the department's guidelines, individuals and councils were free to challenge in the courts any executive that went beyond them. In the Commons Howell said that one of the main purposes of the Bill was 'to discourage city authorities from the reckless course on which some of them have been set, with their excessive commitment to high rates, which destroy jobs with deadly efficiency, and ultra-low fares which destabilise our transport system.'[53] The 'ultra-low fares' referred to were those charged under Fares Fair when the London farebox ratio was still well above the level prevailing in most other large cities, as Table 9 above shows. The Act represented a decisive increase of centralisation of powers with the Department of Transport and a weakening of control of the electorate in the localities; for if the electors opted for a policy of low fares and high investment in public transport, the authority they elected would face a high risk of its grant from the department being withheld or reduced and would also face the risk of having its transport expenditure challenged in the courts. Ultimately the lawyers, rather than the electorate, would determine transport policy, as had happened in the case of the GLC. The comment of the Association of Metropolitan Authorities (AMA) was that 'if the Bill reaches the statute book in its present form local authority freedom in relation to public transport will be dead.'[54]

Under Section 8 of the Act the executives are obliged to seek tenders for the privatisation of bus and ancillary services and can be forced to adopt these tenders if they are 'more effective and cheaper'. The executives have been concerned lest they are obliged to grant charters to private bus operators that cream off the best of the traffic but ignore the unprofitable services, at the same time undermining the commercial viability of established operators.

Indicative of what might happen under the privatisation provisions of the Act was the launching of Mr. Anthony Shephard's Associated Minibus Operators (AMOS) in London early in 1983. Shephard applied to run 400 minibuses on four cross-London routes in direct competition with LT buses. His vehicles, which were planned to run at two-minute intervals, were to have no fixed stops, but could be 'flagged down' anywhere along their routes. The drivers of the sixteen seater minibuses would have deposited with the company a bond of, say, £1,000 and a monthly fee of £500. It would thereafter be up to them to earn as much as they could from fares. The proposal was rejected following an enquiry conducted by the London Traffic Inspector, Geoffrey Holden, at the Royal Commonwealth Society in March. Objections to the scheme were widespread. LT estimated that it would lose £10 million in revenue through the creaming off of some of its most lucrative traffic; the police were concerned with road safety; the GLC and others questioned Mr. Shephard's ability, in London traffic conditions, to keep his buses to the two-minute intervals promised. The GLC was also concerned that random services offered by several hundred individuals would make immeasurably more difficult the task of planning an integrated and efficient transport system for London.[55] However, the chances of a scheme of this kind being backed by a Tory minister were enhanced after the passing of the Transport Act on 23 March 1983.

A month after the general election of June 1983 the new Thatcher government published its White Paper *Public Transport in London* (Cmnd 9004) which revealed that the Tories planned to give Londoners even less control over transport policy in the capital than was given to the electorate in the Passenger Transport Authorities (PTAs) over their transport systems under the Transport Act, 1983. Tom King, the new Secretary of State for Transport, proposed to replace the popularly elected GLC – which in any case the government proposed to abolish by 1986 – by a quango of transport experts appointed by himself and called London Regional Transport (LRT). Financial support for LRT would come direct from government and not from the rates, though ratepayers would not benefit financially since it was proposed that central government rate support grant would be reduced to the extent that boroughs were exempt from GLC precept for LT support. Even Mr. Alan Greengross, leader of the GLC Conservative group, was highly critical of the new proposals which he described as a 'dictatorship from the centre' under which Londoners 'could merely be exchanging an existing hazard for an even greater one'.[56] The LRT was likely to be a less democratically run organisation than the Commons' Transport Committee's proposed Metropolitan Transport Authority, half of whose members would have come from the local councils, the GLC, the London boroughs and the shire counties impinging on the capital.[57]

The government's concern to extend privatisation was made clear in the White Paper. Under the proposed LRT the bus and Underground services would be separate subsidiaries, one of whose tasks would be 'to involve the private sector in the provision of services and to make better use of publicly owned assets'.[58] Robert Hughes, opposition front bench spokesman on Transport, summed up the White Paper as 'a prelude to the privatisation of what profitable parts may be abstracted from London Transport, and the encouragement of local private operators to cream off profitable services.'[59] The White Paper proposed that the London boroughs should take back the responsibility for paying for pensioners' transport passes. The result of such a change would be to ease substantially the rate burden of the wealthiest councils and add to the burden of some of the poorest ones. The big gainers would be the Cities of London and Westminster with relatively few OAPs; they would be able to make a saving of between two pence halfpenny and threepence in the pound. The rates of Wandsworth and Lewisham, by contrast, would rise by similar amounts. Ironically, Bromley, whose councillors initiated the legal proceedings against the GLC because of the cost of the Fares Fair policy to ratepayers, would incur an additional rate burden of £1,182,000 or 2.37 pence in the pound, if the White Paper proposals became law. In the Commons, John Page, Conservative MP for Harrow West, said that 'after the raping of the ratepayers of Harrow by the GLC' his constituents would be delighted with the government's proposals. In fact, under the White Paper plan, they would be called upon to pay 2.26 pence in the pound *more* than they were currently being called upon to pay by the GLC.[60]

The authors of the White Paper were right in stressing that the condition of London's transport services is a matter of national importance. There is also much to be said for their suggestion that LT's, as well as BR's, grant requirements should be met from central government funds. But the big question is, will the funds provided be adequate? All the indications are that they will not. The White Paper states that a primary objective of LRT will be 'to reduce costs and the call on taxpayers' money'. And yet Tom King assured the Commons that the objective was 'a better deal for the London traveller'.[61] In the light of the fact that capital and revenue support for LT is already well below that provided in most major cities abroad the two objectives are contradictory. LT needs greater capital and revenue support, not less. This was stressed in the Transport Committee's Report which called for a '20 per cent increment on total central government support for public transport in London'.[62] If, as the Thatcher government plans, that support is reduced rather than increased, the result will be a further deterioration in London's public transport services.

V

The White Paper: *Rates: Proposals for Rate Limitation and Reform of the Rating System* (Cmnd 9008) published in August 1983 provided a further pointer to the Thatcher government's intentions regarding public services (including transport) in both London and the PTAs. The nub of the proposals is that the government plans to acquire power to set limits to the rates of a small number of councils

– between a dozen and twenty – which it considers have been guilty of 'excessive' spending. Nearly all the councils under consideration for a rates 'cap' to be imposed in 1985-6 were Labour-controlled at the time of the publication of the White Paper. As councils prepare their budgets in the autumn of 1984 they will be assessed by civil servants of the Department of the Environment. Some of those councils will then be given figures for their permitted rate levels and if they defy the department, the Secretary of State will enforce the new guidelines by law. Among the councils described by *The Times* as 'in the firing line' are the GLC, Sheffield, Greater Manchester, Merseyside, Tyne and Wear and the West Midlands.

The PTA likely to suffer most from the government's clampdown on spending authorised under the Transport Act 1983 and expected to be carried further under the policy spelt out in the White Paper on Rates, is South Yorkshire. Until the mid 1970s public transport trends in this region mirrored the decline in usage which was general in the UK. Between 1960 and 1974 a quarter of the passengers were lost from the municipal bus services of the area. With the establishment of the PTA and the re-organisation of local authority boundaries, however, a complete change of policy was adopted. Fares were kept stable, in Sheffield and Barnsley from the first quarter of 1975 and in Doncaster and Rotherham from January 1976. By 1982 the average adult fare was seven pence, fares representing only twenty-three per cent of total costs. Whereas in the country as a whole the number of bus passengers declined by twenty-three per cent and in the other PTA areas by a quarter, in the county of South Yorkshire the number of passengers *increased* by three and a half per cent. In 1981-2 there were 344 million passenger journeys in South Yorkshire; if the trend there had been the same as the national average there would have been only 256 million journeys. Hence in that year South Yorkshire buses had thirty-four per cent more passenger journeys than the national trend would have given. The growth of passenger journeys compared with those in other PTAs and the NBC is shown in Fig: 7. Meanwhile in the neighbouring county of West Yorkshire fares rose faster than the rate of inflation and between 1974-75 and 1980-81 the West Yorkshire PTA lost thirty-nine per cent of its passengers.[63] Lest it be imagined that the heavy rate subsidies required to keep fares unchanged over the years put a premium on inefficiency, it needs to be pointed out that South Yorkshire,

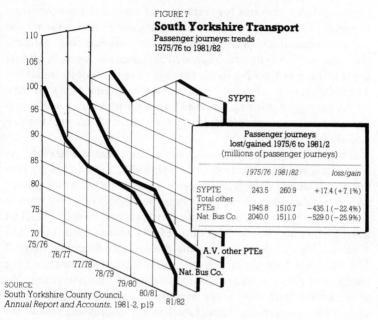

FIGURE 7
South Yorkshire Transport
Passenger journeys: trends
1975/76 to 1981/82

	Passenger journeys lost/gained 1975/6 to 1981/2 (millions of passenger journeys)		
	1975/76	*1981/82*	*loss/gain*
SYPTE	243.5	260.9	+17.4 (+7.1%)
Total other PTEs	1945.8	1510.7	−435.1 (−22.4%)
Nat. Bus Co.	2040.0	1511.0	−529.0 (−25.9%)

SYPTE

A.V. other PTEs

Nat. Bus Co.

SOURCE:
South Yorkshire County Council,
Annual Report and Accounts, 1981-2, p19

together with Tyne and Wear, have the lowest operating costs per
mile of service and per passenger of any of the PTAs. In 1979 each
South Yorkshire bus carried an average of 240,000 passengers compared with an average of 128,000 for all PTAs.[64] Since 49.6 per cent
of all South Yorkshire households are without cars the cheap fares
policy is popular with most of the electorate, as is shown by the
return of Labour councillors in local elections and Labour candidates in five out of the six Sheffield seats in the general elections of
1979 and 1983.

The big problem inherited by the Tyne and Wear PTA in the early
1970s was the run-down state of the North Tyne Loop railway.
Under the energetic and forceful leadership of the first PTE director,
Tony Ridley, himself a Tynesider, consultants were commissioned
to study the possible options for the transport development of the
area. Their recommendation to adopt a light rapid transport system
was adopted. An enabling Act was obtained in 1973 and the new
Tyne and Wear Metro was in operation in the early 1980s, though
parts of the system still remained to be completed. Notable features
of the new Metro are its well-planned integration with the bus

services; the cheap fares for children and pensioners; the provision of ramps or lifts at all stations to aid the mobility of the disabled and the use of enamel for wall panelling to deter vandals from defacing the stations. The Tyne and Wear Metro is a legitimate source of civic pride and is a monument to the foresight and drive of its initiators. The decision to go ahead with an imaginative plan is being justified by the passenger statistics. In 1983 passenger usage exceeded a million a week – a rate exceeding the thirty-eight million a year the PTE had anticipated.[65]

It is policies such as these which are under threat as a result of the Thatcher government's Transport Act, 1983, and of that government's policy of withholding support grants to PTAs which pursue an active policy of boosting public transport. On 5 July 1983 Patrick Jenkin, Secretary of State for the Environment, 'fined' Sheffield £14.179 million, South Yorkshire £5.584 million and Tyne and Wear £7.379 million for exceeding the targets set by Whitehall.[66] The Sheffield City Council warned that the abandonment of the cheap fares policy would mean that relatives of the elderly and disabled would find visits more expensive; community care would suffer; high fares would limit the choice of schools to less well off families; family links with relatives in 'overspill' estates would be weakened; attendance at evening classes, football matches and other sporting events would decline; bus workers would lose jobs and community life in inner cities would wither.[67] The Thatcherites have tended to exaggerate the rate burden resulting from progressive transport policies. In South Yorkshire only eleven per cent of rates income goes towards transport, and the average domestic ratepayer pays seventy-five pence a week for transport, less than the cost of two average bus journeys in London.[68]

The most serious threat of all was included in the Conservative Party general election manifesto in 1983 where it was stated that the GLC, together with the metropolitan authorities set up a decade earlier, would be abolished by 1986. If this policy was to be implemented the future of the imaginative public transport policies of Tyne and Wear, South Yorkshire and the other PTAs would be in jeopardy.

The Way Ahead in Transport Policy

The Department of Transport has a routine computer programme for assessing the comparative merits of different trunk road construction and improvement schemes. The programme is called COBA – – short for 'cost-benefit analysis'. Among the elements that enter into the calculation are the costs of construction, the anticipated saving in motorists' journey time and fuel consumption, the easing of congestion in towns and villages and the reduced likelihood of accidents.[1] It was after weighing considerations such as these that the department decided to include the proposed extension of the M25 between Swanley and Sevenoaks, costing £42.7 million, as one among many projects to be authorised for completion by March 1985.[2] It has not been found possible, so far, to bring into the calculations environmental factors such as noise, traffic fumes and damage to the structure of buildings. Changes in the quality of social life resulting from the construction of a by-pass or the driving of a six-lane motorway through a built-up area are also difficult to evaluate in financial terms and are therefore left out of the computer calculations, though they may be the subject of discussion in the department and the cause of vociferous protests in the localities affected.

The Cabinet and Margaret Thatcher's trusted economic advisers raised no objections to the Department of Transport's plans to spend nearly £740 million on trunk road schemes in the financial year 1982-3 – an increase of twenty per cent on the allocation for 1981-2. Nor was there objection to Local Authorities spending a further £1.2 billion in 1982-3 on road maintenance and construction.[3]

It was a very different story when the same group of people considered BR's repeated pleas for investment in railway electrification.

No computer programme was pressed into service to give proper weight to the speed, fuel-saving and environmental advantages of railways over road transport. Instead, BR was required to demonstrate that each electrification scheme it submitted was justifiable in purely commercial terms. The Board had to prove that when the electrified line was opened it would yield a return of at least seven per cent on the capital invested. The Leitch Committee put the situation succinctly when it reported that 'in keeping with BR's commercial remit, financial appraisal is used rather than cost benefit methods'.[4] Furthermore, the 'commercial remit' was being made ever more exacting with each year of Thatcher government. Within a month of the publication of the White Paper, *Policy for Roads in England: 1983*, authorising a twenty per cent increase in expenditure on trunk roads within a year, Nicholas Ridley, the newly appointed Secretary of State for Transport, announced that BR's PSO was to be *reduced* from £819 million in 1983 to £635 millions in 1986, a decrease of twenty-nine per cent over three years.[5] The Department of Transport was fully aware that the application of cost benefit analysis to BR's proposals for capital expenditure on electrification and other projects would produce a more favourable assessment than was obtainable using the traditional, purely commercial yardstick.[6] The department was quite content that road and rail schemes should be processed through different hierarchies in Marsham Street. At no time were representative road and rail schemes put side by side and subjected to the same cost benefit analysis. By contrast, in the Federal Republic of Germany, 'all projects for road, rail and waterways are evaluated by a standard procedure from the viewpoint of the overall economy, and put in order of priority'.[7] This is one important reason why, at the end of the 1970s, Deutsche Bundesbahn was responsible for twice as large a proportion of freight transport work within the Federal Republic – thirty-seven per cent of tonne-kilometres carried – as was BR within the UK, carrying a meagre eighteen per cent.[8]

Because different methods of assessment have been applied for road and rail projects over many decades, BR has been consistently under-capitalised and denied the opportunity of carrying as large a proportion of passenger and freight transport as its potentialities would justify. The Department of Transport's attitude to the railways is shown in the comments of E.B.C. Osmotherly, one of its leading officers, on BR's draft for the *Corporate Plan 1983-88*. (Osmotherly had moved from being secretary of the Serpell Committee to the secretaryship of the department's committee for vetting railway finance. This was a significant change in the light of Howell's comment that any action on the Serpell Report 'would be decided in the public forum'.) In a letter to a member of the Board on 22 April 1983 in which the emphasis was on the need for BR to achieve 'commercial viability' he wrote: 'As we see it, tight resourcing is not just a matter of having no slack in resources when facing the planned level of traffic. It goes further than that because it involves accepting that if planned levels of traffic are achieved, the resources will be placed under intense pressure to cope with the load and it may even be necessary to turn away some of the traffic on offer.'

If the UK is to achieve a properly balanced transport policy it is essential that road, rail, inland waterway and coastal shipping sschemes should each be given a fair assessment and that the over-emphasis on the advantages of road transport should be corrected.

II

In weighing up the comparative merits of road and rail improvements account should be taken of the likely consumption of energy using the alternative modes of transport. The Figure overleaf shows that, if the aim is to achieve accessibility with the minimum expenditure of exhaustible supplies of energy, and the journey distance is beyond the radius of urban transport, the well-filled passenger train has an immense advantage over the private car. Of course, energy conservation achievement of the private car and the passenger train varies enormously: in motor cars from the gas-guzzler to the most economical small family limousine, and in trains from the over-crowded inter-city electric to the nearly empty, stopping, dmu. But car petrol consumption assumed is that of the average medium-sized vehicle. Much attention has been directed to the subject of energy conservation recently, but consideration of the subject is far from comprehensive. On 2 November 1983 Peter Walker, energy secretary, launched what was described as the 'biggest ever' energy-saving campaign in which he claimed that out of £100 million worth

FIGURE 8
Transport energy consumption
in Joules/person/100km

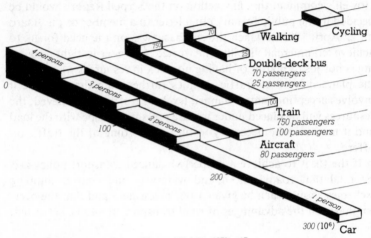

SOURCE N.Pole, *Oil and the Future of Personal Mobility* (1973), p17

of energy consumed daily twenty millions worth is wasted. There were plans for the Secretary of State to visit forty of the largest cities and towns in the UK to spread the message.[10] The biggest loss of energy was in the heating of people's homes and advice was offered on how savings could be made. However, to the relief of the road lobby and the heavily road-oriented Department of Transport, no reference was made to the waste of energy in transport. Thirty-three per cent of Britain's oil consumption is channelled into transport and ninety-seven per cent of the oil destined for transport use is taken up by road passenger and freight vehicles.[11] The fact that in the EEC countries as a whole only twenty-seven per cent of oil consumption is required for transport purposes is a measure of the greater success of countries of continental Europe in keeping a larger proportion of passenger and freight transport on the rails than we have had in Britain. It is also some indication of the scope for fuel economy in British transport.[12] Within a week of his appointment as Chairman of the BRB, Bob Reid told a London conference of over two hundred transport experts that recent evidence showed that 'private cars in cities consume four times as much energy per seat mile as a commuter train or coach and over double the amount of energy per passenger mile'.[13] It is not often realised that the private motor car 'consumes more energy than lorries, vans, buses, coaches, aeroplanes, ships, barges and railway engines put together'.[14]

It would be unwise to assume the imminent exhaustion of world fuel oil supplies. In 1973-4, when the war between Israel and the Arab states shook the complacency which had existed concerning oil supplies since World War II, it was widely predicted that from the mid 1990s available supplies would begin to decline sharply. Even in 1982 'the twelve-fold increase in the price of internationally traded oil since 1972' was noted by a leading expert.[15] But with the world economic depression in 1980-3 forecasts were revised. No imminent threat was envisaged.

It would, nevertheless, be prudent to reduce dependence on a single source of energy. The new North Sea oil fields being developed in the 1980s had smaller reserves than had the giants opened up in the 1970s.[16] The sale of French Super-Etendard aircraft and Exocet missiles to Iraq in October 1983 led to threats from Iran to close the Strait of Hormuz through which up to twenty per cent of the non-communist world's oil supplies passed each year. If such a threat were to be carried out, it would lead to a sharp increase in world oil prices and in the costs of motor transport.[17] Such possibilities highlight the case for the electrification of British railways since electric power can be generated from a variety of indigenous fuels as well as from the harnessing of water power.

If the cost benefit approach was applied to proposals for increasing investment in BR, the fact that road transport costs the community 'almost ten times as much as rail in terms of casualties per passenger mile' would have to be taken into account.[18] Road accidents in Great Britain in 1981 cost an estimated £2.2 billion.[19] In the years 1976-81 inclusive 38,166 persons were killed in road accidents, an average of 6,360 annually.[20] By contrast, the BRB's *Annual Report and Accounts 1981* commented: 'Safety remained a paramount consideration in all railway operations, but to the deep regret of the Board, four passengers were killed in two tragic accidents in December. These were the first deaths in passenger train accidents since 1979.'[21]

Between 1976-81 inclusive a total of twenty-five passengers were killed in train accidents, an average of just over four persons annually.[22] If a sum equal to only half the annual cost of road accidents was invested in BR, it would more than treble the present level of investment in our railways and within a decade could transform the quality of the service and take passengers and freight off the roads.

Although giving due weight to the above facts would strengthen the case for the railways, cost benefit analysis has its limitations. It is a mistake to give too much emphasis to items which are measurable in purely monetary terms. As a former Secretary of State for Transport commented: 'A less noisy, less polluted environment is as much part of the standard of living in its broadest sense as lower prices in the shops.'[23] The difficulty, of course, is that with environmental goods 'their actual price appears to be zero simply becaue there is no market'.[24] This should not be an excuse for inaction. Government has a duty to protect the quality of life as well as to promote economic efficiency. The environmentalist T. Aldous has drawn attention to those traffic engineers whose tunnel vision 'takes account of traffic flows, construction costs and mechanics and road safety, but discourages them from thinking of the devastating social impact of their work'. The orbital motorway, he wrote, 'would bring Chiswick within twenty minutes drive of Greenwich' but would destroy both in the process! A community may still be held together despite – or possibly because of – a railway which occupies a thirty foot cutting crossed by road bridges but may well be completely destroyed by an impenetrable swathe of motorway 200 feet wide.[25] How do you express in money terms the damage to health and social life caused by noise? So far no satisfactory answer to this question has been forthcoming. What is indisputable is that, other things being equal, the less noisy modes of transport should be encouraged. The noise from a trunk road or motorway half a mile away can often exceed that of an electric train passing through a cutting at a distance of only 200 yards.

The railway also scores better than road transport when air pollution is considered. At the time of writing there is great concern in the Federal Republic of Germany at the effects of 'acid rain' on the life of the forests. It is not claimed that the emission of fumes from motor transport is mainly responsible for the sickness of millions of trees, but on the other hand, it is not denied that it has contributed to the threat. In the UK, even in the early 1970s, total pollution from British cars added up to over six million tons of carbon monoxide, 300,000 tons of hydrocarbons, 210,000 tons of oxides of nitrogen, 20,000 tons of sulphur dioxide and 100,000 tons of aldehydes.[26] Trains are virtually pollution-free, are less noisy than road traffic and are visually unobtrusive. A sensible transport policy would encourage greater use of the railways. Instead, the Thatcher government has kept BR in a financial straightjacket while pursuing a relatively open-handed policy toward road improvements.

III

A sound national transport policy should reflect priorities in social policy as well as contributing to economic prosperity. The Thatcher government places its faith in market forces. It is held that if there is a sufficient demand for a bus or train service private businessmen will come forward to meet it. To the economist, demand is expressed in money terms and is not the same thing as what is commonly understood as a 'need'. A millionaire may create a 'demand' for a chauffeur-driven Rolls-Royce; an unemployed person with a basic minimum income and living in a remote rural area may have a need to visit the nearest hospital twenty miles away, but is unable to translate that need into a demand. The Serpell Report was dismissive of the idea of people having a need for transport: 'Those seeking to justify public transport subsidies often rely on an asserted 'need' for transport. Demand is determined by people individually. The concept of need, however, is an elusive one which cannot be defined objectively or without contention.'[27]

Inevitably in a country in which there is gross inequality in the distribution of income and capital, transport policies will tend to reflect society's class divisions unless government intervenes to protect the interests of the less affluent. Increasing traffic volumes should not be equated with increased accessibility for all sectors of the population. As a recent Labour Party/TUC statement made clear: 'Market pricing fails to ensure either the maintenance of an adequately sized transport network for those who depend upon it, the allocation of resources in a way which meets the social needs for various forms of transport or the fullest use of existing transport capacity.'[28]

The question needs asking: is a 'two nations' transport policy one that it is desirable to encourage? At present those living in households without cars, the low income families, the under seventeens and many of the pensioners who find accessibility to relatives, friends, the doctor and places of recreation increasingly difficult, are the 'poor' in transport terms. The families with cars and above average incomes who find accessibility greater than ever before are the 'rich' nation. The National Health Services Act in 1946 reflected the strong feeling in the country that in case of need, access to the best that the health services could offer was the right of every citizen, irrespective of income. The time is overdue for a similar type of decision in respect of transport policy. It should be the responsibility of parliament to ensure that minimum standards of accessibility are maintained throughout the country in the same way as it has ultimate responsibility for ensuring proper standards of health care.

IV

The aim of the next Labour government should be to expand the network of public transport so as to provide a minimum level of service at low prices for the population as a whole. In recent years the proportion of the GNP devoted to public transport has sunk to dangerously low levels. This trend should be reversed so that there is an increase in the amount of resources made available to railways, buses and inland waterways. It should also be the objective to ensure that the energy-conserving forms of transport, such as the electric train and the bulk-carrier waterway barge, are encouraged; and energy-wasting transport, such as the high-powered, tax-subsidised and often foreign-built company cars are discouraged. The aim should be to liberate people from dependence on their cars by making public transport more attractive, widespread and economical and to make rail freight haulage a better proposition to the businessman than private road haulage. It should be seen as part of the policy for improving the quality of public transport that the rates of pay and working conditions of those who provide this important service are such as to attract a dedicated labour force confident of the prosperous future of the industry. From the highest to the lowest levels of management there should be the full involvement of the trade union movement. Every opportunity should be provided for management's consultation with transport users to ensure that customers' complaints are dealt with and their views on policy options given full consideration.

Historically the Department of Transport has been concerned mainly with a national policy for road building and maintenance. It has failed to develop as an impartial adjudicator between the conflicting claims of road, rail and water transport. It has done very little to encourage transport integration in which the various forms of transport dovetail into each other as they do on a regional scale under Tyne and Wear PTA. Under a Labour Government the department would have to assume a wider role than it has done in the past. But it will also be necessary to create a National Transport Authority in order to develop the integration of the different transport modes and 'to bring together producer and consumer groups in a continuous forum'. The authority would 'draw together the operation of road and rail transport without placing it under a single executive'. The day to day operation of passenger transport would be left to the PTAs and the nationalised industry operators.[29]

The agreed Labour Party/TUC policy is that the National Transport Authority (NTA) would be given the following statutory functions: 1. to consider and advise the Secretary of State on the investment needs and specific proposals of the transport industries in relation to the government's policy objectives, including the roads programme; 2. to monitor and report on the provision of local transport services, and to promote co-ordination between transport modes on a county and regional basis; 3. to review and report on the use of transport taxes and subsidies in relation to the government's policy objectives; 4. to advise on the provision of road haulage operator licences and the development of freight planning agreements in keeping with the government's freight transport aims.

A top priority would be the authorisation of a major investment programme for railway electrification. As electrification advanced so would BR be more and more competitive in the freight transport market. Members of the Board told the Armitage enquiry in 1980 that 'given appropriate investment in improving track capacity at bottlenecks and an appropriate increase in train crew numbers, the present traffic volume could be increased by around fifty per cent to 250 million tonnes'.[30]

The effects of such a switch to rail freight transport would be quite remarkable. Even if the switch was of only half the amount that BR envisaged as attainable, the total tonne mileage carried by long distance heavy lorries would be reduced by thirty-five per cent.

A development which the NTA would need to examine would be the establishment of road freight transport transhipment depots in the vicinity of large towns and cities. In the environs of Paris the Sogaris depot on the southern outskirts of the city and the Garonor depot on the north side have had considerable success in freeing the central areas from movements of the heavy lorries. This has been achieved at minimal expense to the customers. In Britain John Horam, Under Secretary of State in the Callaghan government in 1978, told the freight directorate of the Department of Transport that he wanted outside consultants to be engaged on a full-scale enquiry of transhipment depots. The civil servants in the department played for time, raising numerous objections, until the general election of May 1979 brought about a change of government and the dropping of any suggestion of any enquiry. The Paris depots are profitable and bring considerable environmental gains to the city they serve. When a Labour Secretary of State for Transport takes over in Westminster it is to be hoped that a similar initiative to that shown by the French will be taken here.

The NTA would need to sponsor, through BR, a major revival of the railway system. The Serpell Report largely ignored the public expenditure costs, largely in increased redundancy payments and subsequent increases in payments of unemployment benefit, of its options for rail closures and service reductions. The consultants Transport and Environment Studies (TEST) in their report, *Investing in British Rail*, published in June 1983, estimated that these costs would amount to between £2.3 and £2.9 billion in the period up to 1992. This is seen as an appalling waste of public money as well as of human resources. They advanced a high investment Option T as an alternative to Serpell. It is the kind of plan that the next Labour government would need to adopt. Its main features are shown in the figure opposite. Under this plan sixty per cent of the 10,070 route miles of British railways would be electrified; one hundred new stations would be opened; modernisation of equipment, particularly

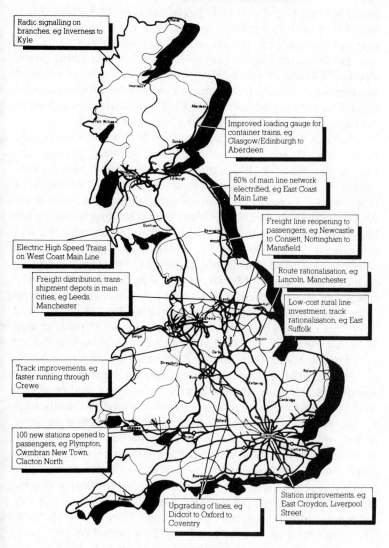

FIGURE 9

Geographical location of some of Option T's components

Radic signalling on branches, eg Inverness to Kyle

Improved loading gauge for container trains, eg Glasgow/Edinburgh to Aberdeen

60% of main line network electrified, eg East Coast Main Line

Freight line reopening to passengers, eg Newcastle to Consett, Nottingham to Mansfield

Electric High Speed Trains on West Coast Main Line

Route rationalisation, eg Lincoln, Manchester

Freight distribution, trans-shipment depots in main cities, eg Leeds, Manchester

Low-cost rural line investment, track rationalisation, eg East Suffolk

Track improvements, eg faster running through Crewe

100 new stations opened to passengers, eg Plympton, Cwmbran New Town, Clacton North

Upgrading of lines, eg Didcot to Oxford to Coventry

Station improvements, eg East Croydon, Liverpool Street

SOURCE: Transport and Environment Studies (TEST), *Investing in British Rail* (1983)

in track; and signalling, would be accelerated; and there would be improved stations and interchange arrangements between train and bus. The cost, spread over eight years, would be £3.9 billion: but it would be a positive capital investment in a vastly improved transport infrastructure for the nation. At the time the TEST proposals were published the Thatcher government had authorised the expenditure of £40 million on the electrification of the lines to Norwich and Harwich – chicken feed compared with the French government's expenditure of the equivalent of £1 billion on the one new project of the Ligne de Grande Vitesse between Paris and Lyon.[31]

A Labour Secretary of State for Transport would have to take quick action to arrest the decline in rural transport services. The NBC, in its report for 1982, expressed 'great anxiety' over the continuing decline of passengers in local bus services. The decline of three per cent in passenger journeys came on top of a much larger decline in 1981. It would have been very much greater had it not been for the fact that the NBC was still operating as 'an integrated business' in which the Express, Holidays and general coaching activities flourished and helped to sustain, from their enhanced earnings, the operation of many local bus services.[32] In default of a reversal of the Thatcher government's policy bus services in both town and country were likely to deteriorate further in 1983 and 1984. The new bus grant was due for phasing out in the course of 1984. Alan Walters' friend Alfred Goldstein was advocating the end of the policy of cross subsidisation and its substitution by a system of 'negative bidding' under which unremunerative routes would be identified and the task of providing the bus service would be offered to the operator prepared to accept the lowest level of subsidy from the government. Although the contracts advocated were for a period of five years there was no guarantee that they would be renewed thereafter. Nor was there any guarantee of satisfactory conditions of employment for the bus crews. Goldstein made no attempt to prove that his scheme would cost less than the existing arrangements through the NBC. He certainly had strange views on the causes of traffic congestion in London and other conurbations. The culprit apparently is the bus. In 1982 the Department of Transport produced a report: *Urban Public Transport Subsidies: An Economic Assessment of Value for Money* in which it was claimed that reducing the number of buses would reduce congestion because 'the increase in car traffic that would result would be more than offset by the reduction of the bus-induced congestion'. No account seems to have been taken of the impact of the level of fares on bus patronage. No doubt if fares are so high that buses run nearly empty it can be imagined that the transference of the passengers by some wave of the wand into private cars would not increase the general level of congestion. But one does not need a pocket calculator to work out that if, through lower fares, a bus has thirty passengers, the private cars they might otherwise occupy would take up far more road space than the bus. Nevertheless Goldstein's paper needs to be taken seriously. He assured his audience that 'The analytical method which produced this result is incorporated in the first comprehensive attempt to examine both the level and the nature of bus subsidies in urban areas, and its application is likely to figure prominently in the Department of Transport's assessments of claims for revenue support from Metropolitan and County Councils.'[33]

Clear priorities for a Labour Government would be to ensure an adequate level of bus services in areas where there is a public need of access to post offices, shops, hospitals, schools, colleges and places of recreation. Full publicity of services and co-operation with local communities to assess need would be essential. The bus grant would have to be restored. Proper integration should take place between bus and train services.

A big effort will be needed if public transport in Britain is to be saved from further depredation and the quality of life in urban and rural areas is to be protected and improved. In this endeavour the trade unions have a vital role to play. With the NUR under the new leadership of General Secretary Jimmy Knapp, there has been a commendable determination to put aside past differences with ASLEF and to work together in future to protect the public transport services. The first Annual General Meeting of the Railway Federation of Unions held on 19 and 20 September 1983 was welcomed as 'a turning point for the rail community'. The executives of ASLEF and NUR pledged themselves and their union's combined resources 'to a full-scale major nationwide campaign to mobilise support for Britain's railways. Over 719 million passenger journeys were made by train in 1981. Over six billion journeys were made by bus.[34] It is in this mass support for public transport, despite its many shortcomings, that there lies potential for action. The unions must win the confidence of the travelling public by explaining the causes of deterioration in services (where they occur) and by pointing out what is needed to remedy the situation. Once the public come to realise that the unions are united in their determination to fight for a decent system of public transport in Britain, the combined demands of the travelling public and the workers in public transport will become irresistible.

In January 1955 – not for the first or the last time – there was a crisis over rail pay. The British Transport Commission claimed that it could not afford the pay rises it saw as justifiable in themselves. Harold Macmillan, the Prime Minister, appointed a Commission of Inquiry under the chairmanship of Sir John Cameron. It gave its opinion on what it called 'the core of the matter': 'The Nation has provided by statute that there shall be a nationalised system of railway transport, which must therefore be regarded as a public utility of the first importance. Having willed the end the Nation must will the means.'

The millions of people who use buses or trains each day have an interest in seeing public transport services maintained and improved. The 'core of the matter' today is that the nation 'must will the means' to sustain a level of public transport services which will meet their needs.

Notes

Chapter 1

1. *Observer*, 25 February 1982.

2. *Hansard*, 5 Ser. Vol 918, Col. 279, 26 October 1976.

3. Department of Transport, *Transport Statistics Great Britain 1981-1981*, London, HMSO (1982), p.76.

4. *Hansard*, 5 Ser. Vol 33, No. 21, Col 264, 1 December 1982.

5. M. Hillman and A. Whalley, *The Social Consequences of Rail Closures*, London, Policy Studies Institute (1980), p.112.

6. Railway Invigoration Society, *Can Bus replace Train?* London 1977 p.16.

7. London Transport Executive, *Annual Report* (1983) p.7. *The Sunday Times*, 15 November, 1981.

8. *The Times*, 11 March 1982.

9. Department of Transport, *Transport Statistics Great Britain 1981-1981* HMSO (1982) Table 1.1. p.9.

10. *New Society*, 6 December 1979. Public Enterprise Group, PEG, Autumn 1982, p.10. British Institute of Management, *Business cars in the UK*, Management Survey Report No. 18 (1978). M.C. Dix and R.H.T. Pollard, *Company Financing of Household Cars*, Transport Studies Unit Oxford University Typescript, May 1980. British Rail Occasional Paper, *Subsidised Car Travel*, April 1976.

11. Peter Gillman, 'Is London choking to death?' *The Sunday Times*, 15 November 1981.

12. Department of Transport, Advisory Council on Energy Conservation *Energy Paper 26*, HMSO (1976). E. Hirst, Research Engineer, Oak Ridge National Laboratory, USA, *Science and Public Affairs*, November 1973; R.G. Harman, 'Fuel in Transport', *Traffic Engineering and Control*, February/March 1974. The Group of Nine Railways in the European Community, *The Future of Transport in the European Economic Comunity*, (n.d., but probably 1980) p.9.

13. Nine Railways in the European Community, *op. cit.*, p.11.

14. Department of Transport, *Transport Statistics Great Britain 1971-81*, Table 3.1 p.99.

15. *Ibid*. 3.26 p.112.

16. *Ibid*. 2.39 p.85.

17. M. Hastings and S. Jenkins, *The Battle for the Falklands*, London, Michael Joseph, 1983, p.316.

18. *Hansard*, 5 Ser. Vol. 987, Cols 515-6, 1 July 1980.

19. Department of Transport, *Transport Statistics Great Britain 1971-1981*, Table 1.12 p.16.

20. *Ibid*. Table 3.4 p.101.

21. See J. Wardroper *Juggernaut*, London, Temple Smith (1981) for the further evidence of the under-taxing of heavy lorries.

22. British Railways Board, *European Railways Performance Comparisons* (1980) Figure 3.2 p.15. The monograph was the outcome of a joint study by economists of Leeds University and British Rail.

23. The case for railway comversion has been stated in P. Hall and E. Smith, *Better Use of Railways*, University of Reading (1975), and by Alfred Sherman writing in *The Guardian*, 26 July 1982. The case against is succinctly presented in British Rail's *Why Our Trains Should Stay on the Rails* (1982).

Chapter 2

1. G. Davies and D. Piachaud 'Jobs: Why Britain's home made record is worst', *The Times*, 22 July 1981. OECD *Labour Force Statistics 1982* Fourth Quarterly Supplement. Unemployment percentages CSO *Economic Trends*, 1982 Edn. p.123.

2. *The Times*, 16 February 1983.

3. ILO, *Yearbook of Labour Statistics*, 1982, pp. 363-75.

4. *The Government's Expenditure Plans*, Cmnd 7746, November 1979, p.1.

5. M. Meacher, 'Four reasons why the Budget strategy cannot succeed', *The Times*, 9 April 1980.

6. Sir P. Parker ' "Sound of music" for the mixed economy', *Guardian*, 3 December 1980.

7. British Railways Board *Annual Report and Accounts, 1980*, p.5.

8. Figures cited in D. Bruce, 'Our idle over-paid: the facts', *The Times*, 12 October 1982.

9. *Financial Times*, 8 April 1980.

10. British Railways Board *Annual Report and Accounts, 1981*, p.26.

11. Central Statistical Office, *Economic Trends: Annual Supplement 1983* HMSO, (1983), pp. 96, 90, 60 and 77.

12. British Railways Board *Annual Report and Accounts, 1981*, p.26.

13. British Railways Board *Annual Report and Accounts, 1980*, p.5.

14. British Railways Board *Annual Report and Accounts, 198.*', p.9.

15. British Railways Board *Annual Report and Accounts, 1979*, p.21.

16. Department of Transport, *Transport Statistics Great Britain 1971-1981*, HMSO (1982), p.100.

Chapter 3

1. N. Fowler, *The Right Track*, Conservative Political Centre (1977), p.21.

2. *Hansard* 5th Ser. Vol. 91, Col. 585, 12 May 1976.

3. Official Report, Standing Committee B, Transport Bill 31.1.1978-18.4.1978 Col. 955.

4. British Railways Board *European Railways Performance Comparisons*, Table 5.3, p.33.

5. H. Duffy, 'Why the track record varies', *Financial Times*, 8 March 1983.

6. British Rail Council Meeting, 17 June 1982, *Minutes*.

7. Norman Fowler, answering a question put by Peter Snape, *Hansard* 5 Ser. Vol. 976, Col. 880-1, 18 January 1980.

8. H. Duffy, *op cit*.

9. Cmnd 7841, March 1980.

10. BRB, *European Railways Performance Comparisons*, Table 5.2, p.32.

11. H. Duffy, *op. cit*.

12. BRB, *European Railways Performance Comparisons*, Table 5.4, p.33.

13. Interview with Mr. Tom Ham, 18 October 1982.

14. *Hansard*, 5th Ser. Vol. 973, Cols. 379-81, 7 November 1979.

15. *Hansard*, 5th Ser. Vol. 975, Col. 472, 10 December 1979.

16. Select Committee on Nationalised Industries, (Sub-Committee A), 19 October 1976, Q 373.

17. Department of Transport British Railways Board, *Review of Main Line Electrification: Final Report*, HMSO (1981) p.1.

18. *Ibid*. p.3.

19. *Hansard*, 5 Ser. Vol. 968, Col. 1313, 20 June 1979.

20. British Rail Council's meeting with the Secretary of State for Transport at Marsham Street, *Report* 29 January 1981.

21. *Hansard*, 5 Ser. Vol. 26 Cols. 21-2, 22 June 1982.

22. NUR, EC Resolution 588 of 29 April 1982.

Chapter 4

1. 'The assault on the nationalised industries', *Labour Research*, Vol. 71, No. 3, March 1982, pp.58-60.

2. *The Economist*, 15 March 1980.

3. *Hansard*, Vol. 974, Col. 1129 et. seq. 27 November 1979. Department of Transport Press Release, 22 August 1979.

4. *Hansard*, Vol. 974, Cols. 1133-48.

5. *Ibid*. Cols. 1211-14.

6. Bus and Coach Council/Rural Voice, *The Country Would Miss the Bus*, February 1983, p.7.

7. *Bus and Coach*, 10 February 1982.

8. National Bus Company, *Annual Report*, 1981, p.9.

9. M. Hamer 'Highway Lottery', *New Statesman*, 13 November 1981. 'The Age of the Coach, *New Society*, 8 July 1982.

10. National Bus Company, *Annual Report*, 1981, p.6.

11. *Ibid*. p.10.

12. *Hansard*, 6th Ser. Vol. 21, Col. 937, 7 April 1982.

13. National Bus Company, *Annual Report*, 1981, pp.10.

14. M. Hamer *op. cit.*

15. Transport and Road Research Laboratory, *Car Sharing and Car Pooling in Great Britain: the recent situation and potential.*

16. *The Country Would Miss the Bus* p.18.

17. *Hansard*, Vol. 981, No. 144, Col. 967, 24 March 1980.

18. National Bus Company, *Annual Report*, 1981, pp.10-11.

19. *Innovation in Rural Bus Services*, HMSO (1979), Financial Times Survey, *Buses and Coaches*, 17 February 1983.

20. *The Times*, 19 January 1982; *Daily Mail*, 17 February 1982.

21. *The Times*, 20 October 1981.

22. House of Commons, Official Report, Standing Committee H, Col. 1635 14 February 1980.

23. *Railtalk*, 1/81, March 1981.

24. NUR, Memorandum on the Transport Bill, 1981 (Typescript).

25. *Guardian*, 11 March 1980; *New Statesman*, 6 June 1980.

26. *Guardian*, 27 February 1980.

27. *Hansard*, Vol. 988, Col. 1056, 14 July 1980.

28. *Hansard*, Vol. 996, No. 24, Col. 1252, 13 January, 1981.

29. *Hansard*, Vol. 988, Col. 1058, 14 July 1980.

30. *Hansard*, Vol. 996, No. 24, Col. 1252, 13 January 1981.

31. *Hansard*, Vol. 996, No. 24, Col. 1244, 13 January 1981.

32. House of Commons, Standing Committee E, Col. 832, 5 March 1981.

33. *Ibid.*

34. *Hansard*, Vol. 996, No. 24, Col. 1283, 13 January 1981.

35. BTH *Annual Report and Accounts*, 1970-9.

36. I am indebted to Ann Laverick, hotel and refreshment staff representative on the executive committee of the NUR, for much of the information contained in the above paragraph. See also *Transport Review*, 19 June 1981; *Financial Times*, 20 November 1982 and 25 February 1983; *The Times*, 25 February and 8 March 1983, and *The Sunday Times*, 13 February 1983.

37. M. Brown and S. Winyard, *Low pay in hotels and catering*, Low Pay Unit, London, (1975). L. Dronfield and P. Soto, *Hardship Hotel*, Counter Information Services, London (1980).

38. *Financial Times*, 24 October 1981.

39. *Hansard*, Vol. 988, Col. 1064, 14 July 1980.

40. *Hansard*, Vol. 974, Col. 1122, 27 November 1979.

41. *Hansard*, 6th Ser. Vol. 17, Col. 867, 9 February 1982.

42. *Ibid*, Col. 873.

43. *Ibid*, Col. 891.

44. *Ibid*, Col. 867.

45. *Ibid*, Col. 879.

46. *Ibid*, Col. 894.

47. *Ibid*, Col. 927.

48. D. Howell, *Freedom and Capital: Prospects for the Property-Owning Democracy*, Oxford, Blackwell, 1981, p.116.

186

Chapter 5

1. *Hansard*, 5 Ser. Vol. 971, Col. 403, 24 January 1979.

2. *The Sunday Times*, 21 September 1980.

3. University of Leeds/British Rail, *A Comparative Study of European Rail Performance*, London, British Railways Board 1979, Table 3.6, p.19.

4. *Ibid*, Table 3.17, p.25.

5. *Ibid*, Table 3.18, p.25.

6. *Ibid*, Table 3.19, p.26.

7. British Rail, *European Railways Performance Comparisons*, London, March 1980, p.5. (An abbreviated version of the *Comparative Study*.)

8. University of Leeds/British Rail, *A Comparative Study of European Rail Performance*, London, British Railways Board, 1979, para 6.19, p.52.

9. Sir P. Parker, '1983: Watershed for the Railways', *Sunday Times*, 12 December 1982.

10 British Railways Board, *Corporate Plan 1981-85*, British Rail Publications, 1981, p.9.

11. *Ibid*, para. 2.5, p.13.

12. *Ibid*, Table 8, p.33.

13. *Ibid*, para. 3.6, p.14.

14. *Ibid*, para. 2.10, p.21.

15. *Ibid*, paras. 3.1 to 3.3.

16. *Ibid*, para. 3.11, p.24.

17. British Railways Board, *Annual Report and Accounts, 1982*, p.7.

18. British Railways Board, *Annual Report and Accounts, 1982*, p.7.

19. British Railways Board, *Annual Report and Accounts, 1982*, p.7.

20. *Ibid*, p.8.

21. British Railways Board, *Corporate Plan 1981-5*, Table 8, p.33; *Annual Report and Accounts 1982*, p.23.

Chapter 6

1. NUR *Proceedings and Reports 1979*, December p.25.

2. NUR EC Resolution 1635, 13 September 1979; *Transport Review* 13 February 1981.

3. NUR *Proceedings and Reports*, December 1980, Appendix D8, pp.932-40.

4. *Discussion paper for consideration by railway trade unions* NUR Research Dept. File JEK 1980, pp.8-9.

5. NUR Research Department, file JEK.

6. *Transport Review*, 24 October 1980.

7. NUR EC Resolution 2184, 2 December 1980.

8. Railway Staff National Council, Minute 840 of meeting held on 13 April 1981.

9. Tim Owen, *Wrong Side of the Tracks: Low Pay in British Rail*, Low Pay Unit. Pamphlet No. 14 1980.

10. Railway Staff National Council, Minute 840 of meeting held on 13 April 1981.

11. Railway Staff National Council, Minute 841 of meeting held on 13 April 1981.

12. Railway Staff National Council, Minute 843 of meeting held on 13 April 1981.

13. Railway Staff National Council, Minutes 844 and 845, 14 and 15 July 1981.

14. TSSA and NUR evidence, Railway Staff National Council, Minute 844 of 21 July 1981.

15. NUR *Proceedings and Reports*, 1981, EC Resolution 1181 of 4 August 1981.

16. Paragraph 3, *Understanding on Productivity*, Appendix to RSNC Min. No. 848 20 August 1981.

17. NUR *Proceedings and Reports, 1981*, EC Resolution 1386 of 21 August 1981.

Chapter 7

1. BRB, *Annual Report and Accounts 1979*, p.20.

2. *Royal Commission on Trade Unions and Employers' Associations*, Minutes of Evidence 14.

3. *Sunday Times*, 21 September 1980.

4. *The Times*, 4 July 1982.

5. *The Times*, 14 July 1983.

6. The pay agreement is printed in NUR *Proceedings and Reports*, August 1980, Appendix A17, pp.A52-3. Details of the proposed reforms in goods handling and administration are included in the same volume's Appendix 8 pp.A12-17.

7. BRB, *Annual Report and Accounts 1981*, p.26.

8. *Ibid*, pp.27 and 22.

9. BRB, *Annual Report and Accounts 1982*, p.21.

10. RSNT, Decision 77, para. 140, 7 May 1982.

11. M. Baily, Transport Correspondent, *The Times*, 21 April 1982.

12. Minute No. 843, RSNC, Watford, 14-15 July 1981.

13. NUR EC Resolution 832, 21 May 1981.

14. NUR EC Resolution 1714, 9 October 1981.

15. NUR EC Resolution 1897, 12 November 1981.

16. NUR Submissions to the RSNT, 3 August 1981 para. 121, p.60.

17. *Ibid*, p.64.

18. NUR EC Resolution 1647, 3 December 1981.

19. NUR Branch circular M.11883/22995.

20. P.S. Bagwell, *The Railwaymen*, Vol. 2, 1981 pp.55-6.

21. BR, *Railtalk Special*, 7 January 1982.

22. Quoted in *NUR submission to a Committee of Inquiry appointed by ACAS*, February 1982, p.27.

23. Information kindly supplied in a letter from G.N. Brothers, Research and Information Department, International Transport Workers Federation, London; R. Gould, letter in *The Times*, 14 July 1982; letter from R.H. Wilcox, BRB, 21 October 1982, enclosing statement.

188

24. ASLEF evidence to RSNT 77, published 7 May 1982.

25. Item 6(i) BR Council Meeting 21 October 1982.

26. NUR EC Resolution 2288, 22 December 1981.

27. See, for example, RSJC (Salaried) Min. No. 5594 25 November 1981 where the principle of flexible rostering was agreed by TSSA, with some reservations..

28. *The Times*, 14 January 1982.

29. NUR EC Resolution 6 8 January 1982.

30. *Dear Commuter*, open letter from Ray Buckton to *The Times* 11 January 1982; *Observer* 25 August 1981, 7 February 1982.

31. NUR Submission to ACAS Court of Inquiry February 1982, Appendix 37.

32. *Daily Mail*, 13 January 1982.

33. *Ibid*.

34. *Observer*, 25 April 1982; *Financial Times*, 3 July 1982; *The Times*, 28 February 1982.

35. *Sunday Times*, 10 January 1982.

36. RSJC (Loco), 25 February 1982.

37. *Daily Mirror*, 22 February 1982.

38. *The Guardian*, 22 February 1982; *Observer*, 21 February 1982.

39. RSNT 77, 7 May 1982, paragraph 77.

40. *Ibid*, paragraph 171.

41. *Ibid*, General Conclusions iii(b) and vi.

42. *Daily Mirror*, 2 July 1982.

43. *Daily Mirror*, 1 July 1982.

44. *Daily Telegraph*, 16 July 1982.

45. BR *Railtalk Special*, 30 June 1982; *The Guardian*, 1 July 1982.

46. *Financial Times*, 16 July 1982.

47. *The Guardian* 16 July 1982; *The Times*, 22 July 1982.

48. BR, *Railtalk Special*, 30 June 1982.

49. *The Times*, 15 July 1982.

50. Interview with J. Stephenson, Secretary of the NUR negotiating committee who was present throughout the negotiations at Congress House, 14 September 1982. Interview with Russell Tuck, Senior Assitsant General Secretary, NUR, who was also present throughout the negotiations, 18 October 1982.

51. *Financial Times*, 19 July 1982.

52. Russell Tuck's assessment.

53. *The Times*, 28 July 1982.

54. NUR EC Resolution 923, 6 August 1982. The full agreement is printed in Appendix 35, NUR *Proceedings and Reports*, August 1982.

55. BR Council Meeting, 21 October 1982, item Freight Business Performance.

56. Interview with Bill Fordham, 13 September 1983.

Chapter 8

1. British Railways Board Typescript *International Comparisons of Railway Performance*, 30 November 1982.

2. British Railways Board, *Annual Report and Accounts*, 1979-82 inclusive, Review of Operations, British Rail Engineering Ltd.

3. NUR Research Department paper *Rationalisation of BREL*, 5 August 1983. D. Foster, *Shildon – a case of unfair competition*, Shildon Works Joint Shop Stewards Committee, 1983.

4. NUR *Proceedings and Reports*, August 1982, p.54 and Appendix 15, pp.A36-7.

5. NUR *Proceedings and Reports*, August 1982, Resolution 588.

6. Durham County Council and Sedgefield District Council, *The Case against Closure: Shildon Wagon Works*, April 1983.

7. Bolton Council, *Horwich Loco Works: The impact of possible closure*, 1983, p.3.

8. *Hansard*, 6 Ser. Vol. 39 No. 84 Col. 757, 22 March 1983.

9. NUR Research Report, *Social Costs of Closures*, 1983.

10. *Hansard*, 6 Ser. Vol. 39 No. 84 Col. 766, 22 March 1983.

11. *Financial Times*, 26 May 1982.

12. T. Owen, *Wrong Side of the Tracks*, Low Pay Unit, 1981, p.11.

13. *Ibid*, p.14.

14. NUR *Agenda and Decisions*, Annual General Meeting, June-July 1981, Resolution 86a.

15. NUR, *Proceedings and Reports*, Auust 1982, Resolution 698.

16. *Transport Review*, 2 July 1982. The General Secretary's front page appeal had been written on 23 June.

17. The above account is based on the *Verbatim Report*, NUR AGM, 28 June 1982.

18. *The Guardian*, 25 June 1982.

19. *Daily Telegraph*, 30 June 1982.

20. *The Times*, 29 June 1982.

21. *Transport Salaried Staff Journal*, September 1982.

22. *Transport Review*, 13 August 1982.

23. NUR AGM, *Verbatim Report*, 28 June 1982, p.1/141.

24. NUR SGM, *Verbatim Report*, 13 October 1982, p.68.

25. NUR SGM, 13-14 October 1982 *Agenda and Decisions*.

26. British Railways Board, *Corporate Plan 1983-88*, August 1983, p.23..

27. *Hansard*, 6 Ser. Vol. 39 No. 84 Col. 764, 22 March 1983.

28. NUR Branch Circular No. M.12050/23319.

29. NUR Branch Circular No. M.12088/24425.

Chapter 9

1. *Investment in Transport* A submission to the Rt. Hon. Norman Fowler, MP, Secretary of State for Transport, 24 February 1981, p.4.

2. *Hansard*, 6 Ser. Vol. 36 Col. 489, 20 January 1983.

3. *The Guardian*, 2 April 1982.

4. British Railways Board, *Rail Policy*, (1981) p.25.

5. *The Standard*, 6 January 1983.

6. *Labour Research*, March 1983, p.62.

7 House of Commons Transport Committee *Second Report*, Session 1982-3. (Hereafter referred to as HCTC, Sir David Serpell's answer to Question 1.

8. HCTC, para 10, p.v.

9. HCTC, para 163, p.36.

10. HCTC, para 15, p.vii.

11. *Hansard*, Vol. 36, No. 54, Col. 460, Speech of Ron Lewis, MP, 3 February 1983.

12. *Financial Times*, *Daily Telegraph*, *The Times*, *Daily Mirror* and *The Standard*, all of 21 January 1983. *Sunday Telegraph*, 23 January 1983.

13. House of Lords Hansard, Vol. 439, No. 56, Col. 1207, 2 March 1983. Although Lord Marsh gave the figure as £627,000, most reports gave the lower total of £552,000.

14. Letter quoted in *Observer Business*, 23 January 1983.

15. *Hansard*, Vol. 35, No. 41, Col. 489, 20 January 1983.

16. *Observer Business*, 23 January 1983.

17. Jane's Yearbooks, *Jane's World Railways*, 1982-3 edn. pp.286-320.

18. HCTC para 259 p.65.

19. *Railway Finances*, Report of a Committee chaired by Sir David Serpell, KCB, CMG, OBE, London, HMSO, (1983) Introduction, para 5, p.5..

20. Script of BBC 2 TV Newsnight, 20 January 1983.

21. *Railway Finances*, p.106.

22. *Daily Telegraph*, 26 January 1983.

23. *Railway Finances*, para 2.12, p.15.

24. *Ibid*, para 2.18 p.16.

25. BR, *Question and Answer Brief on the Serpell Report*. Answer to Q.4.

26. *Railway Finances*, para 5.4, p.27. Robin Cook, MP, Press Statement, 5 January 1983.

27. *Hansard*, Vol. 36, No. 51, Col. 451, 3 February 1983. *Railway Finances* para 6.17, p.31.

28. *Railway Finances*, para 6.10, p.31.

29. HCTC, para 186, p.42.

30. *Railway Finances*, para 6.10, p.31.

31. *Ibid*, para 6.9, p.30.

32. *Financial Times*, 25 January 1983.

33. *Railway Finances*, para 6.39, p.34.

34. *House of Lords Hansard*, Vol. 439, No. 56, Col. 1164, 2 March 1983.

35. *Railway Finances*, para 7.27, p.39.

36. *Ibid*, para 8.18, p.44.

37. HCTC, paras 30-1, p.xvii.

38. *Railway Finances*, para 9.14, p.43.

39. HCTC, p.xvii.

40. *Railway Finances*, para 4.11, p.61.

41. BR, *Question and Answer Brief on the Serpell Report.*
42. *Railway Finances*, para 5, p.61.
43. R. Hope, 'Serpell's options: slow death or quick kill?', *Railway Gazette International*, March 1983, pp.180-2.
44. *Ibid*, p.181.
45. *Hansard*, Vol. 35, No. 41, Col. 500, 20 January 1983.
46. *Railway Finances*, para 14.20, p.78.
47. Hope, 'Serpell's options', p.181.
48. *Hansard*, Vol. 35, No. 41, Col. 489, 20 January 1983.
49. Letter from Michael Bourke, *Daily Telegraph*, 9 February 1983.
50. HCTC, para 229, p.53.
51. HCTC, para 177, p.39.
52. HCTC, p.xvii.
53. *Daily Mirror*, 21 January 1983.
54. *Hansard*, Vol. 35, No. 41, Cols. 489, 499 and 496, 20 January 1983.
55. R. Hope, interview with David Howell, 25 February 1983, reported in *Railway Gazette International*, April 1983.
56. *Report of a meeting between the Secretary of State for Transport and the NUR*, 14 February 1983.
57. HCTC, para 277, 279, p.71.
58. *Sunday Telegraph*, 23 January 1983.
59. TEST, Preliminary Report, 17 May 1983.
60. G.F. Allen, 'Government to take fresh look at "social service" railway', *Lloyds List*, 13 April 1983

Chapter 10

1. House of Commons Transport Committee, Fifth Report, *Transport in London*, (TL) Vol. 3 1982, Q 779, evidence of Rt. Hon. David Howell, p.196.
2. H. Morrison, *Autobiography*, London, 1960, p.120.
3. *Transport in London*, Cmnd 3686, London HMSO 1967.
4. (TL) Vol. 1, p.lx..
5. TL Vol. 1, p.x.
6. GLC, *London Facts and Figures*, 1973 and 1978 editions.
7. TL Vol. 1, p.xiv.
8. TL Vol. 1, p.xxx.
9. TL Vol. 1, p.xiii.
10. GLC Transport Policies and Programme 1982-4, p.74.
11. TL Vol. 2, Qs 25-27, pp.18-20.
12. TL Vol. 2, Q 34, p.21.
13. TL Vol. 1, (Report) p.xvii.
14. TL Vol. 1, (Report) p.xviii.
15. Memorandum submitted by LT, TL Vol. 3, p.103.
16. Memorandum submitted by BR TL Vol. 2, p.71.
17. Memorandum submitted by the NUR, TL Vol. 2, p.284.
18. Paper read by J.E. Allen, *The Urban Transport Future*, University of Nottingham 9 & 10 April, 1981.

19. TL Vol. 2, Q.23, p.18.

20. Letter to the *Financial Times*, 11 January 1982.

21. See Table 8 p.144.

22. TL Vol. 1, (Report) p.xxx.

23. Evidence of Dave Wetzel, TL Vol. 3, Q 727, p.174.

24. *The Standard*, 17 December 1981.

25. *Hansard*, 6 Ser. Vol. 15, Col. 534, 22 December 1981.

26. This was a fact emphasised by Andrew McIntosh 'in Defence of London's Fare Deal', *Time Out*, 20 November 1981.

27. *The Standard*, 5 October 1981.

28. Transportation and Development Department, GLC, *Travel Patterns in London and the effects of Recent changes in London Transport Fares* April 1983, p.4.

29. TL Vol. 3, Q 716 pp.170-1.

30. *Financial Times*, 18 December 1981.

31. *Hansard*, 6 Ser. Vol. 15, Col. 447, 17 December 1981.

32. *The Times*, 18 December 1981.

33. *Financial Times*, 19 December 1981.

34. *Hansard*, 6 Ser. Vol. 16, Col. 37, 18 January 1982.

35. *Hansard*, 6 Ser. Vol. 16, Cols. 896, 897 and 899.

36. *The Sunday Times*, 17 January 1982.

37. This summary of the Law Lords view is based on a photostat copy of the five judgements contained in file HTECD at NUR headquarters, Euston Road.

38. *Financial Times*, 21 December 1981.

39. *Hansard*, 5 Ser. Vol. 775, Cols. 1247-8, 17 December 1968.

40. *Ibid*, Cols. 1254-5 and 1286.

41. Cost of free travel included in GLC document *Initial Comments on the White Paper 'Public Transport in London'*, 28 July 1983.

42. *Travel Patterns in London*, pp.6-7, GLC News Service, No. 252, 28 April 1983.

43. *Hansard*, 6 Ser. Vol. 15, Cols. 540, 545, 18 December 1981.

44. *Financial Times*, 5 February 1982.

45. Report of the LT Rail Consultative Committee, 22 December 1981.

46. NUR Executive Committee, Movements Department report, 21 January 1982.

47. *The Times*, 11 March 1983.

48. *The Times*, 20 March 1983.

49. GLC *Transport in London, The Balanced Plan*, 1983.

50. *Financial Times*, 28 January 1983.

51. *The Standard*, 5 July 1983.

52. TL Vol. 3, Q 740, p.143.

53. *Hansard*, 6 Ser. Vol. 32, No. 9, Col. 42, 15 November 1982.

54. Association of Metropolitan Authorities, *The Transport Bill and the White Paper*, 1982, p.1.

55. Michael Baily, 'Minibuses for London' *The Times*, 17 and 18 February 1983.

56. *The Times*, 27 July 1983.

57. TL Vol. 1, (Report) p.lxviii.

58. HMSO *Public Transport in London* Cmnd 9004, July 1983, p.71.

59. *Hansard*, 6 Ser. Vol. 46, No. 29, Col. 1052, 26 July 1983.

60. GLC, Initial Comment on the White Paper 'Public Transport in London' 28 July 1983.

61. *Public Transport in London*, p.6. *Hansard*, 6 Ser. Vol. 46, No. 29, Col. 1052, 26 July 1983.

62. TL Vol. 1, p.lxviii.

63. P.B. Goodwin, J.M. Bailey, R.H. Brisbourne, M.I. Clarke, J.R. Donnison, T.E. Reyder and G.K. Whiteley, *Subsidised Public Transport and the Demand for Travel: the South Yorkshire example*, Aldershot 1983, pp.11-18.

64. *Labour Research*, January 1982 pp.10-11.

65. Information kindly provided by Professor P. Hills, Department of Civil Engineering, Newcastle University, 25 August 1983.

66. *The Times*, 6 July 1983.

67. City of Sheffield, *Why the City of Sheffield supports the South Yorkshire Cheap Fares Policy*, 1983.

68. South Yorkshire Transport, *Annual Report and accounts 1981-82, 1982-83; Your Transport Service – The Facts*, 1983.

Chapter 11

1. R. Sugden, 'Practical Cost-Benefit Analysis', *The Economic Review* September, 1983, pp.24-8.

2. Department of Transport, *Policy for Roads in England: 1983*, Cmnd 9059 HMSO 1983, Annex B, 'Schemes in Preparation' p.42.

3. *Ibid* pp.7 and 34.

4. *Report of the Advisory Committee on Trunk Road Assessment*, HMSO, 1977, p.123.

5. *Financial Times*, 25 October 1983.

6. *Report of the Advisory Committee on Trunk Road Assessment*, HMSO 1977, p.126.

7. *Ibid*. p.127.

8. Department of Transport, *Transport Statistics Great Britain 1971-1981*, HMSO, 1982 pp.16, 137. J. Wardroper, *Juggernaut*, London, 1981, p.164.

9. *Report of a meeting between the Secretary of State for Transport and the NUR*, 14 February 1983.

10. *Daily Express*, 31 October 1983.

11. Department of Transport, *Transport Statistics Great Britain 1971-1981*, HMSO, 1982, Table 1.25 p.6.

12. TUC-Labour Party Liaison Committee, *Transport Policy*, 1982, p.9.

13. R. Reed, 'Urban Public Transport: Towards 2000', paper read at London Transport Golden Jubilee conference, 20 September 1983.

14. *Transport Policy*, p.9.

15. P. O'Dell, *Oil and World Power*, 7th ed. 1982 p.263.

16. *The Times*, 3 November 1983.

17. *Financial Times*, 19 October 1983.

18. R. Reed, 'Urban Public Transport: Towards 2000'.

19. Department of Transport, *Road Accidents Great Britain 1981*, HMSO 1982, p.xxii.

20. Department of Transport, *Transport Statistics Great Britain 1971-1981*, HMSO 1982, p.86.

21. At p.29.

22. Department of Transport, *Transport Statistics Great Britain 1971-1981* HMSO 1982, p.112.

23. William Rodgers cited in J. Wardroper, *Juggernaut*.

24. D. Pearce, cited in *Ibid*, p.111.

25. T., Aldous, *Battle for the Environment*, Fontana, London 1972, pp.44, 100.

26. National Society for Clean Air Book, 1970-71 cited in ASLEF's reply to the Transport Policy Consultation Document, 1976, p.25.

27. Department of Transport, *Railway Finances* (The Serpell Report) Vol. 1, p.61.

28. *Transport Policy*, p.8.

29. *Ibid*, p.7.

30. Facts cited in J. Wardroper, *Juggernaut*, p.165.

31. K. Buchan. 'A bas la difference', *Transport Retort*, vol 7 No.9, 1983.

32. National Bus Company, *Annual Report*, 1982, p.4.

33. A. Goldstein, 'Buses: Social Enterprise and Business', paper read at the Annual Conference of the Bus and Coach Council, September 1983. Goldstein appears to have been much impressed by the book by S. Glaister and C. Mulley, *Public Control of the British Bus Industry*, Aldershop, Gower Publishing Co. (1983) in which the policy of cross-subsidisation is attacked.

34. Department of Transport, *Transport Statistics Great Britain 1971-1981*, HMSO 1982, pp. 56, 100.

35. Interim Report of a Court of Inquiry into a dispute between the BTC and the NUR (Cameron Report), Cmnd 9352 (1955).

Chronology

1979

3 May — Conservative General Election victory

5 May — Norman Fowler appointed Minister of Transport

9 June — BR announces five per cent cut in rail services

26 June — *RSNT 63* in paras 78 and 79 hints at need for flexible rostering

1980

2 January — BR paper on flexible rostering presented to RSNC

5 January — Norman Fowler entered Cabinet as Secretary of State for Transport

21 February — RSJC (Traffic) Discussion on BR's productivity proposals

11 March — ASLEF, NUR and TSSA agree on joint approach to BR on pay

28 April — BR's offer of twenty per cent from 5 May 1980 accepted. Retail Price Index up twenty one per cent on April 1979

19 June — NBC Chairman warns that enactment of Transport Bill would lead to the withdrawal of many country bus services

30 June — Transport Act privatised National Freight Corporation and opened express coach services to competition.

4 July	House of Commons Transport Committee reported that government squeeze on investment would lead to higher fares or more service cuts
August	BR's letter to rail unions warned that agreement on flexible rostering was a precondition for the introduction of the thirty nine hour week
2 October	Monopolies and Mergers Commission Report on London and South East commuter services
19-20 November	BR Council meeting at Watford produces *Balance Sheet of Change*
16 December	BR's *Corporate Plan 1981-85*

1981

11 February	Department of Transport/BR *Final Report: Review of Main Line Electrification* concludes 'a substantial programme of main line electrification would be financially worthwhile'
28 April	Rail unions reject BR's offer of seven per cent
20 June	Government proposes piecemeal railway electrification paid for by improved staff productivity
16 July	*RSNT 75* awards eight per cent from 20 April 1981 plus three per cent from 1 August 1981
21 July	BR declared it could not implement *RSNT 75* in full but would pay eight per cent from 20 April 1981 and the remaining three per cent only when productivity changes had been completed
31 July	Transport Act. Plans to privatise BTH, NTDB and Sealink
18-20 August	Meeting of ACAS. Then RSNC understandings on (a) Pay and (b) Productivity The three rail unions sign ACAS report
14 September	David Howell succeeds Norman Fowler as Secretary of State for Transport

5 October	'Fares Fair' policy on London Transport inaugurated
30 November	RSNC (Loco) records 'failure to agree' on flexible rostering
15 December	Law Lords outlaw 'Fares Fair' policy of London Transport
22 December	NUR executive accepts flexible rostering for guards
23 December	BR announces withholding of thirty nine hour week and outstanding three per cent pay rise from footplate staff Howell approves railway electrification to Norwich

1982

4 January	ASLEF members ceased voluntary overtime and rest day working
13 January	ASLEF two-day strike begins
14 January	BR undertakes to pay NUR footplatemen the three per cent
19, 22 and 26 January	ACAS talks on ASLEF–BR dispute failed
2 and 9-11 February	ACAS heard evidence
16 February	ACAS report advised ASLEF to call off strike
17 February	Discussion of ACAS report between BR, the rail unions and Len Murray. All parties agreed to the report BR announced its intention to pay the outstanding three per cent. ASLEF called off strike
19 February	Resumption of normal working from 00.01 hours
25 February	RSJC (Loco) 'Failure to agree'

1 March	RSNC 'Failure to agree'
15-16 March	RSNT hearings
22 March	Fares on London Transport double as a result of Lords' ruling
7 May	*RSNT 77* recommended acceptance of flexible rostering
13 May	ASLEF wrote to BR that *RSNT 77* was 'totally unacceptable'
21 May	NUR executive warns BR 'withdraw workshop closures by 7 June or face strike'
28 May	RSNC. BR offers five per cent conditional on productivity
4 June	BR announces postponement of plan to close Shildon and cut workforce at Swindon and Horwich
9 June	NUR calls for strike from 28 June because of unacceptable pay offer
28-29 June	NUR strike
5-18 June	ASLEF strike over flexible rostering
6 July	BR letter to unions. Pay offer withdrawn because of strikes
17 July	TUC advises ASLEF to call off strike
30 July	RSNC. All three rail unions agree to a scheme for flexible rostering
10 September	*RSNT 78* awards six per cent rise from 6 September
6 October	SGM of NUR accepts resignation of Sidney Weighell and accepts *RSNT 78*
28 October	Transport Act. Plans for the privatisation of NBC's express and holiday coaching business

1983

20 January	Serpell Committee Report
28 March	Transport Act. Limitation of powers of PTAs
9 June	General Election. Conservative parliamentary majority increased
12 June	Tom King appointed Secretary of State for Transport
20 June	TEST's *Investing in British Rail* published
September	Bob Reid succeeds Sir Peter Parker as Chairman of British Rail
16 October	Nicholas Ridley succeeds Tom King as Secretary of State for Transport

Appendix

MACHINERY OF NEGOTIATION: RAILWAY CONCILIATION STAFF

The following are the various stages of the negotiating machinery through which applications are considered:

(a) *Matters Arising from Conditions of Service*

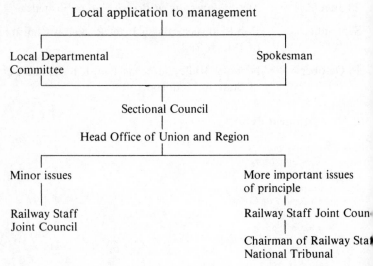

Local application to management

Local Departmental Committee — Spokesman

Sectional Council

Head Office of Union and Region

Minor issues
Railway Staff Joint Council

More important issues of principle
Railway Staff Joint Coun•
Chairman of Railway Sta⁺ National Tribunal

(b) *Proposals to Vary National Agreements*

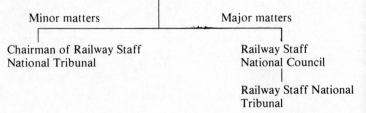

Head office of Union and Railways Staff Conference

Railway Staff Joint Council

Minor matters
Chairman of Railway Staff National Tribunal

Major matters
Railway Staff National Council
Railway Staff National Tribunal

Bibliography

1. Statutes

Transport Act 1980, 28 & 29 Eliz. II, c. 34
Transport Act 1981, 29 & 30 Eliz. II, c. 56
Transport Act 1982, 30 & 31 Eliza. II, c. 49
Transport Act 1983, 31 & 32 Eliz. II, c. 10

2. Government Publications

The Channel Tunnel, Cmnd 5430 1973
Monopolies and Mergers Commission, BRB: *London and the South East Commuter Services*, Cmnd 8046 1980
Public Transport Subsidy in Cities, Cmnd 8735 1982-3
Public Transport in London, Cmnd 9004 1983
Rates: Proposals for Rate Limitation and Reform of the Rating System, Cmnd 9008 1983
Policy for Roads in England, Cmnd 9059 1983
Report of the Advisory Committee on Trunk Roads Assessment (Leitch Committee), 1977
Report of the Inquiry into Lorries, People and the Environment (Armitage Committee), 1980
Department of Transport/BRB, *Review of Main Line Electrification: Final Report*, 1981
Railway Finances: Report of a Committee Chaired by Sir David Serpell, KGB, 1983
Department of Transport, *Transport Statistics Great Britain 1971-1981*, 1982
_____. *Road Accidents Great Britain 1981*, 1982
Advisory Council on Energy Conservation, *Review of UK transport Energy Outlook*, 1982
House of Commons Transport Committee, Reports:
_____. *The Role of British Rail in Public Transport*, 1977
_____. *Main Line Electrification*, 1982
_____. *Review of Railway Finances* (Serpell), 1983
_____. *Transport in London*, 1982

3. Other Published Works

Allen, W.F., *British Railways after Beeching*, London 1966

Association of Metropolitan Authorities, *The Transport Bill and the White Paper*, London 1982

ASLEF, *Transport for the Nation*, London 1976

Bagwell, P.S., *The Railwaymen*, vol 2, London 1982

Bolton Council, *Horwich Loco Works: the impact of possible closure*, Bolton 1983

British Railways Board, *Annual Report and Accounts* 1979-82

———. *European Railways Performance Comparisons*, 1980

———. *Rail Policy*, 1981

———. *Cross Channel Rail Link*, 1982

———. *Why our Trains should Stay on the Rails*, 1982

———. *Corporate Plan 1981-85*, 1981

———. *Corporate Plan 1983-88*, 1983

Brown, M. and Winyard, S., *Low Pay in Hotels and Catering*, Low Pay Unit, London 1975

Bus and Coach Council, *The Future of the Bus*, London 1982

———. *The Country would miss the Bus*, London 1983

———. *The Bus: the key to urban mobility*, London 1983

Dronfield, C. and Soto, P., *Hardship Hotel*, Counter Information Services, London 1980

Durham County Council/Sedgefield DC, *The Case against closure of the Shildon Wagon Works*, Durham 1983

Financial Times Survey, *Buses and Coaches*, 17 February 1982

Fowler, N., *The Right Track*, London 1977

Glaister, S. and Mulley, C., *Public Control of the British Bus Industry*, Aldershot 1983

GLC, *London Facts and Figures*, various dates

———. *Transport Policies and Programme 1982-4*, 1982

———. *Travel Patterns in London and the effect of recent changes in LT fares*, 1983

———. *Transport in London: the Balanced Plan*, 1983

Goodwin, P.B. et al, *Subsidised Public Transport and the demand for travel: the South Yorkshire example*, Aldershot 1983

Goldstein, A., 'Buses: Social Enterprise and Business', paper read to the Annual Conference of the Bus and Coach Council, 13 September 1983

Group of nine railways in the EEC, *The Future of Transport in the European Community*, London 1980

Hillman, M. and Whalley, A., *The Social Consequences of Rail Closures*, Policy Studies Institute, London 1980

Howell, D., *Freedom and Capital: prospects for the property owning democracy*, Oxford 1981

International Labour Office, Inland Transport Committee, *Working Conditions in Rail Transport*, Geneva 1979

International Transport Workers Federation, *Manning of Locomotives and Trains*, London 1968

_____. *We don't hate technology ... but*, London 1977

Jane's World Railways, 1982-3 edn., London 1983

Johnson, J. and Long, R.A., *British Railways Engineering 1948-80*, London 1981

National Bus Company, *Annual Report and Accounts*, 1979-82

National Union of Railwaymen, *A Policy for Transport*, London 1976

_____. *Railway Electrification*, London 1978

O'Dell, P., *Oil and World Power*, Harmondsworth 1983

Owen, T., *Wrong Side of the Tracks*, Low Pay Unit, London 1981

Pole, N., *Oil and the future of personal mobility*, Cambridge 1973

Railway Invigoration Society, *Can Buses replace Trains?*, London 1977

Socialist Environment and Resources Association, *Transport Policies and the Environment*, London 1980

South Yorkshire County Council, *Annual Report and Accounts 1981-82*

_____. *Your Transport Service: the Facts*, 1983

Transport and Environment Studies (TEST), *Investing in British Rail*, London 1983

TUC/Labour Party Liaison Committee, *Transport Policy*, London 1982

Tyme, J., *Motorways versus Democracy*, London 1978

Wardroper, J., *Juggernaut*, London 1981

Locomotive Journal

Transport Review

Transport Salaried Staffs' Journal

Index